OUTSIDE THE BOX

THE HISTORY OF COMMUNICATION

Robert W. McChesney and John C. Nerone, editors

A list of books in the series appears at the end of this book.

OUTSIDE THE BOX

Corporate Media, Globalization,
and the UPS Strike

DEEPA KUMAR

UNIVERSITY OF ILLINOIS PRESS
URBANA AND CHICAGO

First Illinois paperback, 2008
© 2007 by Deepa Kumar
Manufactured in the United States of America
1 2 3 4 5 C P 5 4 3 2 1

∞ This book is printed on acid-free paper.

The Library of Congress cataloged the cloth
edition as follows:

Kumar, Deepa, 1968–
 Outside the box : corporate media, globalization,
and the UPS strike / Deepa Kumar.
 p.   cm. — (The history of communication)
 Includes bibliographical references and index.
 ISBN-13: 978-0-252-03172-4 (cloth : alk. paper)
 ISBN-10: 0-252-03172-5 (cloth : alk. paper)
 1. United Parcel Service Strike, 1997. 2. Mass media—
Political aspects—United States. 3. Globalization—Economic
aspects—United States. 4. United Parcel Service—
History. 5. International Brotherhood of Teamsters, Chauffeurs,
Warehousemen and Helpers of America—History.
 I. Title.
 HD5325.E821997.K86   2007
 331.892'813880440973—dc22   2006022583

PAPERBACK ISBN 978-0-252-07589-6

Contents

Preface

When I first started research on this project, I did so with a sense that something remarkable had happened to the media in the United States during the United Parcel Service (UPS) strike of August 1997. The corporate media, which typically cover strikes in terms unfavorable to labor, seemed to undergo something of a transformation. From national newspapers to television and even the business press, there was real discussion about the growth of class inequality in the era of globalization. Pleasantly surprised by this development, I took it upon myself to understand and explain how it was that a seemingly all-powerful corporate media system could be forced to discuss labor's problems sympathetically.

For much of U.S. history, class inequality has been buried under the myth of the American dream. It is therefore not surprising that the mainstream media paid scant attention to the growth in class polarization in the last three decades of the twentieth century. Since the mid-1970s, most Americans have seen their wages decline or stagnate, while a small percentage has increased its earnings and wealth. In 1978, the average chief executive officer (CEO) earned about 29 times the average worker's wage.[1] By the turn of the century, the differential had increased to 531:1.[2] We find that even during the economic expansion in the 1990s, the gap between rich and poor grew only larger.[3] While the Wall Street elite enjoyed "trophy wines" at almost two thousand dollars a bottle, unemployed and part-time workers, many of whom were hard hit by welfare "reform," had to rely on food pantries and shelters as standard survival mechanisms.[4]

In a democratic society, such disparities should be unacceptable. If we are all meant to be equal and share the same rights, then such class polarization would be the subject of intense discussion and debate. At the very least, we would have a public discussion about why, during a period of economic growth accompanied by increased labor productivity and longer work hours, working people did not receive their share of the profits. The institution vested with responsibility for engaging the citizenry in such dialogue, the media, would be working overtime to shed light on this situation and to facilitate a solution.

Yet, with few exceptions, the media have been silent about inequality. Instead, the corporate media have taken great pains to present the opposite picture. During much of the 1990s, television news and mainstream newspapers gushed about the "miracle economy," asserting that it was a bonanza for all. In reality, the United States is one of the most class-divided societies in the industrialized West. This is not a coincidence. Rather, starting in the early 1970s, the United States has led the world in adopting an economic policy known as "globalization" that restored profitability to corporations at the expense of workers. The elite in the United States can take much credit for crafting strategies that would usher in a new era of global capitalism.

This book is about the power of workers to challenge the dominant logic of this age. Specifically, it is about how the UPS strike of 1997 was able to break through the wall of silence in the mainstream media around the inequality precipitated by globalization. When 185,000 UPS workers across the United States, organized in the Teamsters union, walked off their jobs in the fall of 1997, they made workers and their concerns visible. By withholding their labor, they showed how central they are to the economy. Eighty percent of all packages shipped by ground transportation came to a halt, and UPS lost about forty million dollars for every day of the strike. The strike was fundamentally about inequality. Whereas UPS had made almost a billion dollars in profit the year prior to the strike, its workers had seen paltry wage increases coupled with an attack on full-time jobs, pensions, and safe working conditions. The strike exemplified everything that was wrong economically for workers, and it elevated to national prominence the contradictions at the heart of a booming economy.

Predictably, the mainstream media's initial coverage of the strike minimized its significance while focusing instead on the inconvenience to consumers. However, this would change in the second week of the strike when they were forced to think outside the box. Some sections of the corporate media, such as the *New York Times,* the *Washington Post,* and the ABC television network, began to acknowledge inequality and to discuss the problems of the U.S. working class. This shift happened in a politicized context where individuals and groups were pressured to take sides. In the battle for hearts and minds, the Teamsters and their allies were able to win public support and thus bring into being pressures that normally do not exist on the media. In a sense, the Teamsters were able to break through the limitations of the antilabor framing mechanisms of the "idiot box" and reach out to the outside world. In turn, public support and the world outside would help shape and frame the way the story of the strike was told.

In the immediate aftermath of the strike, the limited concession to labor problems in the national media was further generalized. When the Teamsters won the strike, media across the board, from the business press to news magazines, radio, and local newspapers, attempted to explain how it had happened and, perhaps more important, why the public sided two to one with the workers.[5] What could explain the new prolabor mood in American society and the concomitant failure of antiunion propaganda? In trying to address these questions, the corporate media had to admit, however grudgingly, that a rising tide had not lifted all boats; that is, the working classes had not shared in the promised fruits of globalization.

This book is about the power of collective struggle, of large national strikes, to successfully resist and challenge the corporate media. However, I do not suggest that the media can be permanently reformed under a free-market system. Shortly after the strike was over and its impact assessed, the space that was opened up for a critical discussion of corporate behavior was immediately closed off, and the media reverted to their standard modus operandi. When the pressures that forced the corporate media to discuss labor's concerns dissipated, so did any semblance of an "open marketplace of ideas." This case study shows that the media can be forced to expand the sphere of public discussion but only temporarily. Therefore, I argue that reforming the media is both more difficult than liberal media theorists state and less difficult than political economists expect. A large national strike, or collective struggle in general, in the context of increasing public dissatisfaction with the status quo, has the potential to create the sort of pressure on the media that can dislodge the news from its usual groove. However, once the context of struggle recedes, so does the sustained presence of dissent in the media. Therefore, it is only through radical transformation, and the creation of a society based on equitable distribution of wealth and power, that a truly democratic media system can come into being.

This argument goes against the standard view of the media, which is premised on the notion that, despite their flaws, they do ultimately serve the public interest.[6] Against this liberal pragmatist view, I argue that there is no such thing as "public" interest. Rather, the public is divided into the tiny elite that benefits from globalization policies and the vast majority of workers who do not. Furthermore, it is this same elite that tends to set the terms of public debate due to their effective control over the instruments of mass communication. The interests of workers are thus marginalized in the media.

Much of the research on the coverage of labor emphasizes, and rightly so, the procorporate biases of the media. For instance, William Puette discusses eight lenses through which the media view labor, Michael Parenti arrives at seven generalizations about the media's treatment of labor, Martin Harrison outlines several patterns of antilabor coverage, and Christopher Martin offers five dominant frames of labor news.[7] This research is extremely useful in trying to identify general patterns in media treatment of labor. However, one of the key arguments of this book is that although trends and patterns are useful guides in terms of predicting the larger contours of how the media might cover a strike, it is only through a *concrete* analysis of the *actual* struggle that it becomes possible to understand why certain ideas dominate at the expense of others. In short, while the deck is stacked against labor, I argue that antilabor coverage of strikes is not a fait accompli but rather the product of how the struggle unfolds.

During the course of the UPS strike, UPS and the Teamsters were engaged not only in an economic struggle but also in a battle over ideas in which the interests of labor were pitted against those of corporations. By studying the objective and subjective conditions in which this struggle was fought, this book sets out to explain how the Teamsters won and how the corporate media system can be pressured to represent the interests of labor. Such an analysis is complex and multifaceted. It involves studying objective factors such as the economic, historical, and political conditions in which the strike took place as well as subjective ones such as the level of preparedness of the key actors, their strategies and tactics, the state of public consciousness on economic issues, and so on. For this reason, the book employs an interdisciplinary approach. It draws on the work of economists, political scientists, sociologists, historians, and theorists of the antiglobalization or global justice movement. Such an approach, which situates media coverage of the UPS strike within its larger context, allows us to grapple with the specific ways in which the UPS strike was able to deal an ideological blow to the logic of globalization.

The starting point for this analysis is a concrete examination of the historical conditions that produced the strike. In short, the strike and the issues raised by it are studied within the context of the economy as a whole. Chapter 1 describes the consequences of globalization and neoliberal policy for workers. By looking at the impact of downsizing, wage cuts, attacks on unions, privatization, cuts in social spending, deregulation, and so on, I show how U.S. capitalism regained its competitive edge in the world market at the expense of labor. In telling this story, I have drawn extensively on the work of various economists. Where possible, I have included a flavor of the debates among economists, thus showing why some economic theories are more credible than others.

What became clear to me while doing this research is that when UPS workers went on strike, it was a struggle both against the company and its specific practices as well as the overall strategies of globalization and neoliberalism. The key issues raised by striking UPS workers—part-time employment, stagnant wages, subcontracting, speedups, job safety and health protection, and the pension grab—are not, as I show, unique to UPS. Rather, they are the product of a global corporate strategy, adopted not only by UPS but also by numerous corporations around the world, and workers nearly everywhere have felt the effects of this strategy. This strike therefore serves as a good example of how workers in different corporations scattered geographically across the globe can, by challenging their own employers and building links with other workers, strike a blow against globalization.

Chapter 2 explains why the corporate media system, which has benefited from globalization policies, has tended not to discuss their implications for labor. This reticence is by no means a conspiracy; rather, a for-profit media system is structured to maximize the inflow of revenue and to minimize cost. These priorities translate into a structure and system of organization where the end product, in this case the news, is biased in favor of corporations. Most newspapers have business sections, entire cable channels like CNBC are dedicated to Wall Street coverage, and almost every news outlet has a space for stock market updates and business perspectives on the economy. There are no labor equivalents. A for-profit media system serves not the public interest but the interests of those who make the profits.

However, this chapter also cuts against theories that overemphasize corporate domination and make no space for resistance. Instead, I argue for a model of the media based on a dialectical understanding of the news called the "dominance/resistance model." Since the news is a volatile product, in the process of being made, it is susceptible to various pressures. Under normal conditions, when organized dissent is not present, the news media uphold the status quo. In extraordinary situations, such as mass mobilizations or national strikes, additional, unpredictable pressures come into being. The impact of these pressures cannot be determined in advance. They can be understood only in the concrete context in which the struggle between contending forces takes place, making the news an arena in which the broader struggle is fought out.

Having set up the broad context, chapters 3 and 4 look specifically at how network television and national newspapers covered the strike. Through a textual analysis of 269 news reports on ABC, CBS, and NBC, I show in chapter 3 that the dominant framing mechanism in this strike followed what I call a "nationalist narrative." This narrative, not unique to coverage of the UPS strike, describes American society as a national community whose members are tied together by common economic, social, and political interests. It projects business interests onto the nation by identifying "us" as members of the nation and "them" as the striking workers. The logic of the nationalist narrative, interestingly, runs counter to the economic common sense offered by proponents of globalization. For the most part, free-market ideologues argue that nation-states no longer have the power to control multinational corporations or to insist upon labor and environmental standards. Yet at certain times, such as during strikes, they ask workers to sacrifice for the "national interest." This contradiction conveniently allows capital free rein, while workers have to temper their interests in the name of national well-being. This construction was not uncontested, however. Ron Carey, the president of the Teamsters union, challenged the nationalist narrative by arguing against corporate greed and for a vision of the nation based on cooperation and the sharing of profits. This chapter highlights both the attempt to contain the meaning of the strike within the nationalist narrative and attempts to break out of this frame.

Chapter 4 explores the struggle for ideological hegemony in major national newspapers, particularly the *Washington Post, USA Today,* and the *New York Times.* A detailed analysis of 191 stories published in all three papers reveals that during the first week of the strike (Phase One), the pattern of coverage was consistent with antilabor frameworks. However, during the second week (Phase Two), the *Washington Post* and the *New York Times* switched the tone of their coverage to one that was more inclusive of labor's arguments. Of the three network channels, ABC followed the same pattern as the *Post* and *Times.* After the completion of the strike, in Phase Three, a few stories noted its positive significance for the labor movement. However, as the days passed, there was a decisive movement back toward the status quo.

In sum, out of the six media sources that I studied in detail, three shifted the overall tone of their coverage in Phase Two. In the immediate aftermath of the strike, this limited acknowledgment of labor became more widespread, as radio, television, and local newspapers tried to grapple with the Teamsters' victory and public support. To be sure, media coverage in this period was contradictory: some stories sought to minimize the significance of the strike, while others dealt head-on with issues of inequality in the age of globalization. Nevertheless, it is significant that even the business press recognized that UPS workers had raised legitimate concerns that had larger implications.

Chapter 5 explains how and why this ideological shift in favor of labor took place. It focuses on how the Teamsters and their allies were able to force concessions from the corporate media and to win public support in the battle over ideas. Nothing about this process was automatic. I look at the various aspects that shaped the struggle, such as the Teamsters' and UPS's extent of preparation, their respective internal and external communication strategies, their strategy and tactics, public consciousness in relation to economic issues, the role of solidarity and community support, and the part played by allies on both sides. At the start of the strike, UPS could rely on the corporate media, business ideologues, and politicians, while the Teamsters had the support of other unions, leftist and liberal academics, think tanks, and alternative media. Over the course of the strike, several of UPS's allies would abandon them, thus shifting the balance of power in favor of the Teamsters. By studying the struggle over ideas within a broader historical context, I show that the strike, an act of collective resistance to the policies of globalization, captured the experience of the vast majority of workers in the United States and gave voice to their concerns. The Teamsters won hearts and minds in part because of their interpersonal relationship with the customer base, but in larger part because working people could identify with the strikers. Overall, this chapter explains how the struggle for hegemony was waged during this strike.

Chapter 6 discusses the contributions that this case study makes to the field of media studies. For the reader who is interested in media theory, I strongly recommend this chapter. Other readers might want to skip this chapter and move on to the final chapter. Chapter 6 addresses three areas of scholarly research: cultural studies, liberal theories of the news media, and political economy. Cultural studies, as it emerged in Britain, understood the importance of collective struggle against corporate hegemony. However, the turn toward postmodernism replaced concrete, historical analysis with discursive criticism, and collective struggle with individual textual resistance. Although cultural theorists have acknowledged the limitations of an individualized notion of resistance, I argue that little has been done to rectify the problem and to bring back the vocabulary of collective class struggle, a project that this book takes a step toward.

Liberal theorists of the media, though cognizant of the concentration of media ownership and its detrimental consequences for democracy, tend to assert that the media are, on balance, all right and in need of only minor reforms. Presenting itself as a pragmatic approach to media reform, this approach emphasizes practical solutions. However, as the history of American pragmatism reveals, these "practical" solutions are unfeasible because they go against the logic of the free-market system. The tenets of democracy and the needs of capitalism are fundamentally antithetical, and media reform needs to be thought of within the context of a more fundamental transformation of society.

The area of research that recognizes the contradiction between democracy and capitalism is political economy. However, political economy has tended to focus more on the mechanisms by which the elite control the media and manufacture consent for their policies, and not enough on the role of organized labor in countering and challenging the business assault. The latter is just as important, I argue, if we are to strive for a truly democratic society. Even though, at the time this book was written, unions seemed unable to mount successful challenges to corporate globalization and the proportion of unionized wage workers in the United States had declined to less than 13 percent, the potential of the organized section of the working class to transform society still existed.[8] This is the key lesson of the UPS strike.

Thus, in the final chapter I conclude by drawing the lessons of the UPS strike for the labor movement and for the antiglobalization–global justice movement. The Teamsters showed a way forward for labor in the age of globalization. They also showed that American workers have a role to play in the global struggle against neoliberalism. Too often, activists in the global justice movement have dismissed U.S. workers as being incapable or unwilling to challenge corporate globalization. This strike shows otherwise.

However, at the dawn of the twenty-first century, the corporate assault on the working class continues. Although the labor movement saw other victories in the immediate aftermath of the UPS strike, such as the Bell Atlantic, Bay Area Rapid Transit, and Verizon struggles, it did not reverse the defeats for labor of the past three decades. In each of these cases, future studies might show, media treatment of the strikes was less hostile to labor. At the very least, when the "Teamsters and turtles" united to protest the World Trade Organization (WTO) in 1999, sections of the media did concede some ground to the voices of the global justice movement. However, the leadership of the union movement did not press its advantage, and as a result the neoliberal agenda was reasserted unchallenged.

In 2006, the tide started to turn again when millions of Latino and Latina workers took to the street, protesting racist immigration bills that would criminalize undocumented workers. In so doing, they exposed the hypocrisy of globalization: while corporations freely travel across borders, workers are prevented from doing the same. Some unions have also joined this struggle. Today, the immigrant rights movement has the potential to revitalize the labor movement in the United States.

As I write this preface, workers continue to endure work conditions similar to those of the previous decade. Additionally, social programs that benefit working people, like Medicare, welfare, and Social Security, are under attack, while the wealthy are awarded huge tax breaks. For the first time since the Great Depression, Americans have a net debt, and unemployment is on the rise. In this context, immigrant workers, who bring with them radical traditions of struggle against neoliberalism in various Latin American countries, have shown that workers don't have to take these attacks lying down. In a poetic twist of fate, globalization has come home to the United States.

As the struggle for the rights of immigrant and native-born workers develops in the years to come, I hope that this book will make a small contribution to the process.

Acknowledgments

In the course of researching and writing this book, it became abundantly clear to me that no work of labor, particularly mental labor, is ever the product of just one individual. I have benefited tremendously from the input of many creative, intelligent, and wonderful people. First and foremost, I thank the 185,000 UPS workers who dared go on strike against UPS. Without their efforts this book would never have materialized. It is to them, and the millions of workers before them who have taken on great odds to fight for a better life, that I humbly dedicate this work.

There are two people who have been intimately connected with this project: Carol Stabile and Dana Cloud. Carol's disciplined engagement with my work and her sharp insights have helped me tremendously. Dana gave generously of her time and made valuable contributions to this project at every stage of its development. I thank them both for their confidence in my work and their support, while absolving them of any responsibility for its weaknesses. I also want to thank Richard Oestreicher, Danae Clark, Tom Kane, and Jonathan Sterne.

I have also benefited from the expertise of several individuals who read various chapters. I am grateful to Joel Geier and Jalal Alamgir for their advice on chapter 1, and to Andree Rathemacher for helping me to find several sources and for teaching me the basics of business research. Bill Solomon who read the entire manuscript offered several useful criticisms, particularly of chapter 2. I have presented the research in chapters 3, 4, and 5 at several conferences, and versions of chapters 3 and 4 were published as articles in *Critical Studies in Media Communication* and *Television and New Media.* I am grateful to all involved for their contributions. I want to thank Rand Wilson and Shaun Harkin for reading chapter 5 and for helping to strengthen that chapter. Rand generously made available to me much of the Teamsters' communication materials that I discuss. Douglas Kellner offered several insightful suggestions that have greatly helped the book.

I received three research grants for this project, one from Rutgers University and two from Wake Forest University. The Research and Publication

Fund Award from Wake Forest enabled me to benefit from Julie Edelson's excellent editing and proofreading suggestions. I thank both institutions for their support.

I thank all my friends, my teachers, and my family. I am particularly grateful to my grandmother Kalyanamma, whom I fondly refer to as Amali, for her undying love and encouragement over the years. And finally, I owe a deep debt of gratitude to my partner and collaborator, Nagesh Rao. I thank him for subjecting himself to the painful task of reading the first draft of every chapter and then rereading the chapters again as they went through multiple revisions. He has been a patient editor and has helped me to develop as a writer. Over the years, his keen intellect, sharp wit, and political passion and commitment have been an invaluable influence.

ONE

Globalization and the Media

Globalization and the UPS Strike

Contrary to popular myth, the United States is a society based on vast inequality. The gap between the very rich, who have profited enormously over the last few decades of the twentieth century, and the rest of the populace is truly astounding. In historical terms, the current period parallels the Gilded Age of the late nineteenth century. Characterized by conspicuous consumption, this period marked the heyday of the robber barons, who built mansions and lived like royalty, while the working poor toiled under hazardous conditions for measly wages. The Biltmore estate in Asheville, North Carolina, is an example of the extravagance of those times. Like the mansions on Bellevue Avenue in Newport, Rhode Island, or Long Island's North Shore, the Biltmore estate, modeled on the homes of the European aristocracy, is opulent in the extreme. At a time when most people's homes were yet to be electrified, the estate had a heated indoor swimming pool with an illuminated floor. While hundreds of thousands of children between the ages of ten and fifteen worked in the mines, mills, and factories, the Vanderbilts erected yet another home with 255 rooms.[1]

The Gilded Age has rightly been denounced for its excesses, yet today, under similar conditions, there isn't widespread public acknowledgment that something is wrong. For instance, most tourists who visit the robber barons' estates are encouraged to think of the mansions, and the unequal social relations that correspond to them, as belonging to a bygone era. An unspoken assumption that permeates the air is that while class differences existed a long time ago, today there is far greater equality.

However, a trip to Larry Ellison's San Francisco Bay Area mansion, estimated to be worth one hundred million dollars, will quickly reveal otherwise. Ellison, the CEO of the computer company Oracle, has several homes. The Woodside mansion built on forty-five acres replicates a sixteenth-century Japanese village.[2] Its occupants include Ellison, his wife from a recent marriage, and occasionally his two children—which gives new meaning to the notion that "it takes a village to raise a family." The estate has five guest residences, a forest of cherry trees, streams, waterfalls, ponds, and a lake filled with purified drinking water. Just to maintain the sprawling garden it takes twenty people. Guests are treated like royalty. For instance, they select their food through the click of a mouse, which the numerous house servants then deliver by boat.[3]

The robber barons are back, and extreme differences in wealth are now the order of the day. Economist Paul Krugman argues that the real beneficiaries of the economic growth of the last quarter of the twentieth century are a tiny minority of the population. It is not, as one might expect, the upper 10 percent of U.S. society, but the very top 1 percent. Even among this group, 60 percent of gains went to the top 0.1 percent. In this fortunate group, almost half of the gains found their way to thirteen thousand families, who have almost as much income as the twenty million poorest families.[4]

Any objective evaluation of U.S. census data since the mid-1970s reveals that the gap between the rich and everyone else has widened significantly. Whereas the wealthy have grown rich beyond imagination, most Americans have been working harder for less. Today, the vast majority of people in the United States belong to the working class. Economist Michael Zweig, based on Department of Labor figures, finds that 62 percent of the working population belongs to the working class.[5] Sharon Smith convincingly argues that the figure is upwards of 70 percent of the population.[6] The working-class majority in the United States is extremely diverse, composed largely of white women and people of color.[7] Sociologist Erik Olin Wright shows that close to 60 percent of the working class consists of these groups.[8]

At the lower end of the working class, large numbers of people live in poverty. In 2004, the latest date for which figures are available, thirty-seven million people lived in poverty, an increase of 1.1 million since 2003.[9] In all, 12.5 percent of people in the United States, the world's richest country, live in poverty. Economists argue that the federal poverty line is drawn too low and does not reflect the needs of working families. An Economic Policy Institute study, based on realistic assessments of family expenses, finds that far greater numbers of people are poor. The study estimates that for a family of two adults and two children, annual expenses run between $27,000–$54,000, depending on region. The national median family budget is about $33,500, which is twice the poverty-line figure. The study concludes that at the end of the 1990s, a decade of economic expansion, 29 percent of one- and two-parent families with one to three children did not make enough money to meet the family budget. Almost one in three families of this size cannot meet basic family expenses.[10] The rest of the population has not fared much better, given that the savings rate—the amount of disposable income that is saved—has plummeted to levels last seen during the Great Depression.[11]

The lack of adequate government programs to assist those in need exacerbates economic insecurity in the United States. The limited programs that do exist continue to be eroded. Thus, welfare, or Aid to Families with Dependent Children, was drastically curtailed by the Clinton administration so that today, assistance to poor families is limited to five years. Government medical programs like Medicaid and Medicare are barely adequate to serve the needs of the poor and the elderly. Everyone else is at the mercy of the for-profit health-care system. The growing cost of coverage has fallen on workers so that astounding numbers lack health-insurance coverage: 45.8 million people were uninsured in 2004, which amounted to 15.6 percent of the population.[12] Astronomical medical bills are a key factor in personal bankruptcies. Given this general state of affairs, it is not surprising that between 1988 and 2000, the number of adults taking antidepressant drugs tripled.[13]

At the other end of the spectrum, Dennis Kozlowski, former chairperson of Tyco, a diversified international manufacturing and service corporation, spent $6,000 on a shower curtain, $17,100 for an antique toilet kit, and $15,000 on a poodle-shaped umbrella stand. On his wife's fortieth birthday, he threw a party that cost $2.1 million. This extravagance is not exceptional. As one New York City events planner who serves corporate magnates observed, on average, her clientele spent $1 million on weddings and birthdays.[14] Thus, while a tiny minority lacks for nothing, standards of living for the vast majority of Americans have deteriorated.

Why has this happened? This chapter argues that the depth of class inequality in the United States is the product of a strategy, known as *globalization,* adopted by corporate America in the mid-1970s. Understanding the ways in which capitalism has been reconfigured in the era of globalization is critical to appreciating the causes of the UPS strike. A lot can be said about neoliberal globalization and the ways in which it concentrates power and wealth in the hands of the capitalist class. In this chapter, I will focus only on those aspects that are relevant to this study.

The 1997 UPS Strike: Working Conditions and Management Strategies

Management experts hold up United Parcel Service as a model transportation company. In a 1995 report on the best practices in strategic market management, UPS was described as being on the "front lines of competition."[15] However, the practices that the company has adopted to make it successful have come at a high cost to its employees. If UPS, a corporation with operations in several countries, is a big player on the international scene, it is because its workers have paid a huge price in terms of work conditions and wages. A brief history of the corporation makes clear the mutually antagonistic interests of workers and management.

The company was founded in 1907 as American Messenger Service in Seattle, Washington, by Jim Casey, a nineteen-year-old messenger boy. Casey and a crew of half a dozen on bicycles delivered telegrams, messages, food, and merchandise from local retail stores.[16] A decade later, Casey expanded to California. In 1930, he set up his headquarters in Manhattan, and in 1963 UPS began common carrier service, launching a freight company that specialized in small packages.

To grow from a bicycle delivery service to the digitally coordinated, land- and air-based multinational corporation that it is today, the company adopted several strategies, such as keeping operating costs low while ensuring maximum flexibility. Thus, even in the initial stages, the business was open twenty-four hours a day, seven days a week.[17] While the company's flexibility and efficiency ensured its ability to survive and thrive, they translated into a rigid and controlling workplace for its workers. To be sure, Casey built the success of the company on his workers' loyalty; he even invited the Teamsters union to represent his workers in 1916. However, to ensure that profits remained high, he also adopted the principles of "scientific management" in the 1920s.[18]

Scientific management, or Taylorism, named after its originator, F. W. Taylor, attempts to apply scientific methods to the complex problems of a rapidly growing capitalist enterprise. At its core, it is about effectively controlling labor. It breaks down the production process into distinct, individual parts and then divides them among the workers to minimize time wasted and maximize efficiency. For instance, rather than have one skilled worker produce a chair from start to finish, scientific management suggests that the various tasks involved in chair manufacture be broken down and assigned to several workers, who, working in tandem, could make the chair faster. To this process was added Henry Ford's assembly line, an endless conveyor belt that forced work at a certain pace. Broadly speaking, three principles are at work in implementing scientific management.[19] The first is the process of deskilling; that is, production does not rely on the skills of the workers. The second is the separation of conception from execution; while some do the mental labor, others perform the manual labor. The third is management control over the knowledge of production. This knowledge ensures that managers and supervisors control each step of the labor process, while workers are robbed of autonomy and creativity.

UPS, the "tightest ship in the shipping business," prides itself on its efficiency and employment of scientific management and Fordist principles.[20] Praising UPS's operating methods, Hirshberg et al. write, "Efficiency is the hallmark of UPS. Over the years, UPS developed a comprehensive system of precise operating procedures. Efficiency experts determined how fast drivers should walk (three feet per second), how they hold the van keys (with the middle finger), and even with which foot they should enter the truck (the left). Delivery routes were timed with efficiency in mind."[21]

In addition to delivery, the picking up and sorting of parcels are also carefully calibrated. The workers are then instructed in exactly what is expected of them, and deviations are seldom tolerated.[22] UPS managers and supervisors are entrusted with the task of enforcing workplace rules and making sure that there is little variation from the set pattern of operation. Tim Sylvester, a New York City UPS driver for seventeen years, states that supervisors even go on the routes with the drivers to monitor their activity. He adds that "horror stories abound when it comes to UPS. You can randomly stop UPS drivers anywhere in this country and get similar stories."[23]

Managers willingly adhere to UPS rules because they are rewarded with profit sharing and stock options; these options are generally not available to the workers, resulting in a company where the owners and managers are the same.[24] In addition to enforcing work rules, UPS managers are also instructed to chart worker behavior and determine aspects of their personal lives. Dan La Botz states that managers are given a manual, *Learning to Chart Spheres of Influence*, that instructs them on how to identify informal leaders and how to assess the relationships between various employees. Managers are also asked to find out how workers spend their free time, including the churches they attend, the bars they visit, and the kinds of public transportation they take to work.[25]

Although such methods of ensuring discipline and efficiency are expedient for management, they create a stressful and oppressive environment for workers. C. L. Kane documents the mental and physical stress that he and his coworkers experienced at UPS. We learn about people like Tom Jackson, who started off his career as one of the fastest drivers but ended up needing help from his brother just to complete his route. He suffered several injuries on the job and had to undergo three operations for ruptured and herniated disks. Yet management did not trust Jackson; they visited him at home to check if he was truly in pain and later suspended him for thirty days without pay for having missed too much work. The last time that Kane met Jackson, he was divorced and had started to drink heavily.[26]

Work conditions at UPS have not improved since Kane's book was written. In 1998, UPS worker Robby Hales stated: "Before I started, I always heard it was a real pro-employee place to work. . . . But as profits went up, I guess they've seen more chances to make even more profits. Since I started back then [1986], all I've really seen is immense pressure. . . . It don't matter how much you do or how well you work, it's always never good enough."[27]

In addition to the psychological damage of a stressful workplace, injuries are a regular part of working at UPS. Danny Katch, a part-time UPS Air driver, explains the source of safety problems:

> UPS, like a lot of employers, has hundreds of work rules they expect us to follow. Many of them contradict each other, especially the ones covering safety and the ones covering productivity. If you work safe, they say you're not doing enough stops per hour. If you work fast and get hurt, they say you didn't use proper safety methods. Many of these rules aren't in our contract, but they create an atmosphere where you always feel like if you speak out about something, your manager has some way to nail you.[28]

La Botz and Kane throw light on several severe injury cases. La Botz describes an incident in an Ohio facility, where a worker loading packages suffered a back injury and fell down. Rather than switch off the conveyor belt, the supervisor ordered the workers to continue. The only thing they could do was prevent the packages from falling on the injured man. The man lay there for twenty minutes before he was finally given medical care.

While UPS offers medical benefits, it has done little to address the injury rate at its facilities. On the contrary, it has worked hard to undo Occupational Safety and Health Administration (OSHA) regulations. A study conducted by the International Labor Organization (ILO), a wing of the United Nations, found that UPS violates international standards of occupational safety.[29] The following is an excerpt from its 1997 report on multinational enterprises in the courier-service industry:

Contrary to the principles contained in paragraph 37 of the ILO's Tripartite Declaration which urge multinational enterprises to maintain highest standards of occupational health and safety, UPS had played a significant role recently in seeking to prevent improved safety standards in the domestic workplace. For example, repetitive stress injury (RSI) is regarded as the fastest growing health hazard in the American workplace. To respond to this problem the US Occupational Health and Safety Administration (OSHA) has been working on collecting data on such work-related injuries and has been formulating draft standards or guidelines on ergonomic protection for workers. While, to date, OSHA has only produced an unpublished draft proposal, some members of the US Congress have sought to derail OSHA's efforts by withholding appropriations if they are used by OSHA in connection with this aspect of the agency's work. Many trucking and delivery interests, including UPS and the American Trucking Association, have been among the leading supporters of the Congressional efforts to restrict OSHA's efforts to improve this aspect of workplace safety.[30]

In addition to lobbying against a safer workplace, UPS has sought to employ several cost-saving measures, such as subcontracting, wage freezes, and a tiered workforce. Subcontracting involves employing outside contractors to perform the jobs normally carried out by union members. It relieves the company of paying union wages and benefits and, in some cases, of using company equipment. Another cost-saving strategy is the use of part-time laborers, who are paid almost half the wages of full-timers. This tiered workforce is further segregated: part-timers dominate the sorter jobs (which involves the sorting of parcels), whereas most drivers (who deliver packages) tend to be full-time employees. Prior to the 1997 contract, the hourly wage for full-time sorters, drivers, counter clerks, and vehicle mechanics started at around eleven dollars and in two years reached upwards of nineteen dollars.[31] For part-time employees, wages started at eight dollars an hour and increased to ten dollars. In 1982, the union agreed to freeze the starting wages of part-timers at eight dollars per hour, and they remained at this level, despite inflation, until the 1997 contract. While a starting wage of eight dollars an hour in the early 1980s represented a decent living, when you account for inflation it was barely sufficient to make ends meet in the 1990s.

A number of workers join as part-timers in the hope that they may be promoted to full-time status. However, the trend has been in the opposite direction. Since part-time jobs were first implemented in 1962, the composition of the workforce has changed to 60 percent part-time and 40 percent full-time. Since the 1993 contract, about 83 percent of new unionized jobs were part-time; that is, out a total of 46,000 new hires, only 8,000 were hired full-time.[32] Because the opportunities for full-time jobs are slim, the turnover for part-time workers is high, with as many as three-quarters leaving the company for lack of future prospects.[33] For instance, in 1996, UPS hired 182,000 part-time workers, but by the end of the year, only 40,000 of them remained with the company.[34]

With such a high turnover rate, many UPS workers never qualify for benefits. A study by the Teamsters union found that many part-time jobs could be combined to form full-time positions. Around 10,000 worked more than thirty-five hours a week—the federal figure that classifies them as full-time employees—yet they were still considered part-time by UPS. A Teamsters survey found that 90 percent of part-timers ranked the creation of more full-time jobs as the top bargaining priority.[35]

As the 1997 contract approached, UPS workers found themselves pitted against a multinational corporation whose profits (one billion dollars in 1996) depended on strategies that made their work conditions and wages unacceptable. In particular, they found themselves fighting against the following:

- decreased job security through the creation of more part-time jobs and a tiered workforce
- increased subcontracting
- speedups and Fordist/Taylorist methods to maximize worker efficiency
- decreased workplace safety
- a pension grab (UPS wanted to pull out of the union's multipayer pension plan and replace it with a company plan)

These problems, however, were and are not unique to UPS workers. Rather, as the following sections will argue, they are a symptom of larger trends that have affected workers in the United States and the rest of the world.

Corporate Globalization

Understanding the shifts in the U.S. economy today, and arguably at any point in time, would not be possible without understanding the global economy. Much of this discussion is today taking place under the rubric of "globalization" and what it means for people and the planet. Globalization itself, however, is a much debated concept. Its proponents argue that the global integration of national economies is not only inevitable and automatic but also highly beneficial. They state that the free market guarantees freedom and that by removing obstacles to the flow of finance and trade, countries around the world can prosper. Additionally, since global integration is an automatic and unstoppable process, governments can do nothing to affect it. In short, free trade with limited or no government regulation is the solution to all the world's problems because it creates more jobs at higher wages, leads to greater investment in the environment, automatically raises living standards, and guarantees political freedom.

Politicians and business-oriented academics have vigorously promoted this proglobalization view. In the United States, five Washington-based think tanks have taken the lead: the Heritage Foundation, American Enterprise Institute, Brookings Institution, Cato Institute, and the Institute for International Economics.[36] That these institutions also dominate the discussion in the mainstream media is no coincidence. A study of major newspapers and television and radio transcripts in 1998–99 found that the most quoted think tanks were, in order of prominence, the Brookings Institution, Cato Institute, Heritage Foundation, and the American Enterprise Institute.[37] The Institute for International Economics placed sixteenth on the list. According to this study, taken together, these institutions were cited 7,842 times in 1998 and 7,342 times in 1999. In contrast, center-left and progressive groups like the Center on Budget and Policy Priorities and the Economic Policy Institute were quoted 901 and 995 times in 1998 and 1999, respectively. In all, progressive think tanks make up only 11 and 13 percent of all citations in 1998 and 1999. The proglobalization view, in other words, was given a greater share of time and space in the media during these years.

However, these have not been the only voices on globalization. Several scholars, activists, and journalists have refuted these views based on a study of the actual impact of globalization policy on the world.[38] Perhaps one of the most rigorously researched arguments against the mainstream understanding of the international economy is that put forward by Paul Hirst and Grahame Thompson, who show that its premises are either questionable or downright false. Contrary to the position that global economic integration is a novel development, Hirst and Thompson argue that integration was greater in the period between 1870 and 1914 than it is today. They also maintain that transnational companies (those that transcend nation-states) are rare. Most multinational corporations are nationally based and rely upon the concentration of assets, sales, and production in the home country. Thus, they are not nearly the all-powerful entities, beyond government control, that globalization theorists assert.

Additionally, they argue that the free market system has not led to significant investment in developing nations. Instead, foreign direct investment is
concentrated among the advanced capitalist countries, while the developing
world receives a marginal share. Despite the rise of China, India, Brazil, and
other such non-OECD (Organization for Economic Cooperation and Development) countries, this argument generally remains true, with large sections
of sub-Saharan Africa left to languish. Even in terms of trade, they argue that
developing nations are left out, since the bulk of trade, investment, and finance flows through the triad regions of North America, Europe, and Japan.
Finally, nothing about this process is automatic or ungovernable, since actual
practice shows that global markets are governed by that same triad.

Eric Toussaint similarly argues that globalization is leading to environmental destruction, a growing instability in the financial system, crushing
debt burdens on poor nations, and a deterioration of wages and conditions
for workers all over the world.[39] Joseph Stiglitz, who was chief economist and
senior vice president for the World Bank, changed his views on globalization
after witnessing firsthand what it has done to people around the world. In
his book *Globalization and Its Discontents,* he states, "Globalization today is
not working for many of the world's poor. It is not working for much of the
environment. It is not working for the stability of the global economy."[40] He
adds that although globalization has brought some benefits, international institutions like the International Monetary Fund (IMF), the World Bank, and
the World Trade Organization act in ways that serve the interests of advanced
industrialized nations at the cost of developing nations. He sees a record of
"broken promises" and an utter failure to eradicate poverty and to create generalized well-being.

If globalization, as theory and practice, has failed to make good on its
promises, even by the accounts of insiders like Stiglitz, then what is its real
purpose? Hirst and Thompson argue that it serves the function of a myth emphasizing humanity's "helplessness in the face of contemporary economic
forces."[41] Chris Harman agrees that globalization orthodoxy has been "used
to mean that the world economy has reached a new stage, which governments and workers alike are virtually powerless to withstand."[42]

This myth has been called into question by people's movements around
the world, from the struggle in Chiapas, Mexico, to those in Bolivia, Argentina, and elsewhere. In the United States, the UPS strike showed that American workers have the ability to challenge globalization. Additionally, students at various American colleges joined the antisweatshop movement that
shed light upon the horrendous work conditions that U.S.-based multina-

tional corporations (MNCs) have created for workers around the world. Then in November 1999, the antiglobalization or global justice movement saw its most visible manifestation in the United States when a protest of fifty thousand in Seattle successfully hampered the meeting of the World Trade Organization. Since then, several large demonstrations against the IMF, the World Bank, and other institutions associated with the implementation of corporate globalization have been held in Washington, D.C.; Prague; Millau and Nice, France; Melbourne; Quebec; Genoa; and Cancun. The utter bankruptcy of neoliberalism has also led to large social movements in countries like Argentina, Bolivia, Peru, and Brazil, to name a few.

In the aftermath of the 1999–2001 protests, many scholars, social commentators, and ideologues in the West began to reevaluate the unquestioned faith in the "free market" that had become commonplace after the collapse of the Soviet Union. Francis Fukuyama, author of one of the better-known works of capitalist triumphalism, *The End of History and the Last Man,* had to admit, in an article in *Time,* that there "is plenty about our present globalized economic system that should trouble not just aging radicals but ordinary people as well." He added that "Karl Marx's exhortation 'Workers of the world, unite!' has never seemed more apt."[43] *Business Week* ran a special report titled "Global Capitalism: Can It Be Made to Work Better?" in which the authors, although they defend globalization, concede that too many are being left behind: "The plain truth is that market liberalization by itself does not lift all boats, and in some cases, it has caused severe damage. What's more, there's no point denying that multinationals have contributed to labor, environmental, and human-rights abuses." The report goes on to note that the antiglobalization protests in Seattle, Washington, D.C., and Prague "have helped to kick-start a profound rethinking about globalization among governments, mainstream economists, and corporations that, until recently, was carried on mostly in obscure think tanks."[44]

Thus, the mantra that if countries opened their markets to direct investment and trade, they would experience prosperity, also known as the "Washington consensus," has come under scrutiny as a result of pressure from below. A *Business Week* poll conducted during the Seattle protests found that 52 percent of Americans supported the protestors.[45] An international movement against corporate globalization and the policies of neoliberalism began to develop.[46] As Kevin Danaher and Roger Burbach note, "We can now envision the formation of a truly global movement capable of challenging the most powerful institutions on the planet. . . . The money paradigm that has ruled for so long is now losing public support. . . . [T]he blatant corporate bias of global rule-making institutions such as the IMF, World Bank and WTO have forced the grassroots movement to start planning a global revolution."[47]

In this struggle, the world's working classes have a key role to play. As economist William Tabb observes, only "organized opposition with class-conscious awareness of what is at stake can reverse these developments. The problem is not that we are part of a globalized society, but that we are a part of a global *capitalist* society."[48] The following section will examine the logic and structure of this global capitalist society, with a particular emphasis on the United States.

Class Polarization

It is estimated that the wealthiest 20 percent of the world's population now receives 86 percent of the world's gross domestic product (GDP), the poorest 20 percent receives 1 percent, and the middle 60 percent gets 13 percent.[49] In the United States, a significant number of people have been affected by declining or stagnant wages since the early 1970s, with male workers being affected disproportionately. As table 1 shows, males in the bottom 80 percent have taken cuts in real wages, and overall household income has declined for the bottom 60 percent, despite a greater number of married women entering the workforce. Women with young children, who, in previous decades, had worked primarily at home, became the fastest-growing group entering the paid workforce after the 1970s. By 1993, working women in families contributed 41 percent of the family income, and most families needed two earners, working longer hours, to maintain their living standard.[50] However, as the table shows, it has been a losing battle—only the fourth quintile has experienced positive income growth, whereas for the bottom 60 percent, house-

Table 1. Changes in real wages and income, 1973–92

Quintiles	Males Year-Round (Wages) Full-Time Workers	Household Income
Bottom	–23%	–3%
Two	–21%	–3%
Three	–15%	–0.5%
Four	–10%	+6%
Top	+10%	+16%

Source: U.S. Bureau of the Census, *Current Population Reports: Consumer Income* (Washington, D.C.: Government Printing Office, 1973, 1992), 137, 148. In *The Future of Capitalism: How Today's Economic Forces Shape Tomorrow's World,* by Lester Thurow (New York: William Morrow, 1996), 23.

hold income has continued to fall. The upshot is that most families and individuals are earning less while working longer hours.[51]

A number of economists have arrived at similar conclusions.[52] David Gordon calculated "real spendable hourly earnings," which is the amount left over from a worker's hourly wages after deducting income and Social Security taxes and adjusting for inflation, and concluded that average wages have fallen by nearly 1 percent yearly since the early 1970s. From 1992 to 1997, the year of the UPS strike, the picture did not improve significantly. Wage stagnation and deterioration continued, although wages did improve after 1997. Although the figures show real wages increasing 0.2 percent per year between 1989 and 1996, many economists estimate that this growth is due to longer working hours. When Lawrence Mishel, Jared Bernstein, and John Schmitt factored in these extra hours, they found that real wages actually declined.[53]

The picture is not that different for family income. For instance, between 1989 and 1996 middle-income families took on three extra weeks of work, and for this 3.8 percent increase in the number of hours worked, they received a mere 1.1 percent increase in wages over seven years. Mishel, Bernstein, and Schmitt conclude that until 1997, wages and income decreased, while working hours increased.[54] Furthermore, job security lessened, and groups who had previously not seen wage drops, such as middle-wage women, college-educated workers, and white-collar workers, were no longer spared.

For a few years after 1997, wages went up modestly. However, since 2000 real median household income has fallen for five years in a row.[55] In contrast, the fortunes of the wealthy have soared. In 1978, the ratio of CEO to worker salary was 28.5 to 1; by 1997, it was 115.7 to 1.[56] In other words, a CEO worked half a week to earn what an average worker earned in fifty-two weeks. Another estimate puts the wage differential in the late 1990s at 531 to 1.[57] Paul Krugman shows that in the 1970s, the average real compensation of CEOs of the top one hundred corporations was thirty-nine times the pay of the average worker. In 2002, these CEOs earned one thousand times the average worker's pay.[58] If that was not enough, in 2005 their incomes soared again, increasing by 25 percent over the previous year.[59]

Income and salary, however, do not tell the whole story. This rise in inequality and class polarization is seen most clearly in wealth distribution. Wealth is defined as the value of assets minus liabilities divided by debt. At the end of the 1980s, the "greed decade," the total wealth of the top 1 percent of society was greater than it had been in the previous sixty years.[60] Between 1983 and 1989, the top 20 percent of wealth holders received 99 percent of the total wealth gain. The trend continued in the 1990s. In 1995, the top 1 percent held 39 percent of total wealth, and the top 20 percent 84 percent of all wealth.[61] The other 80 percent of American society held a grand total of 16 percent of all wealth.

This gap is even more stark when one examines financial assets, where the top 1 percent control 47.2 percent, while the bottom 90 percent have 17.1 percent. The richest 10 percent almost exclusively own income-generating assets like stocks, bonds, private business equity, and other financial assets, whereas the type of wealth held by the bottom 90 percent primarily consists of homes and life insurance.[62] Thus, the economic growth of the 1980s and 1990s, reflected in GDP increases, accrued to the wealthiest. Commenting on this situation, Lester Thurow states, "At no other time since data have been collected have American median real male wages consistently fallen for a two-decade period of time. Never before have a majority of American workers suffered real wage reductions while the real per capita GDP was advancing. Something very different was at work in the American economy."[63]

There are several explanations of what was at work in the American economy. Gordon points to the two standard ways of explaining the wage squeeze: skills mismatch and globalization. The skills-mismatch theory tries to explain a decline in wages in terms of supply and demand, claiming that low-skilled workers outnumber demand and that advanced technologies, such as computers, have left many workers behind. The second argument claims that in a globalized economy, as companies move to countries with cheaper labor costs, U.S. workers have to either grant concessions to their employers or risk the wholesale loss of jobs. Gordon rejects these prevailing explanations, based on traditional neoclassical economic theories of market competition, because they blame the victims while shielding corporations. He adds that as more economists reject the traditional explanations, they have been able to "lift the veil on corporations and to examine directly their preferences, strategies, and actions about wages." Such an examination, according to Gordon, reveals a conscious "management offensive," an all-out corporate attack on the working class.[64] Doug Fraser, president of the United Auto Workers (UAW), declared in 1978 that a "one-sided class war" was being waged by the employing class.[65] This war involved not only wage cuts but also speedups, loss of pensions and benefits, layoffs, the creation of tiered workforces, and various government policies aimed at slashing social programs.

The Employers' Offensive

During the 1950s and 1960s, the "golden age" of the American economy, all measures of prosperity were high. The gross domestic product grew by 5.25

percent a year in the 1960s, productivity grew by 2.9 percent a year,[66] and between 1950 and 1965 the average weekly earnings for manufacturing workers rose by 84 percent.[67] This context allowed President Kennedy to talk about a "rising tide, raising all boats," although certainly not everyone benefited from the postwar boom—racism prevented the advancement of African Americans and other minorities, and, even at that point, poverty was not eliminated.

However, after 1965, profits began to decline and failed to recover their peak levels. As a result, the net investment in plants and equipment fell, and productivity suffered.[68] At the same time, American capital lost ground in the global economy. The U.S. share of world trade declined 16 percent between 1960 and 1970 and by 1980 fell another 23 percent. Whereas in 1959 111 of the top 156 multinational corporations were U.S. based, by 1976 only 68 U.S. firms were among the top 156.[69] The relative decline of U.S. capital and global hegemony was further exacerbated when the Bretton Woods agreement collapsed in 1971.[70]

In the face of this crisis, U.S. capital desperately needed a new strategy, which, I will argue, was two-pronged. The first part of the strategy involved state intervention in the creation of conditions favorable for capital (neoliberalism), and the second was internal corporate restructuring. Together, this dual strategy has created the present globalized economy. This is not to suggest that a global capitalist economy is a new phenomenon. Capitalism has been a global system for a substantial part of its history.[71] Rather, this is an argument for a particular understanding of globalization as the restructuring of capitalism based on a management offensive, which runs counter to the fatalistic view of globalization as the inevitable internationalization of capital led by technological development. I use the term *globalization* in this sense to avoid the theoretical ambiguity associated with it. As Doug Henwood correctly points out:

> I think [the term *globalization* is] very imprecise and used to mean many things. On the left, "globalization" is used instead of "capitalism," or "imperialism," or some combination of the two. In some ways this is an uncritical embrace of vocabulary that comes out of the ruling class. Look at the World Bank or mainstream pundits; they all talk about the "inevitability of globalization." Many on the left just take that term—whatever exactly it means—and put negative signs in front of it. They don't really sort through what the term itself means or what the critical approach of an oppositional movement should be.[72]

I have tried to avoid an uncritical use of the term, instead using it to discuss the changes in capitalism prompted by particular and *conscious* strategies used by capitalists and the state to regain profitability over the last quarter of the twentieth century. It is beyond the scope of this chapter to discuss all the changes in capitalism over this period; rather, I will focus on the key aspects that have had a devastating impact on labor.

Daniel Singer explains the process of globalization as the calculated attempt by the capitalist class "to impose and extend the rule of capital on a world scale." Specifically, he suggests that "globalization is a response to the crisis [of the early 1970s]. Faced with the declining rate of profit on the one hand, and the crumbling of a monetary mechanism resting on the absolute, unquestioned hegemony of the United States on the other [Bretton Woods], capital took to the offensive on both fronts. Restructuring and globalization are twin weapons wielded by a capitalism struggling to recover its raison d'être, its very essence—profitability."[73] It is no coincidence, Singer continues, that the ideas of economists such as Friedrich von Hayek and Milton Friedman, who preached the virtues of free enterprise and a market guided by the invisible hand, became fashionable when the last attempts to restore profitability through government expenditure failed and resulted in stagflation (a slowdown in production and increased inflation).

The resulting neoliberal doctrine led to an attack on government interference in the market through regulation on public forms of ownership, cuts in social spending, and increased tax cuts for corporations. This attack on government interference, however, is more rhetorical than real, since governments all over the world have played an active part in promoting neoliberal policies. For Eric Toussaint, "Globalization is not a purely economic process. It has been dramatically accelerated by policies consciously pursued by a growing number of governments in the wake of the Reagan and Thatcher experiences in the early 1980s."[74] In other words, without the active collusion and intervention of various governments, the project of neoliberalism would not have been realized.[75]

The policy of neoliberalism, adapted to various national contexts, has taken different forms and proceeded at different paces. For instance, the United States lifted all restrictions on the movement of capital in 1974, but Britain did the same only in 1979, under Margaret Thatcher. In developing countries, neoliberal policies have been forcibly introduced through the World Bank and the IMF in arrangements tied to financial-aid packages.

The American version of globalization, the "American model" or the "Washington consensus," crafted during the mid-1970s and realized by the 1990s, sought to restore profitability on the back of labor. In 1974, *Business Week* summarized the crisis of world capitalism and the U.S. solution:

The U.S., like the world around it, is in sad shape today. Having borrowed too much in the expectation of perpetual plenty, Americans are desperate for answers to questions for which there are no pat answers. . . . Some people will obviously have to do with less, or with substitutes, so that the economy as a whole can get the most mileage out of available capital. . . . Yet it will be a hard pill for many Americans to swallow—the idea of doing with less so that big business can have more. It will be particularly hard to swallow because it is quite obvious that if big business and big banks are the most visible victims of what ails the Debt Economy, they are also in large measure the cause of it. . . . Nothing that this nation, or any other nation, has done in modern economic history compares in difficulty with the selling job that must now be done to make people accept the new reality.[76]

To meet the challenge of selling this "new reality" and to craft a new economic agenda, business required a new strategy. This led to the growth of think tanks and political action committees, the further expansion of the public relations (PR) industry, and the formation or revival of various business organizations.[77]

The Business Roundtable led this effort. Founded in 1972, the Roundtable was an activist organization consisting of more than 1,000 firms led by representatives of 125 corporations in finance, industry, and commerce. The Roundtable and other probusiness think tanks arrived at an agenda for the decade that included labor-law reform, deregulation, restraints on government spending, and the restructuring of the tax system to benefit corporations.[78] A good deal of this agenda was accomplished under President Carter, when Democrats controlled both houses of Congress. However, President Reagan can be credited with bringing a new zeal to the implementation of policy that favored business and crushed labor. His administration's economic policies decisively shifted the balance of power to the employing class, as the labor movement simultaneously was crippled by the conservatism of its leadership.[79]

Corporate America's response to the structural crisis of capitalism consisted of two related aspects. The first focused on measures that the state could enact, such as deregulation, privatization, rolling back labor-movement gains, cutting social spending, and increasing tax breaks to corporations (neoliberal policy). The second was a shift within corporations to "lean" production.

Neoliberal Policy

In the mid-1970s, as *Business Week* put it, workers were going to have to make do with less so that business could have more. Following this prescription, the government reduced spending on social programs and increased tax breaks for business. In 1978, Congress passed a tax-reform bill that cut capital-gains taxes by 40 percent, while Social Security, a regressive tax where everyone pays the same amount, increased substantially, and income over a certain amount was not taxed.[80] The highest marginal income tax rates for the richest individuals, which were 95 percent in the 1950s and 70 percent in 1980, fell to 38.5 percent in the early part of the twenty-first century due to the Bush administration's tax reforms. Thus, whereas taxes on corporations and the wealthy decreased, those on the average person increased.[81] Using figures from the Internal Revenue Service, journalists Donald Barlett and James Steele show that in the 1950s, the corporate share of total income taxes collected in the United States was 39 percent; by the 1980s, it had dropped to 17 percent.[82] By 2003, corporate taxes fell to 7.4 percent of government receipts. A study by the General Accounting Organization found that 61 percent of U.S.-owned companies and 71 percent of foreign-owned firms paid no taxes in the United States from 1996 to 2000.[83] At the same time as the corporate share of the tax burden was being lowered, welfare payments were also under the chopping block. They dropped under Carter, fell even more during the Reagan-Bush era, and were slashed during the Clinton administration.

Privatization schemes have been less drastic in the United States than in other parts of the world, as its public sector is marginal. The little that is publicly owned—the airwaves, schools, and public services such as welfare and health care—has been or is in the process of being privatized. Deregulation began with the airline industry in 1978, trucking in 1980, and telecommunications in the 1980s and 1990s. UPS lobbied hard for trucking deregulation.[84] Large corporations have been the prime beneficiaries of this process. They seized this opportunity to consolidate by either buying up or merging with smaller or equivalent corporations. Contrary to the claim that deregulation would spur competition in a "free" market and therefore reduce prices for consumers, precisely the opposite has occurred. For instance, deregulation depressed competition in the airline industry, and ticket prices have gone up, particularly in cities where a single airline has a stronghold.[85] The media industry has also benefited tremendously from privatization and deregulation, a point to which I will return in the next chapter.

While large and multinational corporations have benefited from privatization and deregulation, the same cannot be said for workers. Stanley C. Wisniewski notes that in the telecommunication industry, privatization and deregulation have led to "massive lay-offs and dislocation, and there has been a serious erosion in worker morale associated with potential job insecurity.

Similarly, fundamental restructuring in the transportation industries has produced major dislocation, wage cuts and job insecurity which has placed the burden of such 'privatization' squarely on the shoulders of employees."[86] While corporate profits have grown, the employment conditions for workers have deteriorated. The deregulation process has also created the conditions for overproduction.

These neoliberal policies have been enthusiastically supported by Democrats and Republicans alike, who have passed legislation favorable to business, marginalizing and even subverting the interests of labor in the process. For instance, the Carter administration targeted labor income as one of the causes of rising inflation, despite the fact that labor costs had, in fact, declined throughout the 1970s.[87] In 1978, the administration issued a wage and price guideline that pressured unions to refrain from "pattern bargaining," a practice by which the contract reached with one employer in a particular industry becomes the standard for others. Under Reagan, collective bargaining received a further blow: the 1981 firing of air traffic controllers represented by the Professional Air Traffic Controllers Organization (PATCO) sent a clear signal that the administration would aid business by undermining labor.

In addition to these legislative changes, corporate America learned that it had to reorganize itself from within to better compete internationally and boost profitability. The restructuring process emphasized "flexibility" and adopted a mode of capitalist exploitation called "lean production." Ideologically, this shift put an end to some of the concessions granted to labor in the 1950s and 1960s. During the postwar boom era, labor could expect wage increases tied to productivity and state-subsidized home ownership and higher education programs, but not after the early 1970s.[88]

A telling indication of this shift was the success and proliferation of union-busting agencies. Union-busting firms were active in the 1950s, but they were not very pervasive. In the 1970s, these firms grew and were sabotaging most union organizing drives. By 1979, more than one thousand antilabor consulting firms were earning an estimated half-billion dollars.[89]

At the same time, management sought to elicit as many concessions as possible from unions. These concessions were consistent with the management logic of "teams," whereby management and unionists supposedly united to make the firm more efficient and profitable. At its core, lean production was about reorganizing the system of production materially and ideologically so that the balance of power would shift more decisively toward the employing class. This paradigm stands in contrast to the postwar years, when union leadership could expect a less hostile employer and unionized workers saw real wage increases. In the aftermath of the crisis of the 1970s, the rising tide would not again lift all boats.

Corporate Restructuring

The scramble to regain profitability led to the restructuring of capital both internally and externally. External changes associated with the supply of services and products are referred to as lean production, whereas internal changes are marked by the shift to "teams" and the concept of teamwork.

Lean Production

Lean production is associated most closely with the automobile industry, but it has also been adopted by a wide range of firms involved in both goods manufacturing and services, from Xerox, Honeywell, Best Foods, and General Electric to AT&T and UPS. Lean production originated in Japan in the post–World War II era after militant trade unions had been successfully beaten down. The system's supporters claim that it is an efficient, decentralized method of organization that allows for maximum flexibility based on cooperation and mutual respect between workers and managers. Critics point out that although it has reduced costs and improved flexibility for corporations, it has also increased class polarization and involuntary contingent employment. Furthermore, the Japanese model did not and could not come into existence until the militant trade unions had been defeated; that is, it is predicated on labor's acquiescence to management's goals. Much has been written about this new mode of capitalist organization and how corporations in Europe and the United States have selectively adapted it, both by advocates[90] and by critics.[91]

Economist Bennet Harrison suggests that the restructuring that occurred after the 1970s developed a tiered system of production. Large firms entered into alliances and deals with governments, smaller firms, and one another, creating a network of suppliers and subcontractors. The result was a decentralized network that has been compared to a web with the core firm as its spider. Tasks once performed by the core firm are delegated, or outsourced (which is a method of busting unions), to other contractors, establishing several tiers, with work conditions deteriorating down the tiers. In such a tiered, decentralized network, the core firm becomes more "flexible," that is, it can adapt more easily to market changes. Note that decentralization does not loosen power hierarchies and decision-making abilities; rather, suppliers are under the direct control of the core firm without the core incurring their economic responsibilities. Harrison describes the process as follows:

According to a central tenet of best-practice flexible production, managers first divide permanent ("core") from contingent ("peripheral") jobs. The size of the core is then cut to the bone—which along with the minimization of inventory holding, is why "flexible" firms are often described as practicing "lean" production. These activities, and the employees who perform them, are then located as much as possible in different parts of the company or network, even in different geographic locations.[92]

The process of cutting down personnel, or downsizing, is central to the system's leanness. Thus, once the core has been determined, all the other jobs are delegated or contracted out. For instance, in 1980, Toyota had 168 first-tier subcontractors, 4,700 second-tier subcontractors, and 31,600 suppliers in the third tier.[93] The footwear company Nike is headquartered in the United States but at the bottommost level has suppliers who run sweatshops in Indonesia, China, and other developing nations. Nike's success has prompted other shoe companies, such as Vans and Adidas, to follow a similar path.[94] However, this method of production has not been applied uniformly. The tiered workforce at UPS, for instance, is grouped in a single location: permanent part-timers work alongside shrinking numbers of full-time workers. Additionally, key aspects of UPS's services, particularly parcel delivery, cannot be outsourced to workers in distant locations.

This tiered system relies on information technology (IT) that enables core firms to coordinate activities both within their firms and with suppliers. Contrary to the claims of technological determinism, however, most of this technology did not exist when the lean-production model was first developed. Rather, the growth in information technology was fueled by a system that moved beyond Japan and into the West and created a demand for computer software, distance applications, and consistent platforms.[95] As we shall see in chapter 2, the media and information industries have been central to the coordination of multinational corporations.

Additionally, advances in transportation have allowed a practice known as "just-in-time." Contractors can deliver parts and supplies to the core plant as needed, reducing the cost of inventory and preventing excess production. Wisniewski notes:

> Enterprises have sought to simplify their distribution activities worldwide by using only a few delivery modes. Some have resorted to contracting out their entire distribution activities to fully integrate transport companies. As a result, "logistics" constitute an increasingly important segment of the operations of integrators. UPS's five year US $1 billion contract with J. C.

Penney is illustrative of this. Companies can hire a single carrier to handle all of their transportation and warehousing needs.[96]

Furthermore, UPS has carefully positioned itself to cater to regional trading blocs. It introduced a just-in-time logistics management service called "Inventory Express," in which it took responsibility for storing and then shipping merchandise based on the needs of the customer. A more extensive version is called "Worldwide Logistics," wherein UPS not only stores and ships but also performs various services, such as tracking, order processing, and negotiating rates, based on the needs of the corporations that hire them.[97] UPS's new slogan, "Moving at the speed of business," reflects its willingness and ability to meet the needs of restructuring.

It also formed a digital cellular network in the early 1990s, taking advantage of the developments in information technology to make its transportation services more time sensitive.[98] In the process, UPS was able not only to meet the needs of multinational corporations but also to establish itself as an MNC with offices all over the world. Information technology has been vital to this process. UPS both uses IT and provides it to its customers, thus integrating the needs of communication and transportation.[99] By 2003, the trade publication *Traffic World* declared that UPS had established itself as one of two "logistics heavyweights that will continue to dominate global markets." A study on global logistics service providers concluded that the "major package integrators, FedEx, UPS and DHL/Deutsche Post, have led the way in globalization."[100]

As the means of communication and transportation have developed in response to business needs, so has the ability of core firms to seek out suppliers in geographically distant locations, which has given rise to a regional, cross-border production system. The clearest examples are the auto industries in North America, Japan, and western Europe, which have contracted out to neighboring countries. North American auto manufacturers have outsourced to Mexico and South American countries; Japan to South Korea, Taiwan, Indonesia, Malaysia, and the Philippines; and western European companies to Hungary, Poland, and the Czech Republic.[101] International agencies, such as the IMF, World Bank, or WTO, as well as regional trade agreements like the North American Free Trade Agreement (NAFTA), European Union, and Association of Southeast Asian Nations have worked to create favorable conditions for large, first-world multinational corporations and their "strategic alliances" in developing countries. However, these trends should not be exaggerated. For instance, some theorists of globalization have written about the proliferation of the "global assembly line" and the ease of "capital mobility" on an international scale. Although some of this internationalization has taken place, it is important to note that it has occurred at the same time as outsourcing has increased *within* advanced capitalist countries, with corporations moving away from regions with high unionization to those with low unionization.

The upshot of this process is that working conditions and wages have deteriorated. Many people have been forced to accept contingent work—about 25 percent of the total workforce, of which 80 percent are part-time employees. Chris Tilly, who has conducted extensive research on part-time employment, shows that the rise in part-time work since the early 1970s is due to the increase in *involuntary* part-time jobs. In 1993, 5.5 percent of all workers were engaged in such involuntary part-time work; many held more than one job. Though this percentage of the workforce is still small, it should not be discounted, as it indicates a possible future trend. Additionally, the number of involuntary part-time workers would be considerably higher if those considered "voluntary," such as women who also have to care for their children or elderly family members (women make up a significant portion of part-time workers), had access to quality care facilities that gave them the option of full-time work.

Tilly's explanation for the rise in involuntary part-time jobs echoes Harrison's:

> First, the industry composition of employment has shifted away from manufacturing and toward industries such as trade and services that employ a larger number of part-timers. These industries use so many part-time workers because they are predominantly made up of firms that have adopted a low-wage, low-skill, high-turnover secondary labor market. Second, more jobs within almost every industry have been absorbed into this type of labor market. These changes have swelled the ranks of part-time workers even though the workforce's desire for part-time jobs has not kept pace, resulting in the growth of involuntary part-time employment.[102]

As Tilly notes, while manufacturing jobs have decreased, those in the trade and service sector have increased. For example, whereas in 1940 goods-producing jobs accounted for 40 percent of the workforce, by 1980 they accounted for 28 percent[103] and at the turn of the century 18 percent.[104] However, this decline in the percentage of workers involved in production should not be read as a reduction in industrial output, since manufacturing production has actually tripled since the 1950s.[105] Additionally, the actual number of workers involved in production has not changed much since 1950, ranging between 11 million and 14 million.[106] What we have witnessed is not so much a process of "deindustrialization," if the term is understood to mean a reduction in industrial and manufacturing production, but rather fewer workers working harder. Today, following the logic of lean production, fewer, more productive workers are concentrated in smaller workplaces that tend to be located in regions where unionization is low. While the core is cut to the bone and employees worked to the maximum, other peripheral jobs, such as catering, cleaning, security, and accounting, financial, and legal services, are either contracted out or performed at another location by lower-paid and, in some cases, part-time workers.

There are several connections between the decrease in manufacturing jobs and the increase in service jobs. The continued global expansion of goods-producing industries over the past two decades has required the services discussed above. Historically, the rise of service employment has been a function of industrial development. For instance, in the mid-1980s, the federal government reported that fully 25 percent of the U.S. gross national product originates in services that are used as inputs by goods-producing industries.[107] Furthermore, the tendency to reduce the number of workers involved in production is endemic to the capitalist system. As Karl Marx points out in *Capital,* in order to stay competitive the capitalist is driven to increase worker productivity through investment in the means of production and technology. In the process, the number of workers can be reduced. Lean production is only the latest strategy to achieve this aim.

The rise in service-sector jobs is also part of a system that seeks to bring everything under the reign of profit; therefore, services once performed in a nonmarket sphere become commodified. The decline in manufacturing jobs and the increase in service jobs, far from marking the end of the working class, as some have claimed, are products of capitalist restructuring and changes in the occupational character of working-class jobs.

Teamwork

In addition to external restructuring into networks, corporations have adopted internal changes, such as the team concept. It reorganizes work on the shop floor but also has an ideological dimension: it is management's effort to win employees to the corporation's mission. Although application has varied across firms, some of its core features are (1) to organize workers into teams with leaders (either unionists or supervisors), who then meet constantly to discuss how they can improve efficiency and reduce defects (referred to as *kai-*

zen); (2) to encourage workers to perform each other's jobs so that they can be interchangeable *(multiskilling)*; and (3) to create an atmosphere of mutual respect between workers and management, where both groups are asked to maintain a polite and cheerful demeanor.

Those who favor the team concept view it as a more humane alternative to the Fordist mass-production system.[108] In the Fordist system, management holds all knowledge of the process, and workers are reduced to appendages of the machine. Based on Frederick Taylor's principles of "scientific management," Fordism relies on time and motion studies to calculate workers' every movement. In contrast, by giving workers control over their jobs and the production process, lean production supposedly transcends Fordism.

In reality, however, lean production strips workers' control over the shop floor.[109] As Mike Parker and Jane Slaughter argue, "teams" are not really teams at all, but a way for management to elicit knowledge from workers without giving them control over the production process. They suggest that a more apt description of lean production is "management-by-stress," where every phase of the production process, including workers, is stretched to the breaking point. It uses as few materials as possible, and workers must work as fast as they can to make up for their inadequate numbers. Peer pressure is enormous, because if one worker slows or stops the production process, all the other workers are adversely affected.[110]

This process is very much like the UPS assembly line, which does not stop even when workers are injured.[111] In 1995, to win the consent of workers for this scheme and to introduce further changes, UPS implemented the team concept. For UPS it was a way to replace the seniority system with management favoritism and to change workplace rules without involving union leadership.[112] Additionally, working in teams would have meant that instead of facing pressure from the supervisor, UPS workers would have been putting pressure on each other. As Cindy Ward, a UPS worker in Phoenix, put it, "Before it was the supervisor giving stupid orders, you'd get mad at the supervisor." But "now you had other workers with less seniority telling you what to do."[113] The union, however, rejected this effort, and UPS was forced to abandon it.

Nonetheless, many other unionized and nonunionized workplaces suffer under the tyranny of the team concept. As Parker and Slaughter argue, "Management-by-stress is truly a lean and mean system. In tightly connecting all operations, consciously seeking to strip out all protections and cushions, and making all parts of the system almost instantly responsive to change, management-by-stress becomes a highly efficient system for carrying out management policy." If anything, Fordism is elevated to a higher status under the lean-production system. For instance, the process of "multiskilling" breaks down functions into smaller and smaller units that require little skill and can be accomplished in the least time and with the least motion. As Parker and Slaughter note, "Far from a repudiation of scientific management, management-by-stress intensifies Taylorism."[114]

James Rinehart, Christopher Huxley, and David Robertson sought to test the argument that lean production represents a break from Fordism by studying CAMI, a General Motors (GM)–Suzuki joint venture in Ontario, Canada. They found that although on the surface lean production appears to significantly differ from mass production in terms of its techniques, in substance these changes do not transcend mass production. Instead, they "are more appropriately regarded as supplements to or refinements of Fordism."[115] They conclude that the term *post-Fordism* is a misnomer in describing the lean-production system.

At the end of day, capitalism's search for profitability has led to the adoption of structural changes and ideologies like teamwork that attempt to mask the exploitation at the core of the system. As Harrison observes, "Lean production, downsizing, outsourcing, and the growing importance of spatially extensive production networks governed by powerful core firms and their strategic allies, here and abroad, are all part of business' search for 'flexibility,' in order to better cope with heightened global competition. But this very search for flexibility is also aggravating an old American problem—economic and social dualism."[116]

Thus, the very process that capital needs to strengthen itself—that is, globalization as a policy involving government-enforced laws and corporate restructuring—is undermining its foundation by exacerbating class polarization. This contradiction has resulted in a growing anger toward corporations that found expression in the many bitter struggles of the early 1990s. A *Business Week* cover story titled "Too Much Corporate Power?" found that 80 percent of survey respondents stated that corporations have too much power.[117] Although the number of strikes and other conflicts is low, generalized discontent over corporate America's priorities is growing.

Labor's Tame Response

In the context of growing class polarization and class anger, organized labor is well positioned to counter globalization through strikes and other job actions. Yet labor's response to management's offensive has been less than adequate, allowing the class war to remain, as UAW president Doug Fraser inadvertently yet prophetically put it, "one-sided." The union leadership bears much of the responsibility for this state of affairs. For instance, shortly after denouncing the corporate community, Fraser would concede to the terms of the 1978 Chrysler bailout. While the autoworkers were asked to accept wage and benefit cuts, Fraser got a seat on Chrysler's board of directors.[118] This disjuncture between the leadership of the union movement and the rank-and-file workers explains the lackluster fight that has been waged against globalization. The union bureaucracy's unwillingness to hold corporations accountable follows from the fact that they are not impacted by the terms of the contract they negotiate for their members. Unless pressed by the rank and file, they would rather not rock the boat. This is the legacy of "business unionism," a form of unionism that is based on a business model in which revenues are kept high, risks (such as strikes) are avoided, and the price of labor is negotiated with capital under amicable conditions.[119]

Through much of the 1980s and '90s, in the absence of rank-and-file pressure, the labor bureaucracy conceded to the employers' various demands from "partnership" to "teamwork" and the logic of lean production. Labor's timidity meant that by the late 1980s, almost 75 percent of all contracts covering one thousand or more workers included concessions, and the figure was 90 percent for manufacturing workers.[120] If the Chrysler bailout indicated labor's willingness to acquiesce to capital, PATCO showed that management would use any means necessary to achieve its goals. Labor was unprepared to meet the new challenge, clinging instead to the "social contract" ideology of the 1950s and '60s, when unions and management were supposedly involved in a mutually beneficial relationship. Yet, as Nelson Lichtenstein argues, the working class did not really benefit from this "labor-management accord." Although real wages did increase, strikes were ten times more prevalent during that time than after 1980. This is because the rise in wages during the postwar years did not compensate for the increase in productivity. Instead, the vast profits generated by highly productive workers went into the coffers of the capitalist class.[121]

Lichtenstein also argues that the current offensive on labor has its roots in the post–World War II era, when business leaders sought to overturn the gains made by the labor movement in the 1930s and erase from public consciousness any memory of that period.[122] It was in this context that the antiunion Taft-Hartley Act was passed. Couched as a way to rid labor of the "domination" of communists, Taft-Hartley was actually a means by which the Wagner Law and the Norris–La Guardia Anti-Injunction Act, both labor victories of 1930s, were overturned. The Taft-Hartley bill put into place a number of antiunion policies. For instance, it made it possible for employers to break strikes through injunctions against picketing, to refuse to bargain collectively, and to even shut down plants to postpone negotiations. It also put a halt to the practice of sympathy strikes, where workers could strike in solidarity with other workers. Labor's failure to overturn Taft-Hartley, and its willing cooperation with management's postwar agenda, laid the basis for a weakened labor movement that was unable to counter management's renewed offensive during the era of globalization.

To make matters worse, as Sharon Smith argues, labor's political strategy of supporting the Democratic Party has been a dead end. After twelve years of Republican rule, when Bill Clinton was sworn into office in 1992, labor believed that it had an ally in the White House. However, the Clinton administration enthusiastically pursued globalization policies. Despite its many betrayals of promises made to labor, including the passage of NAFTA against labor's wishes, the labor movement continued to support the Democratic Party. Though some in the union leadership have publicly acknowledged the weaknesses of this strategy, they have not reversed their general position. In the lead-up to the 2004 elections, Andrew Stern, president of the Service Employees International Union and head of the New Unity Parnership, voiced modest criticisms of the Democrats. Yet Stern and the American Federation of Labor and Congress of Industrial Organizations (AFL-CIO) would continue to back the pro-neoliberal Democratic Party, sinking tens of millions of dollars into the elections. Overall, the strategy of partnership with management combined with support for the Democratic Party has had a debilitating impact on unions.[123]

Within the Teamsters union, these problems are compounded by the long history of ties to organized crime and rampant corruption. Steven Brill, in his book *The Teamsters,* reveals in some detail the sordid history of the union. For instance, President Frank Fitzsimmons had "limousines, a private jet, servants and chefs . . . an unlimited expense account that provided him and his family first-class entertainment and travel," paid for by the rank and file.[124] Additionally, several leaders had ties to organized crime. Jimmy Hoffa, who was later allegedly murdered by mobsters, played a large part in opening the doors of the union to organized crime. When Ron Carey was elected president of the union in 1991, he inherited a union fraught with violence, corruption, and unaccountability (see the interview with Carey in the appendix).

Although reformers like Carey have done much to overcome the pitfalls in the labor movement, rank-and-file workers have led the way through their actions. In the late 1960s and early 1970s, groups of workers in various industries came together to challenge the corporate agenda. Black autoworkers fought against speedups and racial discrimination. They stood up not only to the big three automakers but also against racism within the UAW.[125] The Dodge Revolutionary Union Movement started in Detroit and inspired rank-and-file black workers to form similar groups elsewhere and engage in unauthorized wildcat strikes.[126] In almost all industries, wildcat strikes grew during the 1960s and reached a high point in 1970.[127] Even the Teamsters went out on strike and stayed out for a whole month after Fitzsimmons ordered them back to work.

In 1972, Miners for Democracy elected a reform candidate for president, and in 1975 Teamsters for a Decent Contract (which would become Teamsters for a Democratic Union [TDU]) was formed. However, by the end of the 1970s, this rank-and-file upsurge, and labor militancy in general, would slow considerably.[128] For instance, in 1974 there were 424 strikes and lockouts.[129] By 2003, the number of work stoppages went down to 14.[130] This decline in rank-and-file activity is the product of a number of factors such as the destruction of the labor Left by McCarthyism in the 1950s, the hesitancy of the New Left of the 1960s to form links with labor, the lack of forces that could bring together the various rank-and-file efforts of the 1970s, and the extirpation of labor traditions from the history and memory of the working class.[131]

However, the 1980s and '90s did see some successes. Coal operators in West Virginia, after an eleven-month strike, were able to defeat many of the demands for concessions. Carey, a reform candidate, with the help of TDU, became president of the Teamsters in 1991. In 1995, John Sweeney, who ran on the promise of reforming the union movement, was elected to the presidency of the AFL-CIO. Although Sweeney has made a few strides in this direction, overall he has failed to reverse labor's long-term decline.[132] By 2005, only 12.5 percent of workers belonged to unions.[133] In this context, the UPS strike of 1997 was a symbol of what was possible if the labor movement adopted a more aggressive posture in its dealings with management.

Conclusion

This chapter has argued that for the last quarter of the twentieth century, class inequality has grown tremendously in the United States. This is true too on a world scale. The promise of globalization, that free markets would lift whole countries out of poverty, has failed to materialize. The vast majority of people in advanced capitalist countries have seen their wages stagnate or go down, while social programs have been cut. In developing countries in Asia and Latin America, the debt burden has been devastating, and in sub-Saharan Africa, conditions have deteriorated with alarming consequences.

Yet not everyone has been affected in the same way. Globalization has benefited some sections of society; in 1997, the wealth of the richest 225 people was nearly equal to the combined annual income of 47 percent of the world's poorest people.[134]

The emerging international movement against corporate globalization has started to question this class polarization and the broader priorities of corporations and global institutions like the IMF, World Bank, and the WTO. Can such institutions be democratized? Can the capitalist free-market system create and sustain a democratic political system? In a world polarized by class divisions, what are the prospects for democracy? What is the role of the media in this process?

Robert McChesney argues that a participatory self-government, or democracy, works best when three conditions are met. First, there should be no great difference in economic status, since this would impede the ability of members of a society to treat each other as equals. Second, the well-being of the individual must be determined by the well-being of the community, since this would prevent individuals from seeking to advance their own interests at the expense of the community. Third, there must be an effective system of political communication.[135] Arguably, the first two conditions have not existed for most of U.S. history, but the last time that classes were polarized to this extent was during the Gilded Age. At that time, the political communication system enabled citizens to demand change. In addition to a thriving alternative press, investigative journalists, or muckrakers, such as Ida Tarbell, Upton Sinclair, and Lincoln Steffens exposed social and economic injustices. For example, in response to Upton Sinclair's book *The Jungle,* President Theodore Roosevelt signed the Pure Food and Drug Act into law in 1906.

Today, while some investigative journalists have the passion and courage to uncover social and economic injustices, they are not supported by the corporate media system, which prioritizes profit over public interest. In the following chapter, I discuss the ways in which the corporate media system has both benefited from and served the process of globalization. The end result is a news media apparatus that has a structural interest in legitimating the status quo and securing consent for a fundamentally unequal economic system. What is truly remarkable in this context is how the UPS strike impacted media coverage of economic issues and opened up a space for deliberation on questions of economic and political inequality. In what follows, I explain how the strike was able to do so.

TWO

Understanding the Corporate Media:
A Dominance/Resistance Model

A popular Government, without popular information, or the means of acquiring it, is but a Prologue to a Farce or a Tragedy; or perhaps both.
—James Madison

If globalization policy has disproportionately benefited a small section of society, while the vast majority has been its victims, we need to ask why, until recently, such information has not received sustained attention in the United States. If the media are truly vehicles of democratic discussion and debate, why have they failed to adequately address the consequences of globalization? Do we truly have a "public sphere"—a space where citizens, as rational actors, can debate issues?

To answer these questions, we must examine the unique relationship between the U.S. media industry and globalization policy. On the one hand, like most other industries, it is currently shaped by privatization and deregulation, which have allowed the consolidation of various sectors of the economy from banking to utilities and airlines. Globalization policy is in large part responsible for the fact that fewer than ten multinational media corporations dominate the world market today. Of these, a significant number are based in the United States. On the other hand, unlike most other sectors of the economy, the media industry has been central to the process of globalization. MNCs depend on media-industry services to coordinate activities across vast distances in a tiered system of production, which, in turn, has stimulated the growth of the media and information industry.[1]

While globalization has benefited the media industry, it has also, at the same time, been the backbone of this process. As Herbert Schiller observes, "The expansion of the cultural-communication industries has become critical to the functioning of a globalized market economy. Media, publishing, advertising, public relations, opinion polling, accounting, consultancy, and market research today constitute an essential protective ring around the activities of the goods and services production center."[2] It stands to reason that, being an integral part of the globalization process, media corporations have a stake in presenting the global economy in a manner favorable to corporations.

However, the interests of the owners and stakeholders of media conglomerates are not *automatically* translated into procorporate propaganda, that is, they do not work exactly like a corporation's public relations department. In countries like the United States, where the news media are charged with being the guardians of democracy, profit motives alone cannot blatantly override social responsibility; the media have to make gestures, albeit mostly empty gestures, toward serving the public interest. The corporate media's institutional interests are instead embedded in their structure and method of operation.

This chapter explains how and why the media adopt a procorporate bias in their coverage and treatment of economic issues. I discuss the economic, ideological, and practical mechanisms that set the terms of news coverage. However, these mechanisms of control and dominance are not absolute because the media are contradictory institutions. While for the most part the news reflects and reinforces the status quo, it can be challenged to incorporate critical perspectives, particularly in the context of collective struggle. Building on existing research, I propose a new model of media analysis, the "dominance/resistance model," which accounts for both dominance and resistance.

Media and Globalization

Globalization policy alone did not begin the process of media consolidation. In the United States, through much of the twentieth century, a small number of corporations owned the mass media. However, since the early 1980s, the trend toward concentration has accelerated, much like the mergers in other sections of the economy. In 1996, the volume of all acquisitions worldwide was estimated at $1 trillion, $650 billion of which was in the United States.[3]

The media industry has been at the forefront of this trend. Thus, when the merger between Time-Warner and America Online (AOL) was realized, it was not only the largest media merger but also the largest merger in the history of capitalism up to that point.[4] Media scholar Ben Bagdikian has written about the concentration of media ownership since at least the early 1980s. When he published the first edition of *Media Monopoly* in 1983, about fifty corporations dominated the ownership of television stations, cable, films, recorded music, magazines, newspapers, books, and other media in the United States. In the 2004 edition, that same figure had decreased to five.[5]

This level of media concentration and consolidation has been enabled by privatization and deregulation the world over. The United States, Great Britain, and Japan led the trend in the late 1970s. In the United States, during the Reagan era, media lobbies actively pushed for an end to regulation, a policy consistent with the administration's agenda. The stated goal of deregulation was to create greater competition and enable the industry to "set professional standards," thus improving quality without "needless interference" by the state. The Reagan administration willingly obliged, reducing the standards required by government agencies like the Securities and Exchange Commission and the Federal Communications Commission (FCC).[6]

The most enthusiastic supporter of deregulation was the FCC, under its former chairperson Mark Fowler. As *Business Week* observed, the FCC in the 1980s had "become Washington's most advanced laboratory for the anti-regulation theories of the Reagan administration."[7] As a result, in the 1980s, cable television was deregulated and control over programming and rates placed in the hands of cable providers, the number of TV and radio stations that could be owned by one corporation was increased, the standards for renewing broadcast licenses were reduced, and broadcasting rules about obscenity were weakened.

If the Reagan-Bush administration started the deregulation process, the Clinton administration took it one step further through the passage of the Telecommunication Act of 1996. The core function of this bill was to remove restrictions on firms moving into other communication areas, such as telecommunication into cable, and to remove most, if not all, regulations on their behavior.[8] Contrary to the industry's claims that the Telecommunication Act would spur "genuine market competition" and serve the public better, the outcome has been a consolidation beyond the expectations even of the lobbyists themselves.[9]

Internationally, agencies like the International Monetary Fund and the World Trade Organization have aided in the consolidation of the media industry. As Edward Herman and Robert McChesney note, "The IMF is committed to encouraging the establishment of commercial media globally to better serve the needs of a market economy. The WTO's mission is to encourage a single global market for commercial media, and to oppose barriers to this, however noble in intent."[10] This mission has translated into policies where loans to economically underdeveloped nations are tied to demands that various state-owned sectors, including the media, be privatized and deregulated. The media corporations of the triad regions of North America, Europe, and Japan have consequently established a foothold around the world.

The benefits to media conglomerates of a global system are numerous. Apart from increased profitability, conglomeration and concentration have led to the creation of an oligopolistic market, that is, a market dominated by a handful of corporations, where the barriers to entry are extremely high. As capital outlays for media products tend to be high, only in markets with reduced or diminished competition are the returns on investment guaranteed.

In addition, consolidation has allowed conglomerates to downsize their workforce and outsource low- to moderate-skill labor while coordinating their activities from national headquarters. In other words, lean production and the creation of a tiered workforce are not unfamiliar to the media industry. As Gerald Sussman and John Lent note, "The 'information society' is based on a new international division of labor of men and women sharing a production platform but dispersed into segmented zones of industrial, semi-industrial, and Third World societies." From the production of computer and electronic components to data entry and information processing, aspects of the production process in media industries have been outsourced to regions with lower labor costs. For instance, Lent shows that corporations from the triad regions, particularly Disney in the United States, have shipped out animation work to countries in Asia where, due to antiunion laws, workers are forced to work seven days a week. Additionally, Disney merchandise is produced in more than three thousand factories worldwide, with a significant percentage concentrated in developing countries like Haiti, China, Vietnam, and India, where workers toil in sweatshop conditions. Ewart Skinner demonstrates that the outsourcing of data entry to Caribbean islands has reduced the data-processing budgets for U.S. companies by 50 percent while creating low-wage, tedious, fast-paced, and unsafe conditions for the workers.[11] The net result is superprofits for the media giants and a race to the bottom in terms of wages, work conditions, and union rights for media and information workers around the world.

Consequently, the media have an institutional interest in presenting the global economy in a manner that favors their interests and those of other corporations. A vast body of literature argues that the news media overrepresent the interests of the elites.[12] Herman and McChesney, in their detailed study of the structure and functioning of the global media, make a strong argument that "the global media are the missionaries of our age, promoting the virtues of commercialism and the market loudly and incessantly through their profit-driven and advertising-supported enterprises and programming."[13]

The central premise of the procorporate ideology promoted by these "missionaries" is that the market is the most just means of allocating resources and that a free market, based on the absence of constraints on business, guarantees not only economic but also political freedom. Another aspect of this ideology is that government intervention or regulation unduly burdens business and impedes economic growth. Government ownership or control over resources is seen as extremely inefficient. Thus, state-owned resources are best handed over to business, particularly if they are likely to generate profit. Furthermore, the ideal government does not govern but supports and enhances the market's interests. It can do so by keeping inflation low to enable "sustainable economic growth"; that is, corporations would much rather have slow growth and high unemployment, if inflation is kept in check. Within this framework, economic growth is measured in terms of the gross domestic product, which reflects the prosperity of business, while it hides income and wealth inequality.[14]

This logic underpins much news media economic reporting. Although occasional stories challenge the above assumptions, for the most part the interests of labor are subordinated to those of corporations. As George Lipsitz observes:

> For almost twenty years, working people and their interests have been absent from most public discussions about our national political and cultural life. As deindustrialization and economic restructuring have radically transformed U.S. society, the people and communities most immediately affected by these changes have been virtually erased. Business initiatives dominate the economic, political, and social agenda of the nation, while labor's perspectives and needs remain almost invisible within most of the country's mainstream media and economic institutions.[15]

Robert Goldman and Arvind Rajgopal argue that the mainstream press perpetuates the myth of a classless American society, erasing from public collective memory the history of labor struggles.[16] However, this development is not new; as Walter Lippmann noted many decades ago, "If you study the way many a strike is reported in the press, you will find, very often, that the issues are rarely in the headlines, barely in the leading paragraphs, and sometimes not even mentioned anywhere."[17]

This trend has only been accentuated over the past fifty years with the decline of the labor movement. In the 1930s and '40s, a full-time labor editor or beat reporter was the norm among newspapers with medium to large circulations; today, most labor news is covered in the business pages. By 2002, there were fewer than five labor reporters left.[18] Few reporters are assigned exclusively to cover labor issues. Additionally, though most daily newspapers have business sections, they lack a corresponding labor section. This shift to create a more business-friendly environment took shape largely in the context of the 1970s with the emergence of globalization policy. For instance, in the 1970s the *New York Times* introduced several format changes that would impact labor reporting: labor-beat reporting became less frequent and was assigned to several reporters rather than one or two experienced journalists, and a prominent business section was created to which union news that was not front-page news was shifted.[19]

The picture is not that different in broadcasting. National television, including PBS, offers dozens of business and investor programs but not one regular show on labor or consumer rights. Cable channels like CNBC are completely dedicated to the coverage of Wall Street; CNN, MSNBC, and other channels have slots in regular programming for business perspectives on the economy; similar labor slots or channels do not exist.

That corporate views therefore tend to dominate in the news is not surprising.[20] This raises the question of how the media's institutional interest in corporate ideology gets translated into everyday practice in a system where no formal control mechanisms exist. The dominance/resistance model sheds light on how this process works.

The Dominance/Resistance Model

The model examines both the ways in which the status quo is upheld (mechanisms of dominance) and how critical views might enter the media (mechanisms of resistance).[21] We begin with the mechanisms of dominance, which include the following:

- *economic power* wielded by media owners–corporate parents and advertisers who have the ability to censor media content and create an atmosphere of self-censorship.
- *practical constraints* that flow from how news-gathering practices are organized in a for-profit media system. To maximize profits the media

industry has laid off reporters, slashed budgets for investigative reporting, and thus become more dependent on free or cheap sources of information. These include the standard news services, corporate PR departments, government sources, and corporate-sponsored think tanks, which together have enormous power to determine the content of the news.

• *ideological limitations* of professional journalism and its reliance on official news sources, event-oriented reporting, and taken-for-granted storytelling mechanisms, which reinforce the status quo.

Economic Mechanisms of Control and Dominance

In a commercial media system, the dependence on advertising revenue is one of the key sources of control. Several scholars and media practitioners have noted that advertisers and media owners have a powerful impact on the content of the news media.[22] These and other studies have shown that advertisers constantly pressure journalists, editors, and news executives to censor stories that may affect their interests.

In addition to advertisers, media owners also exercise a fair degree of control over the media. A study conducted by Fairness and Accuracy in Reporting titled *Fear and Favor 2000: How Power Shapes the News* found that journalists "experience pressure from powerful interests, outside and inside the news business, to push some stories and ignore others, and to shape or slant news content. The sources of pressure include the government, which enlists media to support its actions and policies; corporate advertisers who may demand favorable treatment for their industries and products; and media owners themselves, who can use their outlets to support their increasingly various business and political interests."[23] The report cites several examples of a blurring between editorial and advertising content. On March 23, 2000, New York station WCBS-TV earned three hundred thousand dollars for a Web-site ad on a laser surgery procedure. Not coincidentally, the evening newscast that day had a story on the same procedure. Similarly, eight episodes of *The View,* an ABC program cohosted by Barbara Walters, were turned into infomercials for Campbell Soup. In one show, when Walters asked her guests if they grew up eating Campbell's soup, they responded by singing together the "M'm! M'm! good" jingle!

Arguably, these examples are not aberrations in an otherwise public-minded media system. Close to half a trillion dollars a year is spent on advertising worldwide; the United States accounts for almost half of this spending.[24] General circulation magazines obtain about 50 percent of their revenues from advertising, newspapers 75 percent, and broadcasting nearly 100 percent.[25] The media industry has had to tailor its content and structure to the needs of the sponsors on which it so heavily relies. When the Tribune Company bought the Times Mirror Corporation, the logic was to "create a network of regional media hubs where advertisers are matched with audiences through newspapers, television broadcasts and Internet sites."[26] According to the 1997 edition of the *Standard Directory of Advertisers,* which tracks the top 200 advertisers, UPS was number 120 and had spent about eighty-five million dollars in the year 1995–96 on advertising. This amount of spending had a palpable impact on how the media covered the 1997 strike.

Proponents of a commercial media system argue that advertising support enables consumers to have freedom of choice. For instance, if audiences liked and watched a particular television program regularly, then advertisers who are always in search of the largest possible audience would support that program. In reality, the opposite is true; advertisers decide which forms of media content are best suited to their interests, and reaching a large audience is not enough—they must reach the *right kind* of audience, one capable of, and potentially interested in, buying their products. Thus, even shows that have a sizable audience are not guaranteed support. A sitcom like *The Cosby Show,* which presented a successful, middle-class black family, is preferable to shows like *East Side, West Side,* which depicted the grim side of the lives of African Americans and addressed racism. *East Side, West Side* was canceled after one season; a similar show, *South Central,* aired only a few episodes. As Oscar Gandy notes, in "those markets where Black people make up a large share of the primary audience base, high local ratings have not generated corresponding support. This is attributable to low estimates of Black people's purchasing power as well as to conventional racist assumptions."[27]

Thus, in an advertising-sponsored media system, enormous control is handed over to corporate America in choosing media content that suits its interests. Not coincidentally, these interests are similar to those of mass-media owners. Increasingly, owners of the media, due to investments in other sectors, are not a distinct group. In general, trends toward cross-investment and ownership patterns, combined with interlocking boards of directors, have created a class of owners who have stakes in various sectors of the economy. In many instances, media owners intervene to set a tone consistent with their managerial style. For instance, when Rupert Murdoch's News Corporation fired reporters Jane Akre and Steve Wilson for broadcasting information harmful to Monsanto, a major advertiser with Fox, News Corporation was quite clear about the reasons for which the reporters were fired.[28] As a News Corporation executive put it, "We paid $3 billion for these TV stations. We will decide what the news is. The news is what we tell you it is."[29]

However, although this sort of direct intervention by parent companies like Disney, News Corporation, and Time Warner happens from time to time, it is not a regular feature and, arguably, need not be in order to guarantee a procorporate bias. This is because the possibility of such intervention hangs like the sword of Damocles over the heads of print journalists and TV news producers, which could fall any time they cross the line. The mere possibility has a chilling effect that is perhaps far more effective than actual acts of censorship by the owners of the mass media. Rather than face the prospect of being blacklisted and jobless, journalists are driven to exercise self-censorship.

In fact, media moguls rarely peer over the shoulders of journalists or issue guidelines on what should or should not be covered and how. This apparent lack of censorship leads many to conclude that the press is free. However, as Herbert Schiller observes, "[in] truth, the strength of the control process rests in its apparent absence. The desired systemic result is achieved ordinarily by a loose though effective institutional process. It utilizes the education of journalists and other media professionals, built-in penalties and rewards for doing what is expected, norms presented as objective rules, and the occasional but telling direct intrusion from above. The main lever is the internalization of values." Dennis Mazzocco, who worked for twenty years at ABC and NBC, makes a similar observation. He writes that media workers "learn to adopt the owners' views in order to succeed, even when their paychecks or political and social connections may be those of ordinary citizens. No media worker who wants to keep his or her job will ever admit this publicly. Nor will anyone who wants to succeed in U.S. broadcasting publicly confirm that management investment decisions are made to protect the firm's political-economic power and inevitable affect their company's on-air programming."[30] Thus, through direct and indirect mechanisms, owners, corporate parents, and advertisers set the terms of discussion and debate in the news.

Practical and Ideological Mechanisms of Dominance

A corporate media system, driven by the need to make profits, adopts a work culture and practices suited to that primary aim, including the means by which news is gathered and organized.[31]

News-Gathering Practices

A for-profit media system treats news production as a commodity.[32] Just like any other capitalist enterprise, the goal is to keep costs low and revenues high. The result has been major layoffs of news workers, the introduction of new technology, and slashing budgets for investigative reporting. While these trends have a long history, we have seen an acceleration in the era of globalization.

Over the 1990s, a large number of news workers were laid off, and the wages of those who remained were stagnant or depressed. At the same time, the wages of elite journalists—those who dominate the national agenda—have been rising so that there is a vast wage gap between elite journalists and all the rest of the journalists. While Stone Phillips and Diane Sawyer are paid millions of dollars per year, noncelebrity journalists can barely support themselves. Veteran journalist James Fallows states that elite journalists' "earnings go up, with few of the layoffs and none of the 'wage stagnation' that has affected most of America, and they know they have a chance for dramatic windfall earnings if they can establish themselves on the lecture circuit." When the journalists who have a degree of autonomy in deciding what the news is going to be are members of the elite, it follows that they reflect the interests of their class. Thus, Fallows concludes that the "status revolution in big-time journalism has given many reporters a strong if unconscious bias in favor of 'haves' rather than 'have nots.'"[33]

With fewer journalists to cover the news, the trend has been to rely even more on wire services like the Associated Press, United Press International, and Agence France-Presse. Economically speaking, relying on news reports and covering press conferences are easier than conducting an investigative report, where the information is neither readily available nor the sources easy to verify. As Phillip Gaunt argues:

> The tendency toward more homogenous media content is also the result of technological innovations associated with changing patterns of ownership and increased emphasis on profitability. The introduction of new technology, particularly in the print media, has been hastened by

the commercially oriented newspaper groups that have emerged since the 1950s. Electronic news management systems have been viewed as a way to maximize profit in the face of intense competition from other media . . . and a relative reduction of editorial staff have encouraged a greater dependence on centralized electronic news sources, and this dependence tends to result in greater uniformity of content.[34]

Thus, even though the news media have proliferated, news content tends be homogenous.

This trend will only grow in the future. Today, media conglomerates that are not divesting their news holdings are increasingly using news to support "synergy" with their other media companies. For instance, the Tribune Company requires that its journalists contribute news reports to its radio, television, newspaper, and Internet outlets, promoting greater conformity and cross-promotional opportunities for the company without increased pay for its reporters. Other media conglomerates will likely adopt this practice, because hiring fewer reporters and working them harder saves money.[35] As the dean of the Columbia Graduate School of Journalism observed, the Tribune Company is "leading the pack in multimedia journalism."[36] These practices promote not only homogeneity but also a degree of superficiality and a lack of depth in how the news is constructed. It is therefore not surprising that media moguls have deprioritized investigative reporting. When the news as a homogenized commodity can be neatly packaged and used in different media outlets, why bother with complicated, time-consuming, expense investigative journalism?

The two other important sources of cheap and "reliable" information for the news media are corporate public relations departments and the state, with its various departments from the Pentagon to the White House.[37] Vast amounts of information reach the news media through these two sources. It is estimated that anywhere between 40 percent and 70 percent of the news is based on press releases and PR-generated information.[38] Furthermore, with the large number of layoffs among news workers in the past decade, there are now about twenty thousand more PR agents than journalists.[39]

The various agencies of the state also provide large amounts of information. The Pentagon alone employs thousands of people and spends millions of dollars on its public relations every year. The amount of resources allotted by the Pentagon to public information exceeds not only those of the average individual or group who dares to resist the status quo but the resources of *all* such groups in the United States.[40]

Not only does information from government sources inundate the news media, but reporters are also stationed in locations where "news" is known to happen through what is known as the "beat" system. Reporters are assigned beats, that is, they are sent to established locations to cover routine events. For example, a national news media corporation will assign reporters to the White House, the Pentagon, the State Department, and so on. For local news media, the various beats include city hall, the police department, the courts, and other such establishment locations.

The media's reliance on corporations and the government gives the latter two entities enormous powers. For instance, if a reporter were to write an unfavorable story, the source of information might dry up or lead to expensive lawsuits. If the source was a government official who complained about being misquoted or treated unfairly, the reporter could be denied access to further interviews and news conferences, or she or he could simply find that phone calls are not returned. Reporters may also lose their jobs. The *Cincinnati Enquirer* ran a detailed story exposing Chiquita International's unethical overseas practices. Chiquita sued the newspaper because some of the information for the story, based on voice-mail messages, was obtained illegally by the reporter. Although the truth of the story was never disproved, the *Enquirer* fired the reporter, recanted the story, and paid Chiquita ten million dollars. When Gary Webb, who is said to have committed suicide in 2004, exposed the connection between the Central Intelligence Agency (CIA) and drug trade in inner cities, he was eventually forced to leave the *San Jose Mercury News*. When producers April Oliver and Jack Smith ran a story that suggested that the U.S. Army might have used the nerve gas sarin on deserters during the Vietnam War, CNN fired them after retracting the story. Thus, the rational choice for a journalist is to report favorably on those in positions of power and wait to be rewarded through the occasional leak that leads to a story being given importance.[41]

In addition to expanded PR departments, corporations have cultivated "experts" on various issues who are routinely contacted by the media for their expertise. Edward Herman and Noam Chomsky argue that corporations have co-opted experts by putting them on the payroll as consultants, funding their research, and organizing think tanks that will hire them to help spread their message.[42] During the UPS strike, one of the experts often consulted by many news organizations was a professor of management at Emory University, Jeffrey Sonnenfeld, who was also a consultant for UPS. As chapter 4 shows, he was initially presented as a neutral commentator in several media outlets, even though the Teamsters had sent out a press release exposing his connection to UPS.

During the 1970s and 1980s, corporate America developed a media strategy that would ensure the dominance of corporate ideology and overturn the progressive social movements of the past decades.[43] It set up think tanks, such as the Heritage Foundation, American Enterprise Institute, and the Olin and Scaife Foundations, and created media watch groups, such as Accuracy in the Media, the Media Institute, Center for Media in Public Affairs, American Legal Foundation, and Capital Legal Foundation. The media watch groups were created for the explicit purpose of harassing the media if they strayed from the corporate agenda. This harassment, or flak, can range from letters and phone calls to lawsuits and speeches before Congress. The think tanks have been successful in reaching the goals of their corporate sponsors. FAIR has conducted annual studies to determine which think tanks are most often cited in the media. It found that since 1996, when the survey first began, the mainstream media have consistently preferred conservative and centrist think tanks to progressive ones. In 2005, conservative think tanks and "experts" were cited 40 percent of the time, centrist groups 47 percent, and progressives 13 percent.[44]

The upshot is that what constitutes the news is overwhelmingly decided by elite journalists, the standard news services, corporate PR, and government sources. This is then backed up by corporate-sponsored "experts" and think tanks. When journalists dare to cross the line, they are usually disciplined. If not, the media watch groups make sure that they are penalized. Thus, journalists soon learn to stay within the confines of what is allowed.

Nonetheless, media workers have not taken the layoffs, wage cuts, and censorship lying down. From individual forms of resistance—such as writing news stories that question the status quo, among other things—to strikes and other job actions, news workers have fought for their interests.[45] Several large strikes in the past few decades include the strike against the *New York Daily News* in 1989; the Detroit news workers strike of 1995–97 against the *Detroit News,* owned by Gannett Company, and the *Detroit Free Press,* owned by Knight-Ridder Company; and in 1999, the strike against the ABC Network, where workers demonstrated their determination to fight against corporate greed and domination. In some cases, where workers have been successful, programming content has been affected. After the March 1988 Hollywood writers' strike, two well-known sitcoms portrayed labor in a positive light. In an episode of *Designing Women,* not exactly a left-leaning show, the protagonists side with picketing garment workers and stop crossing the picket line when they learn of the workers' horrible work conditions. In an episode of *Head of the Class,* the teacher explains why he supports the teachers' strike, and by the end the class rejects the scab substitute.[46] Overall, however, there have been some victories but more defeats. Another influence that has prevented journalists from fighting back and clouded their struggles is the ideology of professional journalism.

Professional Journalism

Professional journalism arose in the early part of the twentieth century and brought with it, among many other practices, the idea of neutrality in journalism, which formally separated the owner's economic and political interests from the obligations of the journalist, who was to remain above partisanship.[47] However, several scholars have noted that, contrary to its own claims, professional journalism internalized a set of values and ethics that coincided with the needs of business.[48]

Some media historians argue that professional journalism was a response to "yellow journalism" and the product of a trend toward "social responsibility." It institutionalized a code of ethics that emphasized accuracy and objectivity. Schools, such as the Graduate School of Journalism at Columbia University, introduced programs that inculcated the values of neutrality and objectivity among editors and journalists. In 1923, the American Society of Newspaper Editors also adopted these values. What scholars fail to point out is that newspapers readily adopted these new ideals not because they were committed to the truth; rather, as McChesney argues, "the commercial requirements for media content to satisfy media owners and advertisers were built implicitly into the . . . ideology [of professional journalism]."[49]

During the mid-nineteenth century, newspaper publishing's profit potential became apparent, and the latter half century witnessed the rise of a commercial newspaper system, with fierce battles over circulation like those between William Randolph Hearst and Joseph Pulitzer. McChesney points to two critical developments at the beginning of the twentieth century. First, newspapers grew and reached a concentrated readership, somewhere between 40 percent and 60 percent of the population in a market. Second, advertising became their dominant source of income, and if they were to attract advertisers, they had to reach the largest possible audience. Thus, the new form of journalism had to appeal to all and offend as few people as possible. Professional journalism schools came into being "to make a capitalist, advertising-supported media system seem—at least superficially—to be an objective source of news to many citizens."[50]

Professional journalism developed various codes and priorities by which stories could be deemed newsworthy. One of these was the search for "events" that made a story fit to print. As Michael Schudson points out, a convention of twentieth-century journalism is that a "news story should focus on a single event rather than a continuous or repeated happening, [and] that, if the action is repeated, attention should center on novelty, not on pattern." This convention rules out stories that deal with the conditions that affect workers as part of their normal existence. Thus, gradually declining wages or living standards are sidelined. Schudson also explains that the conventions used to frame stories and make a message understandable take for granted a certain understanding of the world and how things are related. The end result is that "the world is incorporated into unquestioned and unnoticed conventions of narration, and then transfigured, no longer a subject for discussion or a premise for any conversation at all."[51]

Another journalistic code accords legitimacy to those in positions of power. As Mark Fishman, author of *Manufacturing the News,* notes,

> Newsworkers are predisposed to treat bureaucratic accounts as factual because news personnel participate in upholding a normative order of authorized knowers in the society. Reporters operate with the attitude that officials ought to know what it is their job to know. . . . In particular, a newsworker will recognize an official's claim to knowledge not merely as a claim, but as a credible, competent piece of knowledge. This amounts to a moral division of labor: officials have to give the facts; reporters merely get them.[52]

More recently, Brent Cunningham, managing editor of the *Columbia Journalism Review,* made a similar point when he stated that the pursuit of objectivity has exacerbated the tendency to rely on official sources, making journalists passive recipients of the news.[53]

The logic of professional journalism, which includes, among other things, event-oriented reporting, taken-for-granted storytelling mechanisms, and reliance on officials, allows the elites to set the terms of discussion.

In sum, due to the aforementioned economic, practical, and ideological mechanisms of control, the output of the mainstream media has an overwhelmingly procorporate bias, thus ensuring the ideological dominance of the business elite. However, from time to time, stories critical of corporations also find their way into the news because the media are contradictory institutions. As Douglas Kellner observes, "It is true that media culture overwhelmingly supports capitalist values, but is also a site of intense struggle between different races, classes, gender, and social groups, and is thus better theorized as a contested terrain, open to the vicissitude of history and struggle, rather than just a field of domination."[54] In the following section we will examine the ways in which resistance to the corporate media is possible.

Mechanisms of Resistance

To understand how a seemingly all-powerful corporate media system is vulnerable to resistance, it is necessary to begin with the concept of hegemony. In elaborating his theory of hegemony, Antonio Gramsci notes that for a class to maintain power and reproduce the status quo, it must constantly win leadership among the subordinate classes. He states:

> The supremacy of a social group manifests itself in two ways, as "domination" and as "intellectual and moral leadership." A social group dominates antagonistic groups, which it tends to "liquidate," or to subjugate perhaps even by armed force; it leads kindred and allied groups. A social group can, and indeed must, already exercise "leadership" before winning governmental power . . . but even if it holds it firmly in its grasp, it must continue to "lead" as well.[55]

In an advanced capitalist society such as the United States, a Gramscian approach suggests that the capitalist class maintains its power through mechanisms not only of domination but also of intellectual leadership, or what is more often referred to as the manufacture of consent. The instruments of domination (the police and the military) are part of the state, whereas those of consent manufacture (religious institutions, schools, and the media) are a part of civil society.

Gramsci argues that consent is obtained from subordinate classes not because they are "dupes" but because "this consent is 'historically' caused by the prestige (and consequent confidence) which the dominant group enjoys because of its position and function in the world of production."[56] However, as Gramsci also reminds us, this intellectual domination of the class in power is *neither absolute nor complete* but rather a process that must continuously propagate itself. In other words, ideological domination is the product of struggle between various groups, and the outcome cannot be determined in advance. The dominance/resistance model of the media tries to capture this dynamic of domination and resistance.

However, this is not to suggest that struggle is the only means by which dissenting views find a space in the media. Even in the absence of collective resistance, the media sometimes present dissenting views when there is conflict between elites; when the pressures of circulation or ratings force them to reflect, in however distorted a manner, the problems faced by their consumer base; when journalistic ethics contradict the interests of ruling groups; or when a media organization's credibility is at stake. Factors that exacerbate these contradictory pressures on the media are the fast pace of the news production process and the impact of disputes within news organizations.

At times, when sections of the elite disagree over particular issues, the media reflect these debates. For the most part, the permissible range of discussion of any topic is usually circumscribed by the ideological limits set by dissenting ruling elites. For instance, even when polls have shown that a majority of Americans want an immediate withdrawal of troops from Iraq, the debate in the media has been between the Democratic proposal for a phased withdrawal and/or redeployment of troops and the Republican position to "stay the course" and not "cut and run." At other times, to increase their audience share, media organizations, on their own initiative, find ways to relate to the experiences of this audience and run stories on issues such as downsizing, the health-care crisis, or the attack on pensions. In 2005, the *New York Times* ran a series titled "Class in America." Not very timely given the growth of class polarization over the past thirty years, it was nevertheless a step forward in terms of addressing class differences in the United States. Often, the news media also include letters to the editor or op-ed essays that are critical of the status quo. For instance, CNN has a slot in its programming when viewer e-mails are read aloud, and sometimes these e-mails express dissenting views. Also, the *New York Times* editorial page routinely features columns by Paul Krugman and Bob Herbert, both critics of corporate globalization. A collection of Krugman's articles in the *Times* has been published as a book titled *The Great Unraveling,* which is a strong indictment of the economic common sense of our times.

Sometimes, critiques of the status quo arise when journalists' worldview and ethics come into contradiction with the world around them. For instance, in 2005 when Hurricane Katrina devastated the city of New Orleans and neighboring areas, reporters on the ground covering the story found that all levels of government had literally abandoned the people who were not able to evacuate. Witnessing firsthand the terrible suffering of the people, journalists called into question the image of the United States as a benevolent and fair society that cares for the needs of all its citizens. Journalists then explained the crisis in terms of race and class, bringing to the fore the fact of inequality in U.S. society. However, coverage was contradictory, with several media outlets chiding the "looters" and cheering on the National Guard as they tried to restore "law and order." At the end of the day, while the reporters asked tough questions of government representatives, the system that produces inequality was left unscathed. And as the months passed by, the very same politicians who were criticized for their handling of the disaster would again become respected official sources of news.

Occasionally, due to time pressures, news stories that feature critical viewpoints might get through. Unlike other media products, like prerecorded television programs or films, the news is very time sensitive and cannot be planned and coordinated to the same extent. An entire day's events must be processed and fitted into a tight production schedule, especially on twenty-four-hour news channels, which need a constant flow of filtered information to fill airtime. Newspapers, network television news, and scheduled radio news broadcasts have relatively more flexibility. Nevertheless, the fast pace of news production means that some pieces slip through the control mechanisms. For instance, a reporter covering an official press conference on the benefits of welfare reform might include information that counters the claims of the official sources, adding facts or stories about the plight of welfare recipients. Even though the story originated in a government press conference, because of time pressures it could run. Despite the atmosphere of self-censorship, individual reporters do sometimes take such risks and criticize those in power. At other times, journalists pitch stories about government or corporate corruption that sympathetic and bold editors encourage, regardless of the consequences.

In short, critical viewpoints do find a space in the media through many avenues, even when there is not significant conflict among various social groups. *However, these expressions of dissent are not truly significant, because they typically do not set the terms of discussion or impact how the news is gathered, packaged, and sold to the public.* They are criticisms that exist in the margins and are not usually found on page 1 or as part of the headline section on television news. Even if they do manage to grab a headline, they are quickly dropped and rarely influence the way the mainstream media frame a topic.

For instance, during the U.S.-led war in Iraq in 2003, the media reported the Bush administration's case quite uncritically.[57] The two main arguments for war were that Iraq possessed weapons of mass destruction (WMDs) and that it had ties to terrorism that made it at least partially responsible for the events of September 11, 2001. Both these arguments were patently false, yet the media reported on them as if they were the truth, even though some outlets had stories that cast doubt on them. For instance, a *Newsweek* article stated that a high-ranking Iraqi official who defected from Saddam Hussein's inner circle had told CIA and British intelligence officers in 1995 that after the Gulf War, Iraq had destroyed all its chemical and biological weapons.[58] The rest of the media largely ignored this information, although the administration had used the testimony of the very same individual to make the case that Iraq had not disarmed. The media also ignored the historical connections between the United States and Iraq and developed a collective amnesia on the question of WMDs. One of the exceptions was a *Washington Post* story that stated clearly that U.S. involvement with Iraq "included large-scale intelligence sharing, supply of cluster bombs through a Chilean front company, and facilitating Iraq's acquisition of chemical and biological precursors."[59] This front-page story had a negligible impact on the overall framing of the war. In general, though a few sections sounded a discordant note, the media choir was consistently in tune with the Bush administration's propaganda efforts.[60]

Several months later, when WMDs were not discovered, the media began to ask embarrassing questions, not so much because they wanted to get to the truth—after all, the truth was available before the start of the war—but because they wanted to look credible. Failure to question the absent weapons of mass destruction would have exposed the media's complicity in the propaganda war, discrediting their reputation among skeptical consumers, and proving that the antiwar movement was right. In order to maintain the facade of an adversarial press, as well as keep up revenues, they engaged in questioning for a respectable period of time before the issue was again dropped.

The same is true of stories related to the economy. When corporate corruption scandals came to light in 2002 with the spectacular Enron bankruptcy, several news media outlets ran stories that were critical of bloated CEO compensations and salaries as well as the rampant corruption in corporate America. If the media were to ignore these scandals, or attempt to justify such blatant corruption, their ideological function would have become too apparent, leading to a loss of some credibility that could affect the bottom line. However, at the end of day, business news reporting has not changed in any significant way. Professional journalism still accords corporate leaders the same authority, and business and labor stories follow the same pattern. In short, the media will sometimes run stories that are critical of people in positions of economic and political power, but they are rare and usually in response to egregious abuses that the media cannot ignore if they are to maintain credibility with their consumer base.

To impact the overall tone of media coverage it takes a collective struggle. An increase in class struggle or growth in social movements critical of the status quo pressures the media to make gestures toward serving the public interest, that is, the interests of the vast majority of people who are part of the working class. At times, these gestures are simply ways in which to inscribe dissent into already existing media frames as a way to devalue them.[61] At other times, as I show below, when the movements are successful in gaining an ideological advantage the media cannot easily marginalize them. In short, when a society is relatively stable, when the organization and priorities of that society are not questioned, the media, for the most part, reflect this consensus. However, during times of social upheaval, when large movements challenge the status quo, the media are pressured to make note of this dissent. How this movement will be represented depends on the context in which the struggle takes place and how it unfolds. A central part of the dominance/resistance model is *an emphasis on studying these concrete circumstances* as a way to understand the struggle for hegemony.

In several instances in the twentieth century, collective struggle has presented working-class views in the "public sphere." In her study of the early-twentieth-century women's suffrage and labor movements, Mary Triece shows how these movements challenged the dominant media framing of women and their role in society.[62] The mass media relied on three framing mechanisms to silence, trivialize, or otherwise domesticate women's actions as workers and activists. The *Atlantic Monthly,* which was targeted toward the well-to-do, relied on depicting women's roles in the home as "natural." *McClure's,* a muckraking magazine, provided a wider variety of portrayals of women, yet it too relied on the frame of "universalization," which omits a discussion of the ways that class impacted women's experiences. Though women were portrayed as stenographers, senators, and factory workers, through the frame of universalization, the need for a collective class struggle was ignored; instead, common values were shown as sufficient for overcoming class hardships. Magazines targeted toward the working class relied on a framing of "domestication" in order to tame labor struggles. Although these magazines recognized working-class hardships, they presented a happy home, a smile, or offering a "helping hand" as solutions.

Women responded to these hegemonic frames by denaturalizing their roles in the home, showing that gender roles and capitalist workplace relations were "not inevitable but rather the result of deliberate and thought-out actions on the part of owners, bosses and foremen."[63] They took on universalization by pointing out that economic position impacted their lives in ways that well-to-do women could not understand. And they countered domestication by showing that a happy home was not enough to put money in their pockets or food on the table. This resistance to dominant media frames of women took place in the context of strikes and protest movements in which women distributed flyers, gave speeches, and told stories. This alternative sphere of protest rhetoric would impact the way in which economic exploitation and liberation were thought of at the time. I will return to alternative media shortly.

In the 1930s, Michael Denning argues, the world of art and culture were proletarianized, that is, the working class and its interests shaped this world. From the citywide strikes in Minneapolis and San Francisco early in the decade to the sit-down strikes and the formation of the Congress of Industrial Organization in the late 1930s, the labor movement and leftist politics reached a high point. As Denning notes, these strikes and struggles "seared the imagination of young writers and artists." The impact was felt in almost every sphere of cultural activity, from Hollywood to the theater, literature, music, and animation, which acquired a proworker coloring. For instance, in response to the poor working conditions at the Disney Corporation, workers called a strike in 1941. Despite Walt Disney's attempts to quash the strike and present it as a communist plot, the strikers would receive massive support. In the end, the strike was settled in favor of the workers, and many of the radical animators would go on to create a "new language of animation."[64] This innovation would bring together the technical advances that they had made while at Disney with content that was politically progressive and even radical. With a multitude of such examples and cases, Denning shows the role played by workers and artists radicalized by the labor movement in creating working-class culture.

Similarly, George Lipsitz argues that in the post–World War II era, when strike activity was at its greatest intensity in U.S. history, the working class voiced radical demands to democratically restructure society. In so doing, they created a public space for the representation of working-class interests in several mediated spheres. Lipsitz shows that whereas Hollywood films allowed for only a muted discussion of these interests, music was "one of the main vehicles for the transformation of particular working-class perspectives into general mass cultural articulations offering leadership and guidance to all."[65] Although workers' struggles did not succeed in creating a radically re-structured society, it did offer us, Denning argues, a symbol of what collective resistance can achieve, namely, a "rainbow at midnight."

During the era of the cold war, the business class would use every means at its disposal to wipe out the impact of the aforementioned struggles from historical memory. As Elizabeth Fones-Wolf points out, the business assault on labor was multifaceted and determined.[66] Ultimately, as history shows, business was victorious in shifting the terms of debate and establishing a hegemonic position for a procorporate vision. Yet, at several points, workers have fought this worldview, and the mainstream media have been impacted in the process. As discussed earlier, after the 1988 Hollywood strike, several television programs featured stories that were sympathetic to workers and unions. In short, collective struggle sets up the conditions under which the mainstream media and its antilabor bias can be challenged.

Additionally, social movements have created their own media. From the newspapers of the American Revolution, the abolitionist newspapers, and the women suffragette press to the antiwar media during Vietnam and the multiple Internet-based media today, alternative media have played a key role in creating spaces outside the mainstream to put forward progressive ideas. Existing alternative media, not part of movements, also find much larger audiences during periods of social upheaval. This is because ideas critical of society find greater resonance during periods of struggle when large numbers of people have decided to take action against the status quo.

At the beginning of the twentieth century, within the context of rising class struggle, hundreds of labor and socialist newspapers and magazines came into being, with a circulation of more than 2 million.[67] The most prominent of these newspapers, the *Appeal to Reason,* founded in 1895, saw its circulation grow dramatically when it abandoned the practice of simply reporting on news events and started to represent the views of the workers and the socialist movement.[68] As strikes and struggles grew in the early part of the twentieth century, so did the audience for the newspaper. Not coincidentally, in 1912, the year of the great Lawrence Textile strike, the circulation of the newspaper went beyond half a million for the first time in its history. At its peak, it had a circulation base of 750,000, with some issues selling as many as 4 million copies.[69] This is a significant number for the times, especially when we compare it to newspaper circulation figures today. For instance, between 1998 and 2004, the *New York Times* home delivery subscription base ranged between 635,000 and 710,000.[70] Despite the fact that the *Appeal* was a weekly newspaper as opposed to the daily *Times,* and that today print is only one among many forms in which the news is available, when we take into account relative population figures, the aforementioned numbers are noteworthy.

With the growth of the Internet, large sections of U.S. society now have access to alternative sources of news and information online. Though the actual numbers of visitors to alternative magazine and Weblog (blog) sites are still small in comparison to the mainstream media's audience, their role in challenging the status quo should not be underestimated. For instance, after WMDs were not found in Iraq and the case for war started to unravel, vindicating the antiwar movement, many Americans turned to the Internet to find answers. Over the first half of 2004, left-wing blogs experienced a significant increase in traffic.[71] Additionally, documentaries like *Fahrenheit 9/11* and *Outfoxed* had an impact in broadening the limited center-to-right range of debate within the mainstream media.

In short, resistance to the status quo manifests itself in the media through a number of mechanisms. During "normal" times, dissenting views can sometimes find their way into the news—when elites disagree, circulation and ratings pressures force the media to reflect upon social problems, their credibility is at stake, or journalists take risks and critique those in power. However, these moments of resistance are peripheral to the system and rarely impact the overall tone of the news. It is during times of social upheaval, when collective agents such as women, workers, or antiwar activists go into struggle, that dissenting viewpoints have the most potential to impact the media. In this context, alternative or radical media have a significant role to play in disseminating a different worldview.

Conclusion

This chapter began by exploring the connections between the media industry and the policy of globalization. It argued that the media industry has been central to the process of globalization while benefiting from its policies. The outcome has been the creation of giant media conglomerates that profit from, and unabashedly promote, neoliberal, free-market ideas. In particular, this chapter focused on the economic, ideological, and practical mechanisms by which the free-market priorities of the corporate media are translated into a system of operation that frames the news in favor of the status quo.

However, the media occupy a contradictory position in society, and this opens the door for resistance. Occasionally, stories arise from within the industry that critique the status quo. But these stories rarely impact the overall framing of the news. It is primarily in the context of collective struggle that social and economic injustices can gain sustained attention. Still, collective struggle does not guarantee a sympathetic hearing in the media; rather, the process of struggle ultimately determines which side sets the terms of debate.

The dominance/resistance model tries to capture the dialectic of mass media. Such a model allows us to understand both the mechanisms of dominance that justify and reproduce the status-quo, and the mechanisms of resistance that can force through an alternative view. In what follows, I show that during the UPS strike, both dominance and resistance characterized media coverage, with the former giving way to the latter as the strike progressed.

Media Coverage of the UPS Strike

THREE

"Us" and "Them": The Nationalist Narrative in Network Television News

What was good for our country was good for General Motors, and vice versa.
　—Charles Wilson

Theorists of globalization have argued that in a world dominated by large multinational corporations, nation-states have lost much of their power. The global movement of information, investment, industry, and individuals, Kenichi Ohmae, author of *The End of the Nation-State,* maintains, has generated a new form of economy, controlled by region-states rather than nation-states.[1] By setting up international trade organizations, such as the General Agreement on Tariffs and Trade, financial entities like the IMF and World Bank, and regional bodies like the European Union, some argue that states have sacrificed their own interests to those of corporations.[2] Furthermore, with the growth of technology, improvement in communication, and economic integration, it is claimed that the nation-state has lost its authority.[3]

As the previous chapter argues, the mainstream media have uncritically echoed the views of globalization theorists and institutions. The catchall explanation of "global competition" serves to marginalize the interests of labor and environmental groups. Interestingly, while we are told, on the one hand, that nation-states no longer have the power to control MNCs or to insist upon labor and environmental standards, on the other, citizens are routinely asked to sacrifice for the "national interest." This contradiction conveniently allows capital free rein, while workers-citizens have to temper their interests in the name of national well-being. At the heart of this appeal is the merging of "public interest" with "national interest," with the latter being that of the capitalist class.

By their very structure and organization, the corporate media construct the news to favor the business class. This chapter explores the specific ways that the "national interest" was constructed during the UPS strike and how the interests of labor were represented or misrepresented. In particular, I analyze how three of the major television networks—ABC, CBS, and NBC—covered the strike.[4] The news programs on which the 269 stories on the UPS strike appeared and the times when they were broadcast is presented in table 2.

My analysis shows that the dominant framing mechanism in this strike followed the pattern of what I refer to as the "nationalist narrative." That is, the way the strike story was told conforms to a nationalist understanding of how individuals are related to each other and to various institutions in a society. The underlying assumption is that business interests coincide with those of the nation; "we" are seen as members of a nation, and "they" are the striking workers.

Challenges to this construction came mainly from Ron Carey, the leader of the Teamsters union. He brought into the mainstream media a rare and strident critique of corporate practices in the boom years of the 1990s. His

Table 2. News programs on the three networks

	ABC	CBS	NBC
Morning Shows			
5:00 A.M.			*NBC News at Sunrise*
6:30 A.M.	*ABC World News This Morning*	*CBS Morning News*	
7:00 A.M.	*ABC Good Morning America*	*CBS This Morning*	*Today*
Evening Shows			
6:30 P.M.	*ABC World News*	*CBS Evening News*	*NBC Nightly News*
Weekends			
6:30 P.M.	*ABC World News Saturday*		
7:00 A.M.			*Saturday Today*
9:00 A.M.		*Sunday Morning*	*Sunday Today*
10:00 A.M.	*Good Morning America Sunday*	*Face the Nation*	*Meet the Press*
11:30 A.M.	*ABC This Week*		
6:30 P.M.	*ABC World News Sunday*		
11:35 P.M.	*Nightline*		

arguments could have been reinforced by rank-and-file workers whose experiences conflict with the rhetoric of "national harmony" and "national interests." However, network television marginalized the rank and file and cast them in an unfavorable light.

This chapter is divided into five sections. The first examines the *particular* role of television in constructing the nation. The second and third discuss the economic and social aspects of the nationalist narrative. The fourth looks at Carey's arguments, and the fifth the way the rank and file were constructed in the strike narrative.

Television and Nationalism

The rhetoric of nationalism has functioned to bring together the capitalist and working classes as a nation, thereby deflecting their conflicts of interest. Though appeals to nationalism are a constant part of the cultural landscape, they reach a fever pitch during times of war, when fear makes it easier to muffle class conflict and its articulation in the public sphere. As George Creel, who headed the first large-scale U.S. government propaganda effort in the early part of the twentieth century known as the Committee for Public Information (CPI), stated, "When I think about the many voices that were heard before the war and are still heard, interpreting America from a class or sectional or selfish standpoint, I'm not sure that, if war had to come, it did not come at the right time for the preservation and reinterpretation of American ideals."[5] In order to successfully "reinterpret" the American nation along nationalist terms, propagandists like Creel needed mechanisms of mass communication that could reach the majority. These mechanisms did not exist during the early twentieth century, and alternatives had to be found.[6] These alternatives included the printing of millions of pamphlets; using a national network of locally trained public speakers also known as the "four-minute men"; setting up the National School Service, which was meant to promote nationalism and citizenship in the public school system; printing official state bulletins; hiring large numbers of prominent advertising personnel; and flooding newspapers, from metropolitan dailies to rural weeklies, with information; not to mention the use of mail, telegraphy, and newspaper exchange.[7] Among the many lessons that the agencies and individuals who were part of the CPI learned was that having a means of national communication was necessary. The growth of the advertising industry, which received a boost from the success of the committee's Division of Advertising and Division of Pictorial Publicity, also contributed to the interest in developing new national communication technologies. The emergence of radio and then television coincided with the needs of nationalist propaganda.

Many media historians have pointed out that from its very inception, television was thought of in national terms.[8] Jonathan Sterne argues that as early as the 1920s, television was seen as national in scope. By the 1930s, the key players who would determine the shape of broadcasting understood that the nation was to be the basic geographical unit of television. He quotes NBC president Niles Trammel in 1944: "With national coverage we shall be able to attract the national advertisers to support major program productions. Simultaneous coverage of the nation will enable us to bring into the American home leading events as they occur, and to unite the nation as a single audience to hear and see the great personalities of Government, of education, of the arts, and of entertainment."[9]

Historians disagree on exactly when television became a national medium. The dispute hinges on universal access, the language used to discuss the medium versus its infrastructure and distribution problems, and radio's role in its development. However, most would agree that by the 1960s, a national television medium existed and television news had begun to supersede newspapers and radio. In 1963, a Roper poll found that most people obtained their information from television. Douglas Kellner argues that by the 1960s, television had supplanted radio in its unifying role, stating that "television bound the country together in rituals of national mourning and national drama, and demonstrated that it was now the new national force."[10]

We began to witness what Godfrey Hodgson calls the "nationalizing of American consciousness." "Network TV was making people think nationally. But TV itself was thinking nationally, in news terms as well as in entertainment terms, because other "nationalizing" forces were at work. National networks wanted to build national audiences, so that they could sell space to national advertisers, through national agencies, who were targeting national markets."[11] Michael Schudson explains that as television news became "the symbolic center of the national agenda and the national consciousness," the newsroom culture and the ways in which social problems were viewed changed.[12] Even in governmental policy debates on access, television was discussed in national and nation-building terms. Utah senator Frank Moss argued in 1960, "Every American home should be able to receive at least one free television signal and, eventually if FCC policies and priorities can make this possible, every American community should have its own television station. A TV station helps to give a community a voice, and its place in the neighborhood of communities, and in the State and the Nation."[13] Thus, the assumed national structure and content of early television were viewed as a means of uniting the nation. If the quote above indicates that television was to serve in creating a participatory democracy, where every community had a voice, the reality could not have been further from this vision. Instead, a particular idea of the nation, derived from cold war ideology, was being constructed on the news.

Nancy Bernhard's research reveals that the histories of early television news and cold war ideology are "deeply intertwined." The mutually dependent relationship between the government and television news producers explains the content of the news in the early years of television. Government officials, Bernhard explains, were fully aware of television's potential in constructing citizenship, and television news producers needed help from the government, particularly in the form of inexpensive programming, to produce their shows. The result was a complicity that built a consensus for the cold war and put in place an ideology that would outlive the cold war.

Cold war ideology, like the efforts of the Creel committee, constructed the United States and its "way of life" as characterized by democracy and freedom, guaranteed by a free market. As Bernhard observes, television news "portrayed the communist threat to the American way of life through the lens of consumer capitalism."[14] Patriotism and national identification were equated with personal consumption and an appreciation of free-market capitalism. Various corporations, advocacy groups, and trade associations actively promoted the notion that the interests of the nation were coterminous with the success of business.

The research of Robert Giffith and of Elizabeth Fones-Wolf is illustrative on this point. Giffith shows that the Advertising Council's public service campaigns "sought to promote an image of advertising as a responsible and civic-spirited industry, and of America as a dynamic, classless, and benignly consensual society." Fones-Wolf discusses a range of methods used by corporations and industry groups, such as direct lobbying in support of specific legislation and economic education programs in factories and churches. In their attempt to sell the free-enterprise system, businesses explicitly connected the economy with freedom and individualism. This directly challenged the values of class struggle of the previous decade and New Deal liberalism.[15] The rhetoric of these campaigns involved tying corporate self-interest to the broader public interest. It was in this context that Charles Wilson of General Motors could claim that what was good for GM was good for the nation.

This rhetoric persisted over the following decades due to the cold war. During the Reagan era, the escalation of arms spending and the renewed vigor with which the cold war was prosecuted only entrenched this ideology further, and then the rhetoric of globalization was integrated into the definition. The result is that today, even after the collapse of the Soviet Union, the news takes the free-market nationalist frame of reference for granted, and the interests of the working class are subordinated to those of capital on a national and international scale.

In the following section, I will examine the particular ways in which nationalist ideology was used to frame the UPS strike. Even though the issues raised by the strike go to the heart of globalization policy, by presenting the strike in national terms the media tried to minimize its significance.

Media Frames of the Strike

The dominant framing mechanism used in the strike, the nationalist narrative, consists of two sets of arguments. The first has to do with a particular interpretation of the economy and the second with the nature of society. Economically speaking, a strike is a struggle in which workers, by withholding their labor, resist the work conditions imposed by the employing class. The conflict has two clear sides: the workers and the owners-managers of capital. Covering strikes through the lens of nationalism enables the corporate media, and television in particular, to take the owners' side without appearing overtly biased. Nationalism, as an ideology of cross-class unity, thus serves to marginalize strikers by constructing the public as members of a nation who share a common interest with the capitalist class.[16] There are five economic arguments that enable this construction: a healthy business sector means a healthy economy; Americans are consumers, not workers; the free market best defines the nation and its history and traditions; strikes are un-American; and everyone can achieve the American dream.

Healthy Businesses Equal a Healthy Economy

Initially, the prospect of a strike at UPS was news because it had the potential to disrupt "business as usual" and to precipitate a social and economic crisis. A question that was asked and repeatedly answered before and during the first few days of the strike was "What impact will the strike have on the economy?" For instance, on *Good Morning America,* guest Jeffrey Sonnenfeld, a labor relations professor at Emory University and UPS consultant, was asked, "Could this strike have a profound economic impact nationwide?"[17] One answer to this question is that if the working class was the subject of this inquiry, then the response would be that a successful nationwide strike against low-wage, part-time employment could set a trend, both nationally and internationally, for better wages and jobs. However, neither the host nor the guest had this perspective in mind. Instead, Sonnenfeld stated that the strike would have a "huge impact . . . and retail showrooms, factories, warehouses, can get emptied fairly soon."

Responding to a similar question, Alan Murray of the *Wall Street Journal* argued that by the end of that week, there would be a "real effect" on businesses and the economy. Ed Emmett of the National Industrial Transportation League claimed that a "ripple effect" was likely, leaving businesses that relied on just-in-time delivery stranded and leading to shutdowns and job losses elsewhere in the economy.[18]

The "experts" consulted on the strike's impact were overwhelmingly business-related professionals whose explanations were remarkably similar. They argued that a strike, which disrupts the normal flow of business, was detrimental not only to corporations but to workers as well. In short, the health of an economy is based on the health of business. Absent from these discussions was mention of the fact that through much of the 1990s boom, most Americans saw their wages decrease or stagnate, while the new robber barons increased their overall wealth. No one suggested that the most effective way for workers to address this class polarization is through strikes and collective actions.

The argument about a healthy economy being beneficial to all was not restricted to "experts"; rather, it reflected the networks' general approach. For instance, reporters announced that a strike at "America's largest package delivery firm" was of concern not only to UPS workers but also to "millions of Americans," not to mention the impact on "American business." Other businesses were also given a national identity: "America's warehouses" and "America's largest mail-order catalog houses."[19] Thus, corporations, even those like UPS that have operations in several countries, stand in for the nation, and the health of the economy, based on their prosperity, becomes the interest not only of those who own and control the means of production but also of the rest of society. When business interests became the interests of the nation, the striking workers were marginalized, and an alliance between capitalists and consumers was created.

Although all three networks aired a few stories on part-time employment, probusiness stories vastly predominated. During the second week of the strike, ABC and several other news media outlets corrected this problem, as will be discussed in the following chapter. ABC's second-week coverage stands as somewhat of an exception to the broader arguments that follow.

Americans Are Consumers, Not Workers

Another question that framed the strike's initial coverage was "What does the strike mean for me?"—that is, the viewer of the television news program. When asked this question, Tyler Mathisen, editor of *Money* magazine, responded that there was no cause for worry and that packages already in the system would be safe.[20] It would appear that, for both the host and the respondent, the term *me* stood for consumers rather than workers. Thus, the working-class viewer was invited to identify with UPS as a consumer rather than with the striking workers.[21]

An emphasis on the shared inconvenience caused by the strike enhanced this sense of community between customers and businesses. The strike was the proverbial "spanner in the works." The notion that buyer and seller could no longer reach each other meant that for "individual customers, patience may be at a premium during this strike. For businesses that depend on UPS shipments, the strike's impact is likely to be immediate and crippling." Reporters desperately sought other avenues for the shipment of goods. Anchor Ann Curry asked reporter Joe Johns, "What alternatives do Americans have?" to which he replied that Federal Express and the post office were attempting to take up the slack.[22] A number of stories focused on how these two alternatives were handling the extra business in their attempt to patch up a "crippled national delivery system."

Television news also shouldered the responsibility of teaching us how to compensate for the temporary inconvenience caused by the strike, so we could continue to shop: *Today Show* host Matt Lauer asked, "If I were to order something by—or through a catalog today or through mail order, what would be the immediate impact to me?" The guest, William Dean, a "catalog consultant," replied, "It would really have to depend on the individual company . . . so . . . when you call in, you'd have to ask the company, you know, how's [sic] your method of shipping, and what's going to happen to me on the order?"[23]

The implications are that consumers and business owners, both part of a harmonious national community, have an interest in the maintenance of a healthy national economy. If this connection is made with the middle-class consumer base, which consists of about 20 to 25 percent of the population, then it is relatively accurate.[24] However, it is untrue if it refers to working-class consumers, who make up the vast majority of American society and do not share interests with their employers. But television, whose reason for being is to round up a middle-class audience for advertisers, does not distinguish between these two classes of consumers or even acknowledge that one of them exists. The conclusion is that all consumers have an interest in maintaining a "healthy" economy; thus, any action that goes against the free market benefits no one.

Treasury secretary Robert Rubin, the architect of the 1990s economic recovery, explicitly articulated this argument. Substituting the word *Americans* for class, he argued that it was "very important that we have an economy that works for working Americans and that middle-income Americans, lower income Americans, share in the benefits of economic growth." If the rewards of the economy were being distributed unequally, as was the case with UPS, then, according to Rubin, "that needs to be resolved as between employers and employees in the tradition of our country, which is one of market forces."[25] The "market" and "market forces" become mechanisms for the creation of national well-being, conveniently erasing the history of the labor movement; in place of labor traditions, we were offered capitalist "free market traditions."

American Free-Market Traditions

The rhetoric of nationalism rests on the selective reappropriation of history and what Eric Hobsbawm and Terence Ranger refer to as the "invention of tradition." Hobsbawm explains: "'Invented tradition' is . . . a set of practices, normally governed by overtly or tacitly accepted rules and of a ritual or symbolic nature, which seek to inculcate certain values and norms of behavior by repetition, which automatically implies continuity with the past."[26] In the United States, this tradition has defined the nation by consumption and free-market capitalism. By tacitly accepting the integration of capitalism with the nation, Rubin reinvented "America" through the process discussed by Hobsbawm.

Reporters bolstered this view. For instance, reporter John Palmer explained the origins of the antilabor Taft-Hartley Act as follows:

> *Many Americans* had similar feelings [as Russ Berrie, a small business owner interviewed earlier in the show, who was against the strike] just before Taft-Hartley became law half a century ago. There were dozens of national strikes, as workers demanded the pay raises they'd been denied by the wage and price freeze imposed during World War II. Coal miners' strikes, rail strikes, telephone workers strikes, strikes against the major carmakers, walk-outs by taxi drivers, and even coffin makers. That prompted Congress to take action against what *many* thought was runaway labor by passing a labor-relations bill sponsored by Senator Robert Taft and Congressman Fred Hartley.[27]

We notice here the construction of workers as a distinct and unique part of the population who share little in common with the majority ("many Americans"). Defined as classless subjects of the nation, it becomes possible to see why "many" thought it was necessary to "take action" against these striking workers. Along with owners of coal mines, railroads, and car companies, this majority seems to have pressed for laws to prevent "runaway labor" from achieving its aims. Thus, a strike that threatened to disrupt national harmony not only justified but *required* state action to "put the screws on somewhere in order to protect the economy of this country," as Irwin Gerard, a senior federal mediator who followed Palmer in the story, claimed. The rhetoric of nationalism allowed both Gerard and Palmer to defend the interests of the capitalist class without actually saying so.

Palmer's discussion of Taft-Hartley was based on a selective construction of history that failed to account for the fact that the act was passed with the explicit goal of destroying the labor movement. George Lipsitz argues that the 1940s were a period when workers were beginning to solidify a class-based identity and to develop a broader notion of social change that conflicted with the ideas of the capitalist class.[28] In response, business tried to find legislative means through which class struggle could be checked and the gains of the labor struggles of the 1930s rolled back. In this context, the Taft-Hartley bill, written by the National Association of Manufacturers, was passed.[29] Labor historian Jeremy Brecher points out that the "conditions affecting workers in 1946 cut across industry lines, leading to the closest thing to a *national general strike* of industry in the twentieth century."[30] In 1946 alone, 4.6 million workers were involved in strikes, which suggests a significantly larger consensus for the strike wave than indicated by Palmer. Additionally, Taft-Hartley was not popular. President Truman vetoed the bill and later ran on the promise that he would overturn it.

Thus, a selective appropriation of history allowed the strike narrative to "other" the strikers, that is, to draw the distinction between "us" and "them" and, in the process, erase labor history. However, the strikers were not consistently constructed as "other." At the same time that the strike narrative constructed "us" as consumers and "them" as "runaway labor," it also attempted to assimilate the strikers into the narrative by stressing the strike's impact on them. The strike was futile, we were told, and, thus, un-American.

Strikes Are Un-American

A constant refrain in strike coverage from beginning to end was its threefold impact: on businesses (including UPS), consumers, and workers. This position was shared by reporters, anchors, CEOs, and government representatives. When negotiations broke down, we were informed that to the federal mediator, "things did not look good for the *company,* the *union,* or the *customers.*" A reporter stated that "the strike has become a package deal—affecting *UPS,* the striking *Teamsters Union* and millions of *businesses* and *ordinary customers.*" James Kelly, CEO of UPS, commented that the strike was "not good for our *customers . . .* not good for *our people . . .* not good for our *company.* The strike [was] not good for anyone." Echoing Kelly's sentiment, Bill Clinton said, "This strike is beginning to hurt not only the *company,* but its *employees* and the *people* who depend on it." Dan Rather began a report as follows: "This is the end of the second business week since the Teamsters union struck the United Parcel Service. The *company's* hurting, the *strikers* are hurting, and so are the many people in *business* who depend on them. And while both sides were talking again today, there's no end in sight to this strike so far as anybody can see."[31]

Although it is true that strikes do bring businesses to a halt and impact those who depend on them, that is precisely their *intended* effect. From the point of view of labor, the strike is the most effective means by which to negotiate a better contract. It clearly demonstrates to employers that, without the workers, the system shuts down. When workers go on strike, they not only display their collective strength but also make collective sacrifices for the longer-term good. By the second week of the strike, UPS workers were no longer receiving their regular paychecks; instead, the union distributed weekly checks of fifty-five dollars per worker from the strike fund.

No doubt such scant pay was difficult for the workers involved. All three networks interviewed workers on the picket line to investigate the hardships they had to endure. Stories of worker hardship have a dual character. They can be used to demonstrate either resolve and fortitude or that strikes are "irrational." In an instance of the former, Sal Tutelamundo, a UPS driver who normally earned one thousand dollars a week, was asked how he could manage on fifty-five dollars. He replied that the strike was not "just for the drivers. This [was] for every family in America." Although he did not use the term *class,* Tutelamundo generalized the strikers' interests to those of working-class Americans. Another striker explained how personal hardships had "to be set aside to better the cause."[32] In short, the workers argued that they had to put aside their short-term interests for the sake of longer-term goals. It is through this process that American workers have won many of the benefits they have today.

However, this explanation of the importance of strikes in labor disputes was almost incomprehensible to reporters, particularly those who have never been on strike or part of a labor union. Add to this inexperience the absence of labor history in mainstream discourse, including in public schools, and the dominance of the logic of consumer capitalism that promotes immediate gratification, and these prostrike arguments become unthinkable. Thus, when workers expressed concern about their inability to feed their children and pay rent, these hardships were used to make the argument that strikes benefit no one, not even the workers who are on strike. A perfect illustration of this logic is found in the following report:

> Ray Brady: The noose is tightening around UPS customers. In Connecticut, Susan Laing is closing her Postal Center USA, going out of business.
> Susan Laing: Two weeks ago everything was fine. I had an income. And suddenly, now I don't have an income. I have no UPS.
> Brady: And in Orlando, the noose is tightening around Teamsters Local 385.
> Unidentified Woman #1: And the members are beginning to call and say, "There's no paycheck and my baby needs food."
> Brady: So the local has set up a food bank for the strikers feeling the pinch.
> Unidentified Woman #2: I'm trying to get my two—two grandchildren through school, feed them, clothe them. What am I supposed to do?[33]

Adopting a highly sensationalized tone, the story of Susan Laing, a small business owner (run in greater detail by NBC the previous day) was juxtaposed quite unproblematically with the difficulties faced by the workers to make the larger argument that strikes only devastate.

The failure to explain the justification for a strike displaced the focus onto the problems it caused business, consumers, and workers. The assimilation of workers and their hardships into the nationalist narrative and the random placement of hardship stories within an overall antistrike narrative, bolstered by the strike's impact on small business owners or the petty bourgeoisie, made strikes seem positively un-American.

The Middle Class and the American Dream

A significant number of stories contained interviews with small business owners about the impact of the strike. The audience was told repeatedly that although "the strike [was] costing UPS tens of millions of dollars in lost deliveries, it [was] also undermining thousands of small businesses," such as a bakery in Evanston, Illinois, owned by the Hoopers. Mr. Hooper explained that, unable to ship his products, he was faced with the prospect of laying off his workers. Tom Loomis, who made taxidermy supplies, found the very existence of his business threatened.[34] Russ Berrie, a small business owner with merchandise and shipments ranging in the millions of dollars, could not ship his normal load. He stated that the strike was particularly hurting the "small-business person."[35] These stories illustrated the casualties of an act that disrupted "business as usual," and the viewer was invited to identify or, at the very least, to sympathize with the small business owner.

Underlying this invitation is the unspoken logic of the American dream. Its construction is clearest in NBC interviews with small business owner Berrie. In a morning news story, Berrie stated that small business owners "are the heartbeat of the economy and their dreams [were] being shattered by not having merchandise on the shelf." Later, on *NBC Nightly News,* he added that it was "the small-business person that [was] being hurt. It's the dreams of America we all have."[36] In the rhetoric of the American dream, the middle class, particularly the small business owner, is upheld as an example of hard work and diligence leading to the ownership of private property. The small business becomes the means by which the individual entrepreneur can aspire to the doorstep of the capitalist class.[37] Thus, a strike that jeopardizes the chance of realizing that dream is necessarily un-American. Historically, the strength of this logic has served to blunt class consciousness and promote individualism at the expense of class solidarity. As Mike Davis argues, from the early nineteenth century, the possibility of upward mobility through petty production and small property put the brakes on workers finding collective solutions to their problems.[38]

Arguably, the high point of the American dream was the post–World War II era, when large sections of the population did achieve real material gains. Concurrently, commercial television was able to mass-market consumerism through the logic of the American dream. By the mid-1990s, however, after two decades of declining wages, it was clear that for about three-quarters of the country the dream had become a myth. The economic recovery of the 1990s disproportionately benefited the rich. The story being told by television contradicted the reality for the vast majority of Americans.

In summary, the logic of the economic aspects of the nationalist narrative rests on the generalization of the interests of business to that of the nation. American workers are constructed as consumers with a distinct national interest, rather than as members of an international working class. The argument necessarily relies on an erasure of the history of labor struggles and on the promotion of free-market traditions. Also, in place of class solidarity, the logic of the American dream promotes individualism. Yet the economic arguments of the strike narrative only go so far. They do not explain why the strike was initiated in the first place or, more important, what role each member of the nation had to play in resolving this conflict. It is here that the social aspects of the nationalist narrative assume importance.

All in the Family: Home, Work, and Nation

In nationalist rhetoric, the nation is a large community that draws individuals together on the basis of perceived shared interests. Within this community, the relationships between individuals are defined fundamentally by those in the nuclear family. Over the past quarter century, we have witnessed the reemergence of conservative, patriarchal notions of the family and "family values." Orchestrated as a backlash against feminism and gay rights in the 1980s, the "New Right" argued that most of the country's social problems were due to the disintegration of the family and that it was necessary to bolster the traditional nuclear family. Dana Cloud's analysis of family-values rhetoric in the 1992 presidential race shows that they functioned to scapegoat blacks and the poor for social problems. This logic then served to blame individuals for larger societal issues. Barbara Dafoe Whitehead, vice president of the Institute for American Values, expressed this argument succinctly: "The family serves as the seedbed for the virtues required by a liberal state. The family is responsible for teaching lessons of independence, self-restraint, responsibility, and right conduct, which are essential to a free, democratic society. If the family fails in these tasks, then the entire experiment in democratic self-rule is jeopardized."[39] For Whitehead, the nuclear family bears responsibility for democracy with little or no role for social institutions. This notion of the family has a long history in bourgeois democracies. It derives from the understanding that the family, a self-contained unit based on the uncompensated labor of women, is central to the nation and the place where socialization and disciplining occur.

If the family is understood as a microcosm of the nation, the nation is viewed as an expression of the family. Newt Gingrich, who spearheaded the "Contract with America" in the early 1990s, explained his picture of the nation: "Think of America as a giant family of two hundred and sixty million people of extraordinarily diverse backgrounds riding in a huge car down the highway trying to pursue happiness and seek the American dream." The national family does have problems, or, as Gingrich put it, "a crisis of our entire civilization," which is apparently the product of children straying from familial norms: "twelve-year-olds having babies, fifteen-year-olds killing each other, seventeen-year-olds dying of AIDS, and eighteen-year-olds getting diplomas they can't even read."[40] If the ills of the nation are a product of wayward children, then the solution lies in both parents and the state employing harsher disciplinary measures.

The logic of a nation as a family is illustrated most clearly by David Abshire and Brock Brower in their book, *Putting America's House in Order: The Nation as a Family.*

> Americans readily envision the nation operating as one big family. If not all stuffed into Newt's big car, still acting in concert. Everybody pulls together in this country, we often tell ourselves, like family. And when we criticize some aspect of national behavior, such as the escalating deficit, we argue that we should have more sense, most families would not plunge into debt this way. We all know what we mean by "family values." The family represents loyalty, cohesion, religious or moral principles, the care and love of children, pride, even patriotism.[41]

In the nuclear family, parents are accorded legitimate authority to subject their children to the requirements necessary to socialize them, even if this conflicts with the rights or choices of the child, and especially when children are defiant. Since their bonds are supposedly based on love, individual members must give up their rights in the interests of familial harmony. When the nation becomes a family, a similar subordination of individual rights is expected. Thus, the family and patriarchal relations within the family become a way of justifying the existing power relationships within the nation.

The extent to which this rhetoric is reflected in the mainstream media is demonstrated in the way it takes the nationalist antistrike narrative for granted. Television, in particular, has a long history of framing stories through the lens of a family. In the context of war reporting, Dan Hallin observes that "television loves, in fact, to find stories that allow it to celebrate the unity of the National Family. These are essential to the dramatic structure of the news: Evil must stand in contrast to Good, disharmony to the ideal of harmony."[42] In this antistrike narrative, three levels of familial discourse function to exclude other ways of thinking about kinship and community: nuclear, corporate, and national. The nuclear family consists of heterosexual, monogamous parents and children. The corporate family consists of management and workers. The national family consists of consumers, the corporate family, and the state. In each of these cases, the power to discipline in the interests of familial harmony lies with the "parent," usually the father. In the corporate family, the parental disciplining figure is management, and in the national family, it is the state.

The Nuclear Family

The nuclear family appeared in several stories about the picket line. For instance, a reporter announced that it "was a family affair on the picket line today for striking driver Edward Howse. He brought his three-year-old son Alex with him, and his wife Susan and their four-month-old son, Ryan."[43] The aim of family stories was to depict, on the one hand, their hardships and, on the other, the family as a haven against external crises. An interview with the Passaretti family illustrated the latter:

> Bill Ritter (reporter, voice-over): Now the strike is also hitting home for Passaretti's wife, Laura.
> Laura Passaretti: It is scary, but I—like I said, I work, I work for an insurance company, you know, I make a good salary. And we're just going to have to manage.
> Bill Ritter (voice-over): And the Passaretti kids are also pitching in. Twenty-one-year-old Anthony Jr. works as a plumber, and 17–year-old Denise is a clerk at a grocery store.
> Denise Passaretti: I don't make that much money, but if they needed it, like, I would give it to them, I think.
> Anthony Passaretti Jr.: They did it for me for 21 years, I'm willing to give back anything.[44]

This story resonated perfectly with the image of the ideal nuclear family that pulls together during a crisis. Certainly, the nuclear family does protect workers both financially and emotionally from the vicissitudes of the market, but in the antistrike narrative, these familial bonds are stressed over and above those among the workers themselves. Thus, the way in which unions and unorganized workers pulled together in solidarity with the striking workers was not discussed as a metaphor for an extended family, even though in historic precedents, workers refer to each other as family members to show class solidarity.[45]

During this strike, rallies held across the nation brought together hundreds and, at times, thousands of union and nonunion workers who joined and reinforced picket lines.[46] The limited coverage of this public support and the financial contributions made by other unionists, workers, and members of various communities worked to erase this solidarity. Ninety-five percent of UPS workers did not cross the picket line, and 55 percent of the American public supported the strikers.[47] In place of such class solidarity, news coverage focused on the individual strength that derives from the bonds of loyalty among nuclear family members.

The Corporate Family

The corporate family consists of workers and managers whose relationship is based on mutual dependence, teamwork, and the surrender of individual interests for the benefit of the company as a whole. According to this logic, UPS, we were informed, was the ideal corporate family, as one reporter described it:

> Scott Cohn (reporter): This [strike] is almost completely out of character at a company where labor/management relations have traditionally been among the coziest in corporate America.
> Janny Pollock (Striking Employee): With the company and the . . . employees . . . it was like . . . a family thing.
> Cohn: In fact, Jim Casey, who founded UPS, was a teen-ager in 1907—actually invited the Teamsters union to organize his workforce. . . . But in recent years, with competition growing, the company has been cutting costs to stay on top . . . relying on part-time workers and paying them at a lower rate. And so a family feud with UPS managers, many of whom worked their way up the ranks, now on the inside looking out.[48]

From the way the story is told, UPS used to be an ideal corporate family, where workers and management had no conflicts. However, because management, the parental actor, succumbed to the external pressures of competition, work conditions deteriorated. Management had basically reneged on its responsibility to its workers/children, resulting in a "dysfunctional UPS family." However, as with most "family feuds," reconciliation was an imminent possibility, and a solution was extremely likely, thanks to familial bonds. At the conclusion of the strike, Michael Baroody of the National Association of Manufacturers commented: "We're talking about a company and a union that has a 60–year relationship. They worked it out and that's good news for all concerned."[49]

This construction was not left unchallenged. Ron Carey, as will be discussed in the next section, was quoted several times on the hypocrisy behind UPS's veneer of an "ideal corporation," pointing to the huge profits it accumulated at the cost of workers' wages. However, within the dominant narrative, the logic of corporate paternalism was so complete that the bonds between manager and employee were supposed to be forged in love. On one segment, a manager was heard saying, "Remember the people out there on the other side. They're our employees. We love them. We're going to love them when they come back." The company tried to portray utmost concern for its employees. Its representatives constantly referred to UPS workers as "our people." When asked to comment on why 57 percent of the U.S. population supported the strikers, CEO James Kelly responded, "If you were to pit a large corporation against a friendly, courteous UPS driver, I'd vote for the UPS driver, also. I think if you talk about who has the welfare of the UPS people more in minds, UPS or the Teamsters, you get a different response."[50] Kelly's argument allows corporations to express concern about their workers while distancing the union from the workers. Ultimately, father—in this case, UPS management—knows best.

When the strike was settled, a reporter concluded that "in the end, it sounded more like a lovefest than one of the biggest battles . . . on the labor market in the US in more than two decades." Proof of this assessment was presented as follows:

> David Murray (UPS's chief negotiator): To our employees, we hope to welcome you back very soon. And when you are back, we hope that we will join together once again, roll up our sleeves and do what we have to do to rebuild this great company of ours, UPS.
>
> Ron Carey (President, Teamsters Union): The best salesman for the customer, of course, is the UPS package car driver. And as a result, we will encourage our members—and they'll do it on their own—to get out there and to get that customer base back.[51]

For all the animosity between the company and the union, even Ron Carey started to make gestures of reconciliation, a picture-perfect ending for a family that had withstood the trial presented by the strike. This myth is shattered by the fact that soon the company stated that it would not create the full-time jobs to which it had agreed in negotiations. Even after the National Labor Relations Board ruled that UPS had to honor the 1997 contract, implementation was slow.[52]

Tom Tuttle, a UPS driver, became the poster boy for a nonconfrontational solution to the "crisis" that most resonated with the corporate family scenario:

> Whitaker [reporter]: Union man, company man, family man. UPS has afforded Tuttle, his wife Heather and their six children a good life.
>
> Tuttle: It's been a great job. My wife is able to stay at home with our kids. UPS has really provided a—a good living for us.
>
> Heather Tuttle: UPS is great. Where else can you work and make the money—kind of money that Tom makes without a college education?
>
> Whitaker: Now they can't pay the mortgage. If the strike drags on, they could lose the house.

Tuttle: We have worked so hard to buy our home. We love the home. Now the union, along with UPS, has given us so much. So it's—it's both. And I am torn. It's like a family feud.[53]

Unable to understand the need for a strike or to recognize the class nature of the conflict, Tuttle appeared like a child caught in a dispute between his parents, UPS and the union leadership. Placed in a vulnerable situation, Tuttle could not explain why the familial status quo had broken down. He seemed to be the all-American success story—he made a comfortable living, headed a nuclear family with a stay-at-home wife, and owned a home—and both the company and the union, he believes, made this lifestyle possible. Unable to take sides between quarreling parents, Tuttle was in a quandary.

This story was so consistent with the all-American narrative of the strike that versions of this segment were run twice the next day.[54] In many ways, Tuttle was representative of the elitist construction of the strikers. The workers were shown as either deviant children involved in picket-line violence or innocents under the sway of the union leadership; in both cases, they were portrayed as victims rather than self-conscious agents of change.

The National Family

Encompassing the corporate and the nuclear families is the overarching national family. It brings together business, consumers, workers, and the state in a harmonious relationship. When "normal" relations between the first three are disrupted, state intervention is presented as the logical outcome and in the interest of all Americans. That is, when the parents of the corporate family have failed in their tasks or when children have committed deviant acts, the intervention of the paternal state becomes necessary.

The state can intervene in a strike in at least two ways. It can use laws, such as the Taft-Hartley Act, to end the strike, or it can bring labor and management together to facilitate the process of negotiation. The Clinton administration chose the latter course, a prudent choice given that polls taken later showed that the use of Taft-Hartley would have been extremely unpopular.[55] Labor secretary Alexis Herman, who played an active role in resolving the conflict, explained that when "there are differences, it takes real work. It takes hard work to bridge those differences. But when there are shared values and there is a shared commitment at stake, then that work is made easier."[56] This form of reasoning assumes that it is both legitimate and natural for the state to become a family counselor of sorts and act in the interests of "shared" national values. Rather than representing the relationship between UPS and the

Teamsters as fundamentally antagonistic, since the well-being of the employing class is achieved at the cost of the work and living conditions of labor, the conflict is seen as a temporary bump on the road to national harmony.

Treasury secretary Rubin, emphasizing the negotiating process, stated that the labor secretary had been "working with the parties, trying to keep them at the table and working together to get this resolved between themselves." Rahm Emanuel, senior adviser to Clinton, repeated several times that the solution to the strike was to continue negotiation, arguing that "the American people want them to find the differences and . . . a way to bridge their differences and also come to understand that they had to find the solution . . . by negotiating." At the strike's conclusion, John Calhoun Wells, the federal mediator, explained the role of the state: "We had a clear understanding of each other's point of view, and we tried to see not only what our interests were but what their interests were. And our job as the mediator was to try to get people to look beyond their own self-interest to the shared interests that would be good not only for them but for the other party as well."[57]

Herman, who is credited with bringing about the settlement, triumphantly declared that what "we saw working was collective bargaining at its best. They got to the table, they worked out their differences, and that really is how it should be if we're going to honor the spirit of collective bargaining in this country today."[58] In short, members of the national family can be brought together to reach decisions of collective benefit through the dispassionate yet persistent efforts of the neutral paternal state. What is implicit in all these interviews with Herman, Reich, Rubin, and Emanuel is the legitimacy of state intervention into labor disputes in the capacity of a neutral parental arbiter.

The most focused discussion of state intervention took place on August 10. All three networks interviewed various state officials, union representatives, and company spokespersons to determine whether President Bill Clinton should employ the Taft-Hartley Act. UPS argued that Clinton should, while labor representatives John Sweeney and Ron Carey argued that he should not. Neither side questioned the *legitimacy* of state intervention in labor struggles. Instead, the debate centered on corruption, with the charge that Clinton had not intervened because of the Teamsters' financial contributions to his campaign. Sweeney, president of the AFL-CIO, jumped to Clinton's defense, claiming that Clinton had not used Taft-Hartley because he believed in collective bargaining and workers' right to strike.[59] This defense is questionable, given that only a few months prior to this strike, Clinton had prevented American Airlines workers from striking by using the Railway Labor Act. Immediately after the UPS strike, he used the same act to stop Amtrak workers from striking.

Also note that barely a week after the conclusion of one of the most successful strikes for labor in two decades, Carey's election was declared null and void by a government overseer, who claimed that Carey knew about election-finance wrongdoing while offering no real evidence of his direct involvement. After the strike, UPS publicly pressured the former election officer to disqualify Carey from reelection; Republican representatives Bob Barr (Georgia) and Joe Scarborough (Florida), who had attacked Carey during the hearings, are believed to have received donations from UPS. None of the networks broadcast the details of his dismissal. Ironically, at that time, Bill Clinton and Newt Gingrich were both involved in scandals of open violation of election-finance laws yet were not dismissed from office. Furthermore, if state intervention into unions was genuinely about national well-being, why was Jimmy Hoffa Jr., Carey's opponent in the union elections who is reputed to have open ties to organized crime, not investigated for the two million dollars in unaccounted contributions to his campaign that were supposedly raised by "bingo and bake sales"? At the very least, Carey's dismissal opens up the question of the neutrality of the state in labor disputes. Ultimately, in 2001, he was acquitted in the federal case.

In summary, in each of the families discussed, the subordinated members were expected to forfeit their rights for the good of the family, and in each case, the parental figure was assumed to arbitrate in the interests of the entire nuclear, corporate, or national family. We also saw that, from reporters and anchors to government officials, business leaders, and business professors, the nationalist narrative was taken for granted as the natural way of framing the strike. The section on the economic aspects of the nationalist narrative also demonstrates how the conventions of the narrative make certain messages acceptable and others unmentionable. Thus, whereas business interests were presented as being in the national interest, those of labor were marginalized and even subordinated to those of the national family.

However, such a narrative convention did not go uncontested. Ron Carey, who was interviewed several times on all three networks, put forward a powerful attack on the nationalist narrative.

Carey's Nation

As the leader of the Teamsters union, Ron Carey was faced with the task of challenging the nationalist narrative and presenting an alternative framework from which to understand the strike, taking into account the interests of workers. In studying the various news programs on which Carey appeared,

I found that he, like most labor representatives, was limited from making an effective case. There are several ways in which a news organization can filter a message, such as how editors select and place quotes within a larger story, the kinds of questions asked in interviews, and decisions about who speaks last, among others. All these factors had an impact on how Carey's statements were interpreted and inserted by the editors, journalists, and other media personnel. However, despite these limitations, Carey, a skillful speaker, was able to present a powerful prolabor message, carefully constructed and thought through by the union (as discussed in chapter 5). This message took corporate America to task, introducing into the mainstream media the rhetoric of anticorporatism that, until then, had not received such attention.

Labor Nationalism

This anticorporate rhetoric, I argue, is best described as "labor nationalism," because it inverts the logic of corporate nationalism by making labor the most important member of the nation. The key arguments of labor nationalism are presenting the progress of workers as essential for national progress and demonstrating that the interests of labor are really the interests of the nation (a nation of workers); and presenting an alternative set of national traditions based on notions of morality and decency and pitting corporate greed against the American dream (labor is more American than corporations). Labor nationalism refutes and challenges the nationalist narrative almost point by point.

A Nation of Workers

The thrust of Carey's argument focused on the mistreatment of UPS workers. He explained what the strike was about as follows: "It's about corporate greed, a company that has made $1 billion profit. A company that has over 10,000 part-timers who work 35 hours a week on part-time, low-wages. That's wrong."[60] He went on to generalize from this point by arguing that the same treatment was meted out to all American workers at the hands of "greedy corporations." In several instances, Carey was heard emphatically declaring that the strike against UPS was for all workers, in the process redefining Americans as *workers* rather than as consumers. Thus, the strike came to symbolize the struggle of all American workers against corporate greed. The following are examples of his argument:

> This is really a fight about good jobs. This is not just a fight about Teamsters and their families, it is about working people in this country. You have big companies in this country that are shifting to part-time, low-

wage, throwaway, disposable jobs, subcontracting the work out. Those are some of the vital issues. And as I say, it's a shame, and working people have said, "Enough is enough."

This is an issue about America, where America is going, and jobs that are in America—good, decent, full-time jobs.

In this country, big companies like UPS are shifting to these low-wage, part-time jobs, expanding their subcontracting, outsourcing, and here we have a classic example of trying to grab members' pension money. So what workers want in this country is decent jobs, full-time jobs. That's what America needs. This is not just about Teamsters. This is about American families.[61]

In Carey's rhetoric, working people became the main subjects of the nation, and their needs came to define the character of the nation. Thus, the nation's well-being depended on the workers' well-being. In no uncertain terms, Carey denounced big business for frustrating national aspirations for "good, full-time jobs." The specific focus on UPS, which had "made a billion dollars in profit" and failed to adequately compensate its workers, became a launching pad from which to fight all corporations.[62]

Labor Is More American than Corporations

To win support for this argument within a media system that views the success of corporations and high rates of profit as the basis of a "healthy economy" and beneficial to all citizens, Carey made a moral case associated with a different American tradition based on labor's history. If, for Robert Rubin, the tradition of the United States was the free market, for Ron Carey, it was decent jobs for American families. In opposition to Sonnenfeld, Rubin, and others, Carey stated that the U.S. tradition was about "decency" and "what [was] right and wrong" for working Americans. Carey relocated the terrain of the struggle from the monetary to the moral realm.

This is an American issue. This is not just about dollars and cents, it's about what's *right* in this country.

It think this is a fight for good jobs in America. It's a fight that working families have been taking on the chin. Twenty million Americans work part-time and work two and three jobs. That's *wrong*. This is an issue that has to be dealt with. The—creating good full-time jobs is good for our members, it's good for American working families.

This is an issue about America, where America is going, and jobs that are in America—good, decent, full-time jobs.[63]

In fact, this tradition was so important that the very future of the nation depended on whether the union won the strike and stopped the trajectory toward "disposable jobs."

> What Americans want is hope. They want to look to the future. They want to have a decent full-time job, to be able to purchase a home. There are no part-time mortgages; there are no part-time car payments. That's what it's about. It's about the future of where jobs are going. This country is moving more and more towards disposable jobs, towards throwaway jobs, and enough is enough.
>
> This is a fight about America's future. It's a fight about working people in this country.
>
> If UPS is determined to rob the future for American working families, the labor movement will do whatever it takes to fight back.
>
> It's about the future and it's about where these jobs go in the future. Company's position is to expand more part-time jobs. That's not what America's future should be about.[64]

In the above quotes, Carey presents an argument in which the nation's future and its tradition of righteousness and decency rest on the strike's outcome. In short, the nation's history and its future are the history and future of working-class people. This belief stands in stark contrast to "free-market" traditions. Carey's strident anticorporate rhetoric has many strands in common with the arguments put forward by activists in the antisweatshop movement of the 1990s and those of global-justice activists in the antiglobalization movement that would take shape in the United States after the 1999 protests in Seattle.

At the conclusion of the strike, when the union had won a majority of its demands, Carey extended this theme:

> Our fight for good jobs in America marks an historic turning point for working people in this country.
>
> This strike marks a new era. American workers have shown that if we stand up to corporate greed—this victory sends a signal that American workers are on the move again.[65]

These Carey sound bites directly counter many aspects of the nationalist narrative. They question the legitimacy of the idea that business interests are the same as the nation's interests, pointing instead to the interests of working people. They challenge the notion of the corporate family by pointing to its callous and ruthless behavior. In place of free-market traditions, Carey puts forward labor traditions through a discussion of ethics. Public opinion surveys conducted during the strike found that 55 percent supported the union and seemed to reject the corporate nationalist arguments. This was the product of several factors, discussed in greater detail in chapter 5. However, Carey's central role in mobilizing and crystallizing this anticorporate sentiment cannot be discounted.

At the same time, the limitations of labor nationalism as a rhetorical and tactical strategy must be discussed in the interest of future struggles and workers' internationalism. For instance, the November 1999 protests against the World Trade Organization in Seattle presented yet another instance when anticorporate and antiglobalization sentiments came to the fore through the efforts of workers and students, but it was marred, in part, by the nationalist rhetoric espoused by the United Steel Workers union and the Teamsters trying to prevent U.S. jobs from moving overseas. The problem of job loss in the United States is not the fault of workers in other countries but rather corporations rushing after cheap sources of labor. Unions should find ways to protect *all* workers from job loss and deteriorating wages and working conditions. Although appeals to nationalism were a minor part of the Seattle protests, they became a dividing line between most demonstrators and the labor movement in the April 2000 protests against the World Bank and the International Monetary Fund in Washington, D.C. Several unions organized a separate march on April 12 against China's inclusion in the WTO, which diminished the turnout for the April 16 demonstration. Furthermore, by inviting rabid ultraconservative nationalists like Patrick Buchanan to the April 12 demonstration, the union leadership opened the door for a form of hysteria reminiscent of the cold war. Labor nationalism weakens the struggle by dividing workers along national lines.

Carey's arguments, though oppositional, made concessions to nationalism. Labor nationalism is based on a reformist ideology that claims that workers can fully realize their interests under capitalism or, more specifically, within a particular type of nation that ensures the fair treatment of its workers.[66] Thus, even though it offered a critique of corporate nationalism, it failed to go beyond the parameters of nationalism. In all of the quotes above, Carey rarely, if ever, used the term *working class*—instead workers were referred to, almost exclusively, as "American workers," "American families," "working families," and "working people in this country." Thus, an international class-based identity was not counterposed to a national identity.

Ultimately, such an argument accepts capitalist relations of production.

For instance, Carey admitted that, in negotiating the contract, "you have to understand the company's operational problems."[67] Labor nationalism, while endorsing the struggle of the disfranchised against their exploitation, fails to question the very system that produces the exploitation. The clearest demonstration of this concession to capitalist logic was found in Carey's statements about the American dream.

> It's about good jobs in America. It's about jobs that have some hope for the great American Dream.

> Well, I think this country has come to terms with the kind of greed that's out there and what we should be doing—I mean, it's just very short-sightedness. Down the road, people that have good jobs, buy homes, purchase cars, they have an opportunity to the great American Dream, and that's what America is all about.[68]

Recourse to the American dream is a clever rhetorical strategy and a means to justify the union demands, but ultimately it concedes too much ground to the existing system.

After the strike, UPS reneged on some of aspects of the contract, such as the creation of full-time jobs, and it took years in arbitration before any headway could be made. This is because for UPS it makes economic sense to replace full-time workers with part-timers, given that it is competing with other transportation companies and must seize economic advantages wherever it can. For workers, part-time jobs are unacceptable because they do not provide a living wage. These irreconcilable class differences are part and parcel of the current economic system; only by creating a society based on equality can they be overcome.

Note that the recourse to nationalism is not new to the union movement. As Dana Frank suggests, unions have been involved in the politics of economic nationalism for more than a century.[69] At various points, they have either joined existing "buy American" campaigns or launched their own as a means of protecting American jobs. Additionally, the AFL-CIO's complicity with McCarthyism led to attempts to reconstruct unions as true-blue American institutions. More broadly, nationalism as a political philosophy fits perfectly with the conservatism of the union bureaucracy. Its structural role is to negotiate the terms by which workers can be exploited without rocking the system of exploitation. Carey is an exception to this rule. Because he had worked as a UPS driver, he appreciated his members' work conditions. However, he and his team of organizers were not completely immune from a tendency that has been a recurring feature at the top of the union movement.

The Construction of the Rank and File

The 185,000 UPS workers who, by stopping work, brought the company to a standstill should have played a central role in the story of the strike. Instead, for the most part they were relegated to the sidelines on network television (except when they proved useful to the nationalist narrative). This process of marginalization stems from the conventions of news reporting as well as the biases in the nationalist narrative. One such convention is that reporters tend to gravitate to those in positions of power, who are seen as "legitimate" sources.[70] Rank and filers were rarely interviewed; Carey and other union officials were relied upon to represent them. While Carey appeared in about seventy stories, a few of which are extended interviews, sound bites of the rest of the 185,000 workers can be found in fewer than fifty stories, and several of these were repeat airings.[71] Fewer than ten stories on all three networks were exclusively about workers on the picket line and featured their opinions of the strike.

A second convention, a consequence of the first, is that the actions of the "legitimate" sources are viewed as being the most important and, therefore, the proper focus of news coverage. Thus, the negotiation process involving the heads of UPS, the union, and the state became the key focus. Workers on the picket line, involved in the important task of preventing replacement workers from continuing UPS business, were sidestepped unless they proved useful in providing drama. Strike reporting nowhere emphasized that the power that the union representatives had at the negotiating table derived from the economic power of the workers to stop production and prevent the accumulation of profit. This bias combined with the logic of the corporate family meant that rank-and-file workers were presented as mere pawns in a larger game. In short, workers were constructed as objects rather than subjects who can act in meaningful ways.

Common stereotypes of workers as being unintelligent and unable to understand larger economic issues further objectified them. Reporters consciously or unconsciously subscribe to these stereotypes because of the perceived difference between mental labor and manual labor. Mental labor is viewed as being superior to manual labor, and, not coincidentally, reporters perform mental labor. In short, the economic interests or perceived interests of reporters and publishers shape their views of the economy, strikes, and manual workers.[72]

The end result is that the workers were barely covered, and when they were, the story was less than flattering. Most of the appearances of workers in news stories were as brief sound bites within larger stories. Because we do not hear the questions asked, their comments can be edited into preconceived narratives on the status of the strike. For the most part, their comments did not shape a story but were spliced into a story where they confirmed a certain angle. Extrapolating from their answers and those stories in which the questions were part of the narrative, we see that workers were asked three types of questions: the impact of the strike on their lives, their reactions to the negotiation process or the settlement, and their work conditions. All three questions were framed in ways that solicited an emotional rather than a rational response. For instance, answers to the first and third questions evoked responses about hardship, whether mental, physical, or financial. In both cases, when discussing their conditions, workers were shown as being *acted upon* by the strike and their workplace. The second question yielded responses that ranged from tension and stress to joy. Other worker responses included their feeling toward those who had crossed the picket line.

In contrast to the emotionally charged questions asked of the workers, Carey was asked questions regarding the status of the strike, the economy, and politics. Thus, while workers were primarily asked about how they felt, Carey was asked what he thought.[73] In the process, the workers were objectified and shown to be driven by emotional reactions rather than intellect. When people are seen as lacking the ability to think rationally, then their behavior can be explained through emotional motivations. When the workers attempted to prevent replacement workers from taking over their jobs, they were seen as driven by "bitterness," "tension," and "worry," as the following quotes illustrate:

> Bitter confrontations continue along the picket lines at UPS facilities across the country.

> And on the picket lines, it was another bitter day.

> UPS workers got their last paycheck from the company yesterday. Not surprisingly, the tension is showing on the picket lines. Police arrested more strikers in Massachusetts. In that state and at least eight others, UPS has asked for restraining orders to stop picketers from interfering with UPS business.

> Twenty-three Teamsters from this Boston-area picket line have been arrested this week, a sign of how deeply emotions are running in this walkout.[74]

Little effort was made to explain why it was in the material interest of strikers to prevent their jobs from being taken over. Instead, the drama of picket-line conflict was played out. There was no attempt to explain that workers on the picket line must stop replacement workers from taking their jobs; otherwise, they would weaken their own position. The central goal of a strike is to shut down production and use the collective power from this action to demand a better contract. If the company restarts with replacement workers, the striking workers have lost their leverage. Over the course of the 1990s, some of the major strikes, from Staley to Bridgestone-Firestone, were lost because workers and their union leadership failed to make a priority of stopping replacement workers. Had this context been provided, it would have demonstrated that UPS workers were acting in rational self-interest and not simply reacting in emotional ways. Lacking this explanation, the workers were presented as emotional and even violent. A reporter surmised that "when there is worry on the line, of course, there's the question of violence."[75] Thus, an act of self-interest was reduced to emotional outbursts or character flaws:

> Now people we spoke to on the line have mixed feelings. They say they want to keep it calm here, but this is their first week without a paycheck and also the first week that there are no talks about possible new negotiations at the table. That, of course, is going to be very hard for the workers here, and tempers may flare, they say.[76]

> Teamsters Local 25 is a rowdy groups, always has been, and this week's 23 arrests have made these workers even more committed to stopping the trickle of packages leaving this UPS plant in Somerville, Massachusetts.[77]

When the strikers were allowed to explain their activity on the picket line, the sound bites used were consistent with the emotional and nonrational characterizations:

> George Cashman (President, Teamsters Union 25): We certainly don't stand on the picket line like Gumby and just let everybody go by without expressing, you know, our true feelings about what's happening and what the issues are.[78]

At the end of the day, the workers on the picket line looked more like brutish thugs than people involved in the process of struggle to advance their interests. We were presented with a common stereotype of the working class, in line with the popular conception of the Luddites, who cannot process intelligent ideas and must therefore resort to physical violence. The picket line and the initiative of the working class completely lost significance, and the workers were silenced. This characterization is best captured in this quote: "Both sides admit that these skirmishes [on the picket line] are just the noisiest manifestations of the real war going on inside the negotiating room in Washington."[79] When workers are given a marginal role in the story of the strike, the site of struggle can be shifted from the picket line to the negotiating table, where the corporate and national families were hard at work to reach a resolution that was beneficial to the nation.

Conclusion

In a globalized world, the rhetoric of nationalism is used selectively and conveniently by network television to marginalize the interests of labor. The nationalist narrative constructs the "public interest" as being the same as that of business. This understanding of what is in the "national" interest has a long history. Throughout the twentieth century, men like George Creel worked to undo identity formation based on "selfish" class interests and, instead, sought to present all members of the nation as sharing a common goal. Charles Wilson would argue that the success of GM automatically translated into national successes.[80]

The strength of this procorporate story of the American nation lies in the fact that it is still used today, in ways both conscious and unconscious, to frame strikes and labor disputes. Yet this story did not go unchallenged. The UPS strike was significant in that, for the first time in two decades, an anticorporate sentiment was visible on a national scale. This anticorporate mood found its expression not only in the polls, with 55 percent of the population supporting the Teamsters, but also in mass rallies and demonstrations. The most vocal critic of corporate nationalism was Ron Carey. Despite the limitations of "labor nationalism," Carey was successful in introducing anticorporate language into mainstream news channels. As the next chapter will show, the *New York Times* and the *Washington Post* would take this language a step further in exposing the extent to which corporations have failed to deal fairly with their workers.

FOUR

Breaking Through: Newspaper Coverage of the UPS Strike

The nationalist narrative is only one among many framing mechanisms by which the news media marginalize working-class interests. Michael Parenti argues that strike reporting has a distinct antilabor pattern consisting of seven elements.[1] First, strikes are depicted as senseless acts that could be avoided through discussion; second, the impact on the economy and the inconvenience to the public are highlighted, while little is said about the deeper causes of strikes that may also have negative economic and other public consequences; third, offers that reflect favorably on the company are celebrated, whereas take-backs are ignored; fourth, management's large salary increases and stock options are not mentioned, while the supposedly high wages labor would enjoy if it accepts management's "offer" are emphasized; fifth, public support for the strikers is neglected; sixth, whereas the damage caused to the economy is underscored, the damage to workers' interests if they give up the strike is not acknowledged; and seventh, the state is represented as a neutral arbiter whose task is to restart production, regardless of the settlement terms.

To this analysis, William Puette adds that even the language used to describe strikes is biased in favor of management. Thus, labor makes "threats" and "demands," while management "offers." Christopher Martin's analysis of four strikes in the 1990s (plus the WTO protests) reveals that there are five dominant frames in media coverage of labor.[2] First, the media focus almost entirely on consumers ("the consumer is king"); second, the process of production is obscured from the public; third, the economy is presented as being driven by great business leaders and entrepreneurs; fourth, the workplace is presented as a meritocracy where everyone gets what they deserve; and fifth, collective economic action is presented as bad.

Despite the media's negative portrayal of labor, time and again, workers have tried to resist this characterization and present different viewpoints in the media. The dominance/resistance model, discussed in chapter 2, explains how this tug-of-war works. It is based on a dynamic understanding of consent formation and sheds light on the process of hegemony as the *struggle* among groups. The mass media are one arena where this struggle can take place. This chapter explores how the battle over ideas played out in major national newspapers during the strike, specifically, in *USA Today,* the *Washington Post,* and the *New York Times.*[3] Together, they carried a total of about 191 strike-related stories and editorials.[4]

The treatment of the strike in these papers represents, to a greater or lesser extent, the range of thought permissible in the mainstream media. Each paper constructed a narrative that followed the standard patterns for representing labor, but they also deviated from them. I have therefore divided their strike coverage into three parts in order to explain the shifts: Phase One (July 31 to August 9) marks the beginning of the strike, when coverage was fairly traditional; Phase Two (August 10 to August 18), the thick of the struggle, when there was a shift in favor of labor; and Phase Three (August 19 to September 3), after the settlement, which showed a reversion to traditional coverage.

Phase One (July 31–August 9): The Advil Generation— Naturalizing Overwork

On July 31, 1997, the contract deadline between United Parcel Service and the International Brotherhood of Teamsters expired. Agreement had not been reached between the two parties due to several unresolved issues, as shown in table 3. UPS's "last, best, and final" offer included the following proposals: withdraw from the union's multiemployer pension plan, provide a marginal increase in pay, create one thousand new full-time jobs, and secure a five-year contract. The union proposed staying with the multiemployer plan, increasing pay more substantially, creating ten thousand full-time jobs for part-timers, and obtaining a four-year contract.

The union's negotiating points were determined months prior to the strike, through a communications strategy known as the "contract campaign," which is discussed in greater detail in the following chapter. The cam-

Table 3. Prestrike demands

UPS's "last, best, and final" offer	Teamsters' position
1. Create 1,000 new full-time jobs	1. Create 10,000 new full-time jobs
2. Withdraw from the union's multiemployer pension	2. Stay with the multiemployer pension plan
3. Marginal increase in pay	3. Greater pay increases
4. Five-year contract	4. Four-year contract

Note. UPS's "last, best, and final" offer was not public information (Margaret Grynastyl, UPS public relations coordinator, personal communication, May 7, 1999). The union's stance was also unavailable to the press (Rand Wilson, Teamsters communications coordinator, personal communication, March 11, 1999). Adapted from "Teamsters Can Make Big Gains," *Socialist Worker* (August 15, 1997): 15.

paign revealed that the creation of full-time jobs was of utmost importance to a large number of workers. As mentioned in chapter 1, the union had found that since 1993, 83 percent of the forty-six thousand jobs created by UPS were part-time, and base wages for part-timers had stayed stagnant since 1982. The gap between part-time wages (about $8–$10 per hour) and full-time wages (about $19.95 per hour) was significant. Hiring part-timers thus kept wages low, which helped UPS to realize $1 billion in profits in 1996. The union argued that the company did not need so many part-timers and could afford to create more full-time jobs. The union also found that, in an average week, about ten thousand part-timers worked more than thirty-five hours, pointing to the possibility of converting these jobs to full-time status.[5]

UPS countered that part-time jobs made the company more "flexible" within the global market and able to compete with nonunion transportation companies. It claimed that work flows in the company had "peak" and "slack" times and that hiring part-time workers to cover the "peak" periods was economically more efficient. Furthermore, according to its internal surveys, many workers did not want full-time jobs. It contended that a majority of part-timers were students, women with family responsibilities, or others in situations that led them to prefer part-time employment. However, they were silent on whether these groups also "preferred" lower wages and fewer benefits. Thus, the company stressed that the salient differences were pensions and withdrawal from the Teamsters' multiunion plan. It claimed that with its plan, UPS workers would receive as much as 50 percent more in pension benefits than if they stayed with the current plan.[6]

Whereas the company blamed the breakdown in negotiations on differences about pensions, the union sought to highlight the part-time issue, health and safety, subcontracting, and wages and to generalize from them to the condition of working-class Americans in the 1990s economy. After all, the increase in contingent employment, the creation of tiered workforces, the practice of subcontracting, and so on were not unique to UPS but standard corporate practices in the era of globalization. By broadening the issues at UPS and encompassing all American workers, the Teamsters were, in effect, striking a blow at the logic of globalization. In the absence of a settlement on August 4, Ron Carey called a national strike that was to last fifteen days.

In Phase One, the strike or the possibility of a strike was news, because it would disrupt the normal functioning of capitalism. The shutting down of UPS's services meant that about 80 percent of all packages shipped by ground in the United States would stop. This was no doubt newsworthy, and prior to the strike, all three newspapers ran articles on the impact that a strike could have on businesses and the transportation of their goods.

USA Today

USA Today, true to its reputation as the print equivalent of television or the "McPaper," in Michael Schudson's terms, ran stories that were short, sensationalized, and shallow.[7] It focused almost exclusively on the inconvenience that the strike might cause businesses and consumers, with minimal discussion of the issues at stake. *USA Today* does not have a labor reporter. David Field, who wrote a majority of the stories on this strike, is the business travel reporter, who brings with him the culture of business reporting. When asked what the single most important issue in strike reporting was, he replied, "the impact or effects on readers."[8] Whereas union sources were referenced about 8 times in all the stories during this period, UPS and other businesses were quoted about 73 times (see table 4). Thus, the corporation's perspective overwhelmingly dominated the discussion.

In addition to the large number of stories on "inconvenience," *USA Today* actively justified UPS's practices. Early in the conflict, a front-page story in the news section represented UPS as an icon of American society.[9] It argued that from fast food to drive-in restaurants, current society is characterized by its rapid pace, and UPS's overnight delivery services are its lifeblood. Furthermore, a new generation of Americans (consumers), unable to tolerate delays, had developed a set of values embodied by UPS service.

Mainstream commercial culture echoes such rhetoric in what might be called the "Advil generation," from the pain-reliever commercial that captured and extolled the fast pace of working people's lives. This commercial from the late 1990s depicted smiling individuals who performed multiple roles in a day and had "no weekends to call their own" but would not be held

Table 4. Sources of information

	Phase One Total number of stories = 56			Phase Two Total number of stories = 73			Phase Three Total number of stories = 62		
	UT	*WP*	*NYT*	*UP*	*WP*	*NYT*	*UT*	*WP*	*NYT*
	(21)	(15)	(20)	(24)	(15)	(34)	(17)	(13)	(32)
Teamsters	8	20	37	16	12	28	13	11	23
UPS	16	16	16	9	11	17	8	7	10
Other unions	1	0	1	1	3	10	0	6	13
Businesses	57	27	38	37	13	17	10	11	27
Academic —labor	0	0	5	1	0	6	3	1	3
Academic —business	3	1	4	3	1	7	1	0	1
Economist economic institutions	9	0	4	4	3	8	7	3	8
Government	4	18	9	8	12	24	6	18	16

Note. UT = USA Today, WP = Washington Post, NYT = New York Times. The above figures indicate the number of times the most frequently used sources were quoted or cited. It is hard to tell from this table what particular sources say at certain times, as when small business owners express sympathy for the workers in Phase Two or when *USA Today* quotes strikebreakers.

back by a headache. Advil's "niche" is that its medication lasts a long time, suggesting that one need not take a pill every four to six hours and should not take such long-term pain seriously. Thus, speedups, the shift system, and the lengthening of the workweek—strategies intensified in the era of globalization—were portrayed as the "natural" development of American society, a development, moreover, supposedly welcomed by workers.[10] The logical conclusion of this argument was that a disruption of this "natural" process, of the status quo, was a violation of the American story. The article above quotes corporate psychologist Carol Moog: "This strike is a symbolic tear into the fabric of the American flag."[11] Such a construction falls easily into the logic of the nationalist narrative.

Another way that *USA Today* actively sought to justify UPS's practices was by "explaining" the importance of part-time work to the economy and demonstrating that UPS had behaved responsibly. Discussing the creation of a two-tier workforce and a flexible labor market, an editorial argued that the strike made "no sense" and that if "UPS used part-timers the way some other companies have—downsizing their workforces only to hire some back part-time, without benefits at lower pay—the fight would make sense."[12]

The editorial went on to explain that, historically, unions' attempts to limit workplace flexibility had not benefited workers; therefore, it was in their best interest to cooperate with employers. Thus, one of the key arguments put forward by advocates of globalization to justify antiworker corporate restructuring was echoed here by *USA Today*.

The recourse to this kind of procorporate "sense" was reflected in another article that, at least on the surface, tried to be more balanced.[13] Discussing UPS's argument regarding "peaks and valleys," the authors state that "it doesn't make sense to pay [workers] during slack times. Therefore, part-timers make more sense." The ascription of rationality and common sense universalizes the corporation's priorities. What is "sensible," in short, is what benefits the employers. It is not surprising, therefore, that Ron Carey, who "storm[ed] out" of meetings, claiming that "half a job is not enough," came to symbolize the union's irrationality and lack of public responsibility.

In contrast, UPS was lauded for having taken the responsibility to ship urgent packages like blood and perishables.[14] According to *USA Today*'s strike narrative, UPS was a responsible, sensible company, trying to adjust to the demands of the world market by creating part-time jobs. Resistance, like the Teamsters' strike, to this trend within the new fast-paced era was thus not only a grave inconvenience but also inhibited the "sensible" and "rational" progress of society. In short, globalization is a natural outcome of human society, and, in true Borg style, resistance is futile.

Washington Post

Like *USA Today,* the *Washington Post* devoted a good deal of space to the inconvenience caused by the strike, but unlike *USA Today,* it did not explicitly justify UPS's actions. Most of the *Post*'s stories appeared in the financial section. The strike was thus framed in relation to its impact on businesses and the chaos that resulted from the discontinuation of UPS's services. Business sources in these stories outnumbered labor by more than two to one (see table 4). Thus, business perspectives dominated the framing of the strike during this phase. During this period, Judith Evans, who covers local businesses for the *Washington Post,* wrote most of the stories in the absence of Frank Swoboda, the labor reporter, who was on leave until August 12, because, in his words, the "strike was not considered to be of national significance." During his twenty-one-year career at the *Post,* Swoboda, based mainly in the business section, has gone from business editor to labor reporter. He said that, unlike the heyday of the labor movement in the 1930s, today the public "is more interested in the inconvenience caused by a strike and when it will be over."[15]

It seems his reporting of strikes is informed by a belief that the public is not interested in their causes and effects.

A front-page story in the financial section first briefly described the reasons for the breakdown in talks and then contextualized the situation by stating that a strike "would cripple package delivery throughout the country."[16] It went on in great detail about the measures taken by businesses to prepare for this outcome. Once the strike began, several stories focused on the impact on big and small businesses and the role played by other transportation companies in trying to restore order.

Rather than providing a balance to the coverage in the financial pages, stories in the news section offered little explanation of the specific historical conditions that led to the strike, save one article. The standard news-story format—that is, the "five *W*s and an *H*" that give the reader information on who, what, when, where, why, and how and is meant to contextualize and to explain news events—provided only partial understanding of the strike. For instance, one front-page story covered a range of issues, from attempts by businesses to find alternative shippers, to an interview with a part-time UPS worker, to a UPS negotiator's explanation for why the company needed part-time workers.[17] Intended to capture the multiple dimensions of the strike, the five-*W*s story was peppered with various incidents and voices, while skirting the more substantive issues. It did not discuss declining wages, decreased job security, or the price labor paid for the creation of "flexible labor markets," which could have explained the necessity for a strike. The five-*W*s story did not account for these long-term trends because it is a present-centered narrative that fails to foreground information within a broader historical context.[18] This structural shortcoming exacerbates the shallowness of labor reporting. Labor is not a major news theme, and it is covered irregularly and episodically when "events" arise. A study of media coverage of labor from 1946 to 1985 found that increasingly unions were featured in the news during times of strikes, seen as "events," rather than under normal conditions.[19]

In the absence of background information, readers were offered little that would justify the disorder caused by the strike. Constructed as consumers, American workers were asked to believe that the action was unnecessary and irrational, laying the basis for the assertion that strikes benefit no one, a theme that recurred at the end of the strike. In addition, if strikes are irrational and not the product of contradictory class interests, then an explanation had to be found elsewhere. On the second day, an article discussed the investigation into Ron Carey's reelection campaign. Through the skillful use of quotations, such as the one from "an attorney familiar with the Teamsters investigations" who stated that the strike shifted attention away from the scandal, an alternative, conspiratorial explanation for the strike was implied.[20] Overall, the consistency with which the procorporate logic of strike reporting is reproduced in newspapers, whether in comparison to the nationalist narrative, Parenti's seven points, or Martin's five frames, is remarkable.

In summary, the *Washington Post*'s coverage during this phase focused on the strike's effect on "business as usual." In the process, it provided very little coverage of the Teamsters' arguments or the broader historical context from which the strike emerged.

New York Times

The *New York Times* provided the most "balanced" strike coverage. UPS and other businesses were cited 54 times, whereas the Teamsters and other unions were cited 38 times (see table 4). Although a gap remains, in comparison to the *Post* and *USA Today,* the *Times* seemed less biased. Most of its stories were located primarily in the news section, and their length and depth far surpass those of the other two papers. Because of this presentation as well as the paper's stated ideological priorities, the union's view of the strike received the most extensive coverage of any of the newspapers. However, the *Times*'s overall framing during this period was not qualitatively different from that of the *Post*—half the stories were either explicitly about the inconvenience or made reference to it, while the rest were five-*W*s stories.

Stephen Greenhouse, the *Times*'s labor reporter, attempted to provide a balanced look at the issues in the conflict.[21] He argued in a piece titled "High Stakes for 2 Titans" that the UPS walkout stemmed from "the inevitable clash of two powerful forces in the nation's economy."[22] He discussed the overwhelming number of part-time jobs created by UPS since 1993 and the wage differentials between part-timers and full-timers. At the same time, he underlined UPS's need for "flexibility" and the ability to compete. He also gave a hearing to UPS's claims that "a lot" of their part-timers were college students who did not want full-time jobs and to the insinuation that Carey launched the strike to divert attention from the fund-raising investigation.

To be sure, this story is "balanced," with company and union sources given an equal hearing. However, in the process of balancing sources, vital information that could frame the material differently is omitted. Although Greenhouse's story initiated a discussion about stagnant wages, it stopped short of explaining the contradiction between soaring profits—UPS had made a billion dollars in profits the previous year—and wage freezes. Class polarization and rising inequality have been the hallmarks of globalization, impacting not only UPS workers but all workers for at least two decades before this strike. Yet Greenhouse chose not to discuss this trend. Additionally, had he included a discussion of UPS's violations of Occupational Safety and Health Agency standards; its contributions to politicians in favor of limiting OSHA; its lack of concern for its workers' well-being, shown by the arbitrary increase of package weight limits from 70 to 150 pounds (which prompted a one-day strike in 1994); or its tolerance of racism, against which a class-action suit was filed at the time and later settled in favor of the filers, then the article's title would have been significantly different. Perhaps, he might have replaced the reference to "2 Titans" with "David and Goliath." Greenhouse had access to this information from Teamsters' press releases but chose not to use it. The framing of a story has little to do with access but rather reveals the underlying ideological assumptions of the writers and their editors. I will return to the Teamsters' press releases shortly.

Representations of working-class interests entered the *Times* via op-ed articles: Bob Herbert's column focused on the bigger picture of record-breaking profits versus stagnant wages and UPS's history. However, an editorial on the facing page seemed written to compensate for this infraction. It argued that although the Teamsters might be justified in demanding more full-time jobs, the strike held "little significance for the economy or for most other companies."[23] Part-time jobs, we were informed, were not on the rise, despite "anecdotes to the contrary."[24] The editorial ended by speculating that Carey motivated the strike in an attempt to divert attention from the scandal.

This theme was expanded in a front-page story on the same day. In it, Greenhouse suggested that the strike could have been the result of Carey's need to deliver to his support base, the rank and file, and to divert attention from the fund-raising scandal.[25] Although it tried to position Carey as a militant reformer by stating, "Carey's aides acknowledge that he and the entire 1.4–million-member union have planned for this showdown ever since he was elected president of the International Brotherhood of Teamsters in 1991," it also gave voice to the allegations that the strike was a diversionary plot. Thus, in the broader scheme, the *Times*'s lip service to Teamsters' arguments was neutralized by its overall tone toward the strike.

The way a story is framed by the media derives in large part from the institutional conditions under which it is produced and the taken-for-granted methods of storytelling bequeathed by professional journalism (see chapter 2). Much of this operates at a level that is unconscious, but some decisions are more conscious. For instance, it is arguably a conscious act to sideline the Teamsters' press releases. One wonders to what extent the reporters covering this story even sought out these press releases based on the coverage in Phase One.

On August 2, the Teamsters put out a press release with details about the rise in part-time employment, health and safety issues, the pension grab, and subcontracting.[26] Yet few of these issues were discussed in any depth. The same is true of the support that the Teamsters received. On August 6 another press release stated that postal workers, in an act of solidarity, had refused to hire emergency workers to compensate for the extra volume resulting from the strike. Additionally, FedEx workers had joined the picket lines in Indianapolis, and Houston police officers had issued a "zero tolerance" policy for management-driven UPS trucks, stating that they would pull them over for any violations.[27] Yet these acts of support and solidarity went largely unreported.

But perhaps the most egregious disregard for the Teamsters' press releases was the treatment of the source Jeffrey Sonnenfeld. On August 4, the Teamsters put out a press release with information that Sonnenfeld, an Emory University professor, had presented himself as a neutral "expert" on labor management relations, when in reality he was a consultant for UPS (see figure 1). The press release stated in no uncertain terms that Sonnenfeld was the director of an organization that had received $1.125 million in grants from the UPS Foundation. Yet the very next day, *USA Today* ran three stories that quoted Sonnenfeld, without mentioning this connection to UPS. Instead, Sonnenfeld, the director of a group that receives millions in grants, was presented as a former UPS worker. In one story about management at UPS rising through the ranks, Sonnenfeld was identified as "a management professor at Emory University." In another story, Sonnenfeld's professorial authority was used to make UPS's case about the key issues in the strike: "While the Teamsters say part-time work is the key issue, 'the real issue is union politics about pensions,' says Emory University management professor Jeff Sonnenfeld, a former UPS worker."[28]

No doubt, identifying him as a "former UPS worker" rather than a current UPS consultant adds further credibility to his testimony. What is interesting is that the previous day on an ABC news program, Sonnenfeld had stated that he had worked as a UPS driver for a "short time" while he conducted research.[29] Yet *USA Today* did not report this information. A front-page story identified him as follows: "Aside from its effect on American culture and business, the strike also could have a profound effect on the culture of UPS, whose 'top managers were union members once,' says Jeffrey Sonnenfeld. The Emory University business professor worked as a UPS delivery driver for a year. 'Management is just so low-key and unwilling to mud-sling' but that may change, Sonnenfeld says." By combining his current academic affiliation with a humble past as a UPS driver, the story is able to present UPS as a meri-

Media Advisory for
Monday, August 4, 1997

For More Information Contact:
Cynthia Kain or Nancy Stella
Phone 202-624-6911

MEDIA ALERT

"NEUTRAL" EMORY UNIVERSITY ACADEMIC RECEIVES UPS MONEY

Emory University management professor Jeffrey Sonnenfeld who has portrayed himself to the media as an objective commentator on the Teamster strike at UPS is director of an organization that receives UPS Foundation money.

Since 1992 the Center for Leadership and Career Studies at Emory University has received $1.125 million in grants from the UPS Foundation.

The ties between the Center and UPS are strong. UPS Chairman and CEO Kent Nelson was a founding sponsor of the Center and its CEO college. In 1996, the Center gave Nelson its Legend in Leadership award.

####

International Brotherhood of Teamsters, AFL-CIO
25 Louisiana Avenue, NW Washington, DC 20001 (202) 624-6911

Printed on recycled paper

Figure 1. Teamsters press release exposing Jeffrey Sonnefeld's connections to UPS.

tocracy, and by extension the American dream as a reality. Needless to say, revealing that Sonnenfeld was conducting research at the time that he was a driver would only muddy this story. In all, Sonnenfeld was quoted in five stories in *USA Today,* but only once was his business connection stated. That story identified him as "an Emory University professor who runs a research center that is funded by 90 companies, including UPS," thus minimizing the connection to the extent possible.[30]

Overall, Phase One reveals the ways in which the corporate media, intentionally and unintentionally, marginalize the voice of labor. Yet this method of representing the strike would change in Phase Two. Labor was able to break through the dominant frames and create, for a brief period of time, a space from which to discuss the problems of the globalized economy.

Phase Two (August 10–19): Striking Down Globalization's "Rosy Rhetoric"

Even though the story told about the strike by the mainstream press (and network television) was that it was a major inconvenience and was intended to divert attention from a corrupt leader, the public had a different response. It should be noted that the news media were not the public's only source of information.[31] Other ways to learn about the strike included interpersonal contact with UPS employees, coworkers, friends, and family. Alternative media sources ranged from informational leaflets distributed by the union to the Internet. Local print media and television coverage of various Teamster events, discussed in the following chapter, is also likely to have played a role in shaping public attitudes during the early part of August.

A *USA Today*/CNN/Gallup Poll found that 55 percent of the public supported the workers, as opposed to 27 percent in favor of the company.[32] Despite negative coverage in the media, a large section of the public sympathized with the striking workers. Indications of such support existed from the start of the strike, but it was polled only toward the second week. Chapter 5 explains how and why this support for workers was generated; I outline how by the second week of the strike an important political moment had emerged. An active citizenry, or, more specifically, a class-conscious working class along with its allies, was able to exert significant pressure on politicians and the mass media.

However, despite these pressures, the media were hardly guaranteed to turn a critical eye on their corporate sponsors. In the absence of organized action by news workers, the outcome of new pressures is not predictable. In this case, it forced the media to alter their mode of operation in one direction or the other. They were either going to open up a space for the discussion of labor issues or reinvigorate their support for UPS. Around August 10, the tone of the *New York Times* and *Washington Post* coverage switched to better accommodate labor interests. On network television, ABC did the same. *USA*

Today took the opposite route. In addition to stories on the effects on business, it ran a series of articles that focused on UPS workers and how the company best understood their needs.

USA Today

In Phase Two, *USA Today* continued to cover the strike in terms favorable to corporations. Though stories about the impact of disrupted services continued, they were fewer than in Phase One (note the reduction in the number of business and UPS sources and increase in Teamster sources in table 4). Yet this would not mean more sympathetic coverage of the workers' side. Instead, they now attempted to argue that UPS workers were more loyal to the company than to the union. Quoting company surveys, one article highlighted a finding that 75 percent of part-timers did not want full-time employment and that 40 percent of part-timers were students who "supported management."[33] The article concluded that without unity among the unionists, the picket lines would not hold. It conveniently failed to mention that when the strike vote was taken 95 percent had voted to go on strike.

Other articles about the workers contained interviews with those who had crossed picket lines[34] or were antiunion.[35] The disproportionate focus on these workers served to falsely amplify dissent within the union. Letters to the editor claimed that the union was holding both the workers and its customers hostage.[36] The only time that unionists who had not crossed the picket lines were mentioned was when there were incidents of picket-line violence.[37] Overall, *USA Today* seemed to try to undermine the class solidarity that was beginning to emerge by exaggerating discontent within the union.

The paper also ran a series of four stories under the headline "'Family' in a House Divided," consistent with the logic of the nationalist narrative.[38] The stories interviewed an atypical part-timer who earned forty-six thousand dollars and was not willing to cross the picket line, a unionist who approved of UPS's offer and wanted an opportunity to vote on it, a nonunion employee who opposed the strike, and a Teamster who had crossed the picket line, who represented merely 5 percent of the strikers. Obviously, these interviews were not only unrepresentative of the workers but also disproportionately favorable toward UPS's stance. In all, the only reference to the solidarity among the 185,000 white, black, Latino, male and female, part-time and full-time workers were in stories of picket-line violence, where their unity was given a brutish quality.[39] *USA Today*'s treatment of UPS workers made no attempt at balance or neutrality during this phase.

It is interesting to note that *USA Today* did not resort to demonizing the

UPS workers and representing them as greedy and overpaid, a conventional antilabor mechanism in strike coverage. This is not an indication of its own restraint; rather, the newspaper took its lead from UPS. The company had made a conscious decision not to smear its workers' reputation because they were its public representatives. UPS had invested substantially over the decades in cultivating a positive image for its drivers and saw them as a "strategic, competitive asset."[40] Instead of criticizing their workers, the company presented itself as the best guardian of the workers' interests. Once it had dissociated the workers from the union, UPS tried to demonize the union. *USA Today* cooperated by constructing UPS as a "family" and running interviews with antiunion workers.

When the aforementioned public-opinion survey cosponsored by *USA Today* was released, the paper did its best to ignore it. In general, if a newspaper sponsors a poll, it is likely to report the results prominently, as that would give the paper an edge over its competition. However, *USA Today* instead chose to downplay the significance of the survey. The story on it merely reported the findings without any analysis of its significance. In fact, in all of *USA Today*'s coverage during this period, only one story discussed the strike's proportions and implications for the labor movement.[41] That article missed no opportunity to minimize the strike's significance.

Washington Post

On and after August 10, the *Washington Post*'s strike coverage, previously concentrated in the financial section, began to be more evenly distributed between the news and financial sections. The overall tone in both sections was now more favorable to the workers (the number of business sources was reduced by half—see table 4). Whereas in Phase One the workers' demands were glossed over in favor of the strike's impact on consumers, in Phase Two, the problems of workers as producers began to be discussed.

The "inconvenience" stories included quotes from economists who argued that the strike's impact on the economy was not enormous. David Wyss, an economist at DRI/McGraw-Hill, Inc., said that calling the strike "devastating" was an overstatement. Another story described how business executives were blaming UPS rather than the workers for the inconveniences, concluding that business would henceforth be more cautious about relying exclusively on UPS.[42] By this point, other corporations had started to distance themselves from UPS. This is significant given that such public displays of splits among the elites happen rarely, and workers are almost always blamed for the inconvenience caused by strikes.

In another noteworthy reversal, labor issues and discussions of working-class solidarity appeared on the front pages of the news and financial sections. A story by Frank Swoboda discussed the declining membership in unions, pointing to AFL-CIO efforts to improve this situation. An entire story focused on John Sweeney, the president of the AFL-CIO, when he threw the weight of organized labor behind the Teamsters by offering the union ten million dollars a week to sustain the strike.[43]

A front-page story in the financial section put a human face on the strike by describing the unionists' difficulties. It quotes Rachel Howard, a part-time driver: "I've been very dedicated to this company. I worked up until I was eight and a half months pregnant. I was delivering packages in a blizzard, and this is the thanks I get." It tells the story of a family unwilling to cross the picket line, despite being under pressure to pay the tuition costs of two children. A worker, J. P. Wade, was quoted: "If I have to give up everything to fight this David and Goliath battle, so be it. I'll do everything it takes—I'll sell my truck, let them foreclose my house. . . . [W]e won't give up."[44] In contrast to typical strike coverage, this level of self-sacrifice and courage was not mocked as "irrational," nor were the workers constructed as senseless "dupes" blindly following their leadership along a path that leads to their own destruction.

During Phase Two, the central contradiction of the economic expansion of the 1990s and the real consequences of globalization policy—that is, the unequal distribution of profits—was exposed. An article by Jeff Madrick, author of the book *The End of Affluence,* appeared on the first page of the Outlook section. The article, titled "UPS Strikers Deliver a Message: Rosy Rhetoric Aside, the Boom's a Bust for Many," discusses how labor did not benefit from the profits generated by the 1990s boom. Madrick states: "Most troublesome in recent years is that labor has not even received its share of this slow-growing pie. The income that goes into the pockets of America's workers has fallen as a proportion of GDP in the past few years. By contrast, the proportion of GDP going into corporate profits has risen."[45] He went on to argue that the reality for working people could not be more different from the "rosy rhetoric" about the economy. This theme was taken up again more generally by numerous media outlets after the conclusion of the strike.

The *Post,* in this phase, moved away from the focus on inconvenience and introduced a sympathetic discussion of UPS workers' plight. But if the *Post* opened up a space for the discussion of economic disparity, class polarization, and the problems faced by workers in an era of globalization, the *New York Times* took this perspective several steps further.

New York Times

In Phase Two, the *New York Times* shifted its emphasis from "inconvenience" to a broader discussion of how the economy affected labor. Table 4 shows that business sources were cut by more than half, and other unions entered the picture. As in the *Post,* workers were constructed as producers rather than consumers, and even the five-*W*s story accommodated labor interests to a much greater extent.

In contrast to *USA Today,* the *Times* ran proworker letters to the editor. On August 11, four letters addressed the part-time question. One, by a UPS worker, titled "Corporate Greed," put the lie to UPS's claim that it needed part-timers due to the peculiar nature of work at UPS. The worker pointed out that he regularly worked "37 1/2 hours a week, often in back-to-back shifts," two and a half hours beyond what would characterize him as full-time, but was still considered part-time by UPS. He concluded that with its billion dollars in profits, UPS could afford to convert jobs like his into full-time jobs with corresponding pay increases. He added that UPS's failure to do so reflected its greed.[46]

Many of labor's problems cut right to the key contradictions of the 1990s economic expansion, an outcome of decades of globalization policy. Journalist David Johnston wrote about the struggle for better pensions, showing how, over the previous twenty years, companies had downgraded retirement benefits and reduced spending on retirement plans. Greenhouse wrote about the burgeoning number of service-sector jobs, "especially low wage ones," and discussed the AFL-CIO's efforts to shift focus toward these workers. Speaking about the "contingent economy," he admitted, in contrast to the earlier editorial, that "downsizing, the rise of part-time and temporary jobs, and the trend toward businesses offering fewer workers health insurance and pensions" had become problems. Although he provided corporate America's justifications for these practices, he also gave the Teamsters equal space, drawing from their concerns the broader implications of the strike. Louis Uchitelle characterized the strike as, in part, a protest against the "Age of Downsizing."[47] This article argued that the profits of the 1990s had been generated not by increased productivity but rather at the expense of wages, justifying the strike. Taken together, these articles represented one of the most sustained criticisms of the policies of globalization and their implications for workers.

The argument about the inequalities at the base of a flourishing economy was expressed in its sharpest form in an article by Mark Levinson, chief economist of the Union of Needletrades, Industrial, and Textile Employees. Commenting on the state of the economy, he argued that what was at stake in the UPS strike was "how our society share[d] prosperity." He stated that "if what historians see when they look back on the early 21st century is a broadly shared prosperity and a more equitable society, they may be able to point to the teamsters' strike at U.P.S. as an event that defined the period."[48] Though similar to Madrick's article in the *Post,* this piece went even further to discuss the future of American society based on the shared distribution of wealth. It is a remarkable departure from the standard free-market rhetoric that stresses that equal opportunity does not mean equal entitlement; that is, when everyone has the same chances, those who are wealthy deserve to be so. People like Levinson and Madrick were able to expose the fallacy in this argument and to point to the injustice of class polarization.

During this phase, the *Times* gave union sources legitimacy. Greenhouse took up several of UPS's arguments and used union and prolabor sources to discredit or, at the very least, cast doubt on the validity of the company's claims. A front-page article discussed UPS's argument about the nature of work and the necessity for part-time workers at UPS hubs.[49] Greenhouse explained the actual functioning of a hub in New York City that demonstrated the reasoning to be true. However, the article went on to cite union sources, who showed that UPS could combine back-to-back shifts and multiple tasks performed by different workers to create full-time jobs. In short, the article gave UPS a hearing, but it also showed that part-time positions were not requisite and that many could be combined into full-time jobs.

Another article examined UPS's argument about keeping wages low to ward off competition from nonunion companies. It cited the union's argument that this claim was untrue because the package-delivery market was dominated by two unionized workplaces: UPS and the post office. Other shippers, they argued, were not much of a threat. To add legitimacy to the union's case, Harry Katz, professor of industrial and labor relations at Cornell University, was quoted: "It's wrong to say that U.P.S. suddenly is facing non-union competition. Federal Express has been around a long time, and it can't say it suddenly has to keep costs down to face nonunion competition."[50] Thus, rather than accept a corporation's argument with only cursory mention of labor's side, this article actually gave labor a fair hearing.

UPS's claim that the union was being undemocratic by not allowing its workers to vote on the "last, best, and final" offer was also discussed in the *Times.* Although the article represents both sides, the union's argument seemed more accurate. According to the union, the call for democracy was "a cynical ploy, aimed at winning public sympathy and at diverting members' attention from the main issues . . . in the hope of driving a wedge between the workers and their union leadership."[51] The article seemed to be in tacit agreement with this position. It exposed the hypocrisy of UPS's claim by citing union procedure and quoting pro-Carey members of the reform caucus, Teamsters for a Democratic Union (TDU). The irony of a corporation complaining about the lack of democracy at a moment of heightened mass participation in a national event should be noted. If nothing else, it points to the conflicting interests of the employing and working classes.

By the middle of Phase Two, public support for the strikers was too overwhelming to ignore. Unionists flooded picket lines, and the *Times* printed a few photographs demonstrating this solidarity. Unlike *USA Today,* which glossed over the poll conducted by itself, CNN, and Gallup, the *Times* placed the poll results in a front-page story with the headline, "In Shift to Labor, Public Supports U.P.S. Strikers."[52]

Rather than try to rescue UPS's worsening image, as *USA Today* set out to do, the *Times* offered a more accurate appraisal. An article stated that while UPS posed as a company with enviable labor relations, the strike had cast a shadow on this image. The author went on to denounce the company for its greed and its failure to share profits with its workers. He stated: "The U.P.S. story illustrates how, in the current economy, even a company where all executives once carried teamster union cards and still eat in the employee cafeteria can be torn apart. For U.P.S. is *only one of the many companies* that, saying that their customers would rebel at higher costs, have made this economic expansion one of the *stingiest, least forgiving on record.*"[53]

The author chastises UPS in quite harsh terms, but he has an even more scalding critique of corporations in general. Implicit in the article is the argument that if at a rare company like UPS, which allows upward mobility, workers could be mistreated, then workers at all other companies are in dire straits. Thus, the UPS strike opened up a space for criticism about the unfair aspects of corporate policies in the press. Even though several articles did not talk explicitly about globalization, they were an indictment of corporate restructuring.

In the face of this sort of denunciation, corporate ideologues, such as James A. Champy, author of *Re-engineering the Corporation* and head of consulting at the Perot Systems Corporation, abandoned UPS. In an op-ed article, he stated that behind its ideal image was a "mismanaged" company that had "ignored its customers' needs and misunderstood the important role employees play in its profits."[54] Given that UPS's treatment of its workers had been exposed by this point and earned the disapproval of American workers, it was in the interests of corporations to distance themselves from UPS and its business practices. Thus, rather than generalize the issues in this strike to the plight of the American working class, as the union had done, Champy attempted to localize its significance and construct UPS as an anomaly among corporations. In the struggle for ideological leadership, UPS had started to lose the battle, and it made more sense for corporate America to scapegoat one company than to take responsibility for a set of practices that are typical among corporations. In the aftermath of the strike, others would follow Champy's lead and construct a novel narrative of "UPS exceptionalism." The upshot for UPS was that cracks began to appear even on its own side that would play no small role in Phase Two coverage.

At the outset of Phase Two, it was apparent that UPS was starting to lose the battle. The company tried several tactics to regain the upper hand, from threatening the union with layoffs and replacement workers to increasing pressure on Clinton to intervene and running full-page advertisements in major newspapers. None had the desired impact. Instead, AFL-CIO president Sweeney promised the Teamsters both moral and financial support. As shown in the following chapter, by August 14, it was clear that ideologically and materially, the balance of power had shifted irreversibly toward the union. James Kelly, CEO, indicated that UPS was willing to change its offer, stating that the "last, best, and final" offer was indeed negotiable. The strike was settled on August 18. Table 5 presents the highlights of the contract.

Although the union compromised on certain points, particularly the length of the contract and the terms under which full-time jobs were to be created, it was clear that it had won on the major issues—from the creation of full-time jobs to pensions and wages. Furthermore, within the larger context of the labor movement and its numerous defeats over the previous decades,

Table 5. Comparison between prestrike and poststrike offers

Issue	UPS's "last, best, and final" offer (prestrike)	The settlement (poststrike)
Full-time jobs	1,000 new full-time jobs	10,000 new full-time jobs
Wages	Marginal increase proposed by the company	About twice the amount
Pensions	Switch to company-controlled plan	Stay with the current union-controlled plan
Length of contract	5 years	5 years

Source: From "What We Won by Striking" (September 1997), Teamsters in-house publication.

the contract was a decisive victory for labor. It was proof that if workers organized and struck, it was possible to win, an assessment that had been hard to make in the years after President Reagan fired members of the Professional Air Traffic Controllers Organization in 1981.

Phase Three (August 19–September 3): The Nationalist Resolution

On August 18, the only source of information regarding the settlement was a press conference with Ron Carey. Here, UPS officials stood on the sidelines and did not make an official statement.[55] The contract itself was unavailable to the press. Although Carey hailed the strike's outcome as a victory for labor, this triumph was not evident in the tone of stories the next day. Rather, the term *victory* was defined in ways that reconstituted the status quo and affirmed a sense of national solidarity.

In Phase Three, we witness a partial reversion to the Phase One narrative. All three newspapers, to varying degrees, converged in framing the settlement as a much awaited outcome that ended the strike and restored order. If a return to the status quo was the desired state, then the credit for the outcome went to actors whose efforts resulted in the *settlement,* rather than the workers who forced concessions through a strike. By this logic, the negotiation process became central, leading to the conclusion that the only real winner was Department of Labor secretary Alexis Herman, whose role was to urge both sides to continue discussions.

At this point, the definition of what constituted a victory took several forms. Bill Clinton constructed his own version of the victory when he claimed that "it is a victory for the proposition that you can have good strong labor relations and treat your employees well and make money in this economy of ours."[56] On the one hand, he took credit for himself, and on the other, he tried to bury the discussion of inequality and irreconcilable class interests that emerged in Phase Two by praising the negotiation process. Clinton's "proposition" erases the fact that UPS workers had to strike in order to be treated better by the company.

USA Today

USA Today sought to downplay the outcome of the strike and to minimize its significance. In an editorial titled "Few Winners at UPS Strike," the author argued that neither UPS nor the union had won because both sides lost money, one in the form of lost business and the other in wages. The article contradicted Carey's claim that the outcome was a "victory for all working people." Instead, *USA Today* constructed other victors, such as Alexis Herman, who was credited for her role in the negotiations, and other trucking companies.[57]

An article by John Alden, vice chairman of UPS, echoed a similar sentiment. He argued that despite the "incredible drama" of the strike, the impact was devastating and motivated by "issues other than the welfare of UPS employees." He concluded that there were no winners in the strike. Of all the coverage in *USA Today,* only one story admitted that labor did win but hastened to add that the "headline-grabbing settlement is expected to have little impact on the economy, on the power of unions or on crucial labor negotiations in the next year."[58] The union was given credit for improving its image from "thick-necked ruffians" with Mob ties to an organization interested in the welfare of its members.[59] An accompanying timeline showed the history of the union, with an emphasis on corruption at the upper levels of the bureaucracy. Although the Teamster bureaucracy is notorious for Mob connections and corruption, it is significant that there was no corresponding story that delved into UPS's history or mentioned the "model company's" racist practices and blatant violation of safety standards. There were no interviews with the victorious unionists, but one with a scab concerned for his safety![60]

In all, *USA Today* could not wait to end the discussion of the strike, as evidenced in the placement of this quote from James Kelly at the beginning of a front-page story: "The strike . . . will be ancient history."[61] The paper ensured public amnesia by almost entirely dropping coverage of the strike and its significance after August 22.

Washington Post

The *Washington Post* employed more subtle means to contain the strike's impact. The front-page article the day after the settlement quoted Carey extensively and declared the strike a victory for workers, but an editorial went on to argue that "no one ever comes out of a strike unscathed." It tried to tone down labor's victory by stating, first, that the economy showed no trend toward part-time work and, second, that part-time work was not necessarily evil. Another article argued that the strike would be significant only if labor could organize a higher percentage of the workforce; otherwise, competitive pressures would make its gains short-lived.[62] Although this observation is true, Swoboda's article set a pessimistic tone rather than appreciating the possibilities for a revival of the labor movement.

As a beltway paper, the *Post* emphasized the state's intervention in the strike, claiming that the settlement was a victory for both Alexis Herman and Bill Clinton.[63] A current that ran through various stories in the poststrike period was the construction of amicable relations and nationalist unity between UPS, the union, and the state. Herman, who was depicted as a neutral arbiter, said that the agreement restored UPS's image as a "model workplace," with "good wages, but also healthcare benefits and retirement security."[64] The negotiation process was upheld as crucial to the settlement and the behavior of the participants termed "polite."[65] The article described an incident that epitomized this camaraderie. During the negotiations, a surprise party was thrown for John Calhoun Wells, the federal mediator, where both "sides joined in for a rowdy rendition of 'Happy Birthday.'" The sentiment of unity was best expressed in the words of Bill Clinton, who stated that the agreement "represents the [negotiators'] hard work and determination to reconcile their differences for the good of the company, its employees and the customers they service."[66] Ultimately, the conflicts at the heart of capitalism and globalization policy that were brought to the fore in Phase Two were magically transformed into amiable processes of communication, negotiation, and goodwill among capital, labor, and government.

New York Times

New York Times coverage in this phase was contradictory, with a gradual movement back toward maintaining "balance." For days after the strike, stories discussed its significance for workers. One article talked about the future of work and the possibility of further "class antagonisms." That the word *class* was used in a mainstream newspaper is striking, let alone *class* and *antagonism* used in the same sentence, perhaps the closest that a mainstream newspaper will come to talking about class struggle and the antagonistic relationship between workers and capitalists. Another story, in a stark reversal from conventional antiunion propaganda, explained how unions benefit workers. Two articles lauded the Teamsters' communication strategies. At the same time, employers' stories, such as the one by Jeffrey Sonnenfeld, the UPS consultant, titled, "In the Dignity Department, UPS Wins," drew lessons for the employers from the strike.[67]

The day after the settlement, the front-page story was hesitant to declare a labor victory. Instead, it stated that "the agreement was a triumph for the new Labor Secretary." Another article, titled "A Victory for Labor, but How Far

Will It Go?" exemplified the guarded tone toward the settlement. Whereas this article expressed the views of labor leaders, it also accommodated the opinions of business analysts, who made a case for "UPS exceptionalism," arguing that the strike would have few effects beyond this specific case. The article concluded that the UPS settlement would have ramifications only to the extent that labor leaders started to "fight concerted battles the way the Teamsters did."[68] Although this prospect is undeniable from the labor movement's point of view, it presents the possibility of future struggles as somewhat remote. Like Swoboda at the *Post,* Greenhouse reached a rather pessimistic conclusion after one of the biggest victories for labor in more than twenty years.

On the same page as the previous story, another, titled "U.P.S Says Fears of Bigger Losses Made It Cut Deal," quoted Kelly: "The bottom line is that we have a contract that is good for our people, gets us back in business, and will keep us competitive." The article went on to say that the workers' victory celebrations were dampened by threats of layoffs, followed by a quote from a company representative claiming that the strike benefited no one. It led easily to the reassertion that Herman was the only "indisputable victor." An editorial acknowledged a labor victory but predicted that "the country's current sympathy for the problems of some workers does not necessarily open a new chapter in industrial relations." Furthermore, we were offered Clinton's statement discussed above.[69] His self-serving assessment was repeated because it fitted perfectly into the nationalist narrative, thus giving the biggest labor struggle in two decades a nationalist resolution.

The Phases on Network Television

On national television, only ABC changed the tone of its coverage in Phase Two. Of the three networks, NBC was the most unsympathetic toward the workers, ABC was the most sympathetic, and CBS was in the middle. During Phase One, ABC's coverage was fairly conventional, focusing on the strike's effects on businesses and consumers. Several stories contained interviews with business owners and customers; others focused on how packages were being shipped by alternative means, such as the post office. The part-time question was fairly well covered early in the strike,[70] but it was merely one focus among several, the most important being the disruption of business as usual.

This approach changed around August 11. An ABC-conducted poll released on August 13 showed that large numbers of people did not want Clinton to interfere with the strike. Additionally, 82 percent of those polled said that part-timers should receive the same wages and health insurance as full-timers for the same job.[71] Combined with the other factors discussed in the following chapter, poll results seem to have changed ABC's strike coverage.

The focus on inconvenience was replaced by a day-by-day assessment of negotiations. Far more picketing workers were interviewed,[72] and there were stories on other unionists joining them.[73] Poststrike coverage was as mixed as in the *New York Times,* from anchor Peter Jennings's hesitant declaration of a "lop-sided victory for labor," to reporter Bill Redeker stating that by "almost every measure, the tentative settlement appears to be a victory for the union." In another piece, *Money* editor Tyler Mathisen said, "It is a win not only for the Teamsters Union but, in the long term, a win for organized labor."[74]

NBC's treatment of the strike was the most superficial and sensationalized, rivaling *USA Today*'s coverage. Sporadic and isolated instances of picket-line violence were the focus of many stories. In others, just the prospect of violence set a tone more appropriate to a suspense thriller than a report on a serious labor dispute. The few stories that focused on the part-time issue and the problems faced by workers were overwhelmed by stories on the strike's effects on small business owners. When Clinton failed to intervene, NBC insinuated that the Teamster's $2.6 million gift to the Democratic Party was the cause. By consistently harping on inconvenience, NBC added its voice to the corporate drumbeat for state intervention. Like *USA Today,* NBC defended UPS. In an August 5 report, Sonnenfeld was identified as a "labor expert" who defended part-time employment. In contrast, in an August 4 program on ABC, Sonnenfeld was identified as both a former driver and a current consultant for UPS. It is in this report that Sonnenfeld quickly added that he was a driver for a short time while conducting research.[75]

CBS positioned itself in between the stance taken by NBC and ABC. Although it understood the strike's importance and the concerns that it raised about "labor-management" relations, its coverage of the causes was shallower than ABC's, although deeper than NBC's, particularly on the part-time and pension questions. However, its treatment of picket-line violence was the most dramatic. CBS ran more stories on violence than all other types of stories.

Conclusion

If media coverage of the conflict began with the assumption that a strike was a disruptive act that threw consumers and companies into chaos, then it concluded that negotiation was preferable to strikes and that what happened at

UPS had little relevance for American workers. What was omitted in this discussion was that without a strike—the act of stopping production and preventing the accumulation of profit—the outcome of the contract would have been vastly different. In the absence of an economic battle, labor would have had little or no bargaining power at the negotiating table. This assessment is supported by contracts negotiated in the 1980s, when workers were afraid to strike or union leaders failed to call strikes. As discussed in chapter 1, by 1987, in the midst of the Reagan boom, almost three-quarters of all contracts covering one thousand or more workers included concessions; for manufacturing workers, the figure was 90 percent. The two-tier wage system that became the focus of the 1997 UPS strike was instituted because of concessions made by the Teamsters' leadership in the 1980s.

Although the mainstream media tried to tone it down, the strike's significance was felt far beyond the Teamsters union. The very next year, several large struggles, including the strikes at General Motors, Bay Area Rapid Transit, Northwest Airlines, Philadelphia Transit, and Bell Atlantic, were successes for the labor movement. I am not suggesting that all labor struggles after UPS were successful. Several failed, primarily because of the dead weight of business unionism. Labor leaders invested in the logic of "partnership" with corporations sought to appease the employers rather than confront them. However, labor historians have noted that the UPS strike was a milestone for the labor movement in that it catalyzed other disputes. If nothing else, it gave organized labor the confidence that strikes can succeed in gaining concessions from the employers.

What this analysis demonstrates is that organized labor does indeed have the ability to create, however temporarily, an open marketplace of ideas and to force a democratic representation of strikes in the media. In the battle for hegemony, the working class successfully altered the way the strike was framed; Phase Two media coverage of the UPS strike significantly deviated from conventional reporting patterns. In the aftermath, as the next chapter will show, several leading media outlets, including the business press, had to acknowledge that U.S. workers did not benefit from the 1990s recovery. The chapter also points to the larger democratizing influence that a politicized working class can exert. For a brief period, organized labor demonstrated its ability, first, to galvanize public opinion by appealing to class identity and raising class consciousness; second, to create a more responsive and accountable press; third, to restrain corporate excesses; and fourth, to democratize the political process by preventing political elites from stopping the strike.

However, not all media were impacted the same way. *USA Today* positioned itself decisively on the side of UPS. Phase Two strike coverage was an extension of UPS's public relations campaign. *USA Today,* owned by Gannett Corporation, a large media conglomerate with operations in several countries, waged a battle on behalf of corporations. Gannett's support for UPS can be explained by their many similarities. Like UPS, which dominates package delivery via ground transportation, Gannett dominates the newspaper market, with about a hundred newspapers in the United States. Like UPS, it has a poor record of labor relations. Its rise to prominence as a media giant was based not on labor cooperation but on its unrelenting attitude toward disputes. In 1995, when twenty-five hundred workers—reporters, typesetters, printers, and delivery drivers—went out on strike against the *Detroit News,* owned by Gannett, the company dragged the strike on until 1997 and refused to compromise. Gannett's own history of labor relations and its corporate practices influenced the unsympathetic way it handled the strike.

On the other hand, at corporations like the New York Times Company, whose image and marketing are tied to claims of high journalistic standards and community service, such a stance was unlikely. One could also argue that when Disney bought Capital Cities–ABC in 1995, ABC workers were sensitized to the implications of conglomeration on their conditions of work, which made them more sympathetic to UPS workers. However, it is not the *specific* conditions at media corporations that impacted their coverage of this strike. These conditions and particular editorial decisions do matter, but they are not the focus of this study since, as the following chapter will show, the strike's pressure was felt far beyond ABC, the *New York Times,* and the *Washington Post.* Something far bigger had occurred during this strike; we witnessed a brief moment when culture itself, as Michael Denning puts it, was "labored."[76] Thus, although it would be fruitful to investigate newsroom practices that help us to understand how the news media decide which step to take next after they have made an initial report on a topic, when they become aware of public opinion and how that impacts their editorial stance, when they recognize that a particular angle on a story resonates with the public, and so on, my focus is less about these institutional decisions and more about the broader struggle for hegemony.

For instance, after the strike, the game show *Wheel of Fortune,* produced by Sony Pictures, included union workers on episodes that ran for a week. "*Wheel of Fortune* Salute to America's Working Families" began on Labor Day. The producer, Harry Friedman, stated that "Americans are working harder and smarter than ever before. . . . We think a salute to workers, their unions and the products and services they provide our society is a fitting tribute to offer." All the contestants were either union members or their families, and the major prizes were union-made and identified as such, with prominent displays of union labels. The AFL-CIO's seal was seen in the center of the stage floor, and several thousand union members were present in the audience, wearing their union T-shirts and carrying signs. During one show, AFL-CIO president John Sweeney stated, "American workers have made personal sacrifices and investments to improve the products and services they produce. They're the most productive and efficient workers in the world. They deserve the highest possible respect for their major contributions that make our country the economic power that it is."[77] Such a ringing endorsement of the union movement on a popular game show would have been unthinkable prior to the UPS strike. It represents a considerable reversal for a culture that has long reviled distinct worker organizations.

The moment was short-lived. As time passed, the dominant hegemonic position was restored, and labor influences were all but purged. Although the strike proved that resisting the dominant framing mechanisms is not futile, the status quo reestablished itself rather easily in the absence of a continuous and ongoing struggle. The main classes of society cannot be continuously involved in struggle, since the system relies on class peace in order to exist and flourish. Short of a complete transformation of the economic system, strikes have to end at some point, after which the status quo is resumed. This reversal raises larger questions of how we understand resistance and the process of democratization under a fundamentally unequal economic system. In other words, based on this study, it does not seem possible to permanently reform the media in ways that make them more democratic under a capitalist system. However, even under the present system, it is important to learn how labor can take advantage of the media to put forward its ideas and interests. The following chapter explains specifically what the Teamsters did, and what UPS failed to do, to gain the upper hand.

FIVE

The Battle for Hegemony:
How Did the Teamsters Win?

When *Business Week,* the voice of the corporate elite, admits to the problem of rising inequality, one begins to grasp the impact that the UPS strike had on the terms of public discussion. In an article titled "A Wake-Up Call for Business: The Teamsters' Win Means That Workers Can No Longer Be Taken for Granted," the magazine drew out the lessons for the employing class as follows:

> More important than the union victory is the way the Teamsters' campaign captured what seems to be a new mood in America. For the first time in nearly two decades, the public sided with a union, even though its walkout caused major inconveniences. Polls showed the public supported the 185,000 striking workers by a 2-to-1 margin over management. The message: After a six year economic expansion that has created record corporate profits and vast wealth for investors, Americans are questioning why so many of their countrymen aren't getting a bigger piece of the pie.[1]

It went on to suggest that businesses could no longer take their workers for granted and had to address the sense of discontent that the UPS strike brought to the fore. The secret of inequality lurking beneath the surface of a booming economy was now out in the open. In this context, the guardian of capitalist globalization, *Business Week,* chose to forewarn the business community of future class tensions that might erupt if it did not address the "new mood" among workers.

Business Week was not alone in raising the alarm about class disparities and its impact on public opinion. A study of poststrike coverage in newspapers, magazines, television, and radio demonstrates, as I show below, that the discussion of the economic injustices of the 1990s went far beyond *Business Week*, the *New York Times, Washington Post,* and ABC. To be sure, coverage was contradictory. Some stories downplayed the strike's significance, arguing that it was a flash in the pan with no larger consequences. Others tried to explain why the public supported the strikers and what this support said about inequality in the United States. On balance, the number of stories that focused on questions of inequality is striking. Of particular significance is the *breadth* of the discussion across the various media, rather than the *depth* within particular news organizations. Several news media outlets, including the business press, general news magazines, radio, and regional and city papers, acknowledged economic inequality as a problem. They also attempted to explain the widespread discontent at corporate practices and the new prolabor mood created by the strike. I discuss a cross-section of these stories below.

In a tone similar to *Business Week,* the *Financial Times* pointed out that "UPS seems to have misjudged the mood of its employees, and of the public," which was "broadly in sympathy with the strikers." Despite its skepticism about labor's renewed power, the *Wall Street Journal,* in an article that barely concealed the authors' contempt for the "working stiff," acknowledged that "the unsung hero—or, rather, sucker—behind the current boom is the docile American worker, too cowed to demand a pay raise despite surging corporate profits."[2] The article wondered if the union victory heralded the possibility that workers' attitudes were changing.

Traffic World, a trade publication, editorialized that although Ron Carey "tapped into the welling anxiety that many middle- and lower-class Americans feel about job security and the issue of part-time labor and diminishing benefits," UPS could have avoided the strike had it responded better to the part-time question during negotiations. On CNNfn, a channel that caters to business interests and is not normally given to discussing inequality, viewers were treated to the following:

Varney (host): There is a strong feeling in the country at the moment, is there not, that capital has been well rewarded for 15 years; labor has taken second place in the pecking order, but now it's time for a reversal—and a justified reversal? That is the feeling in America, isn't it?

Valliere (guest): I think one of the—yes—I think one of the biggest surprises coming out of the strike is public opinion polls showing overwhelmingly the public supported the workers. They sure didn't support the baseball players, and they didn't support the air traffic controllers, but this was really different.[3]

Had it not been for the strike, neither the host, Stuart Varney, nor the guest, Greg Valliere, managing director of Charles Schwab Washington Research Group, would likely have discussed the unequal distribution of wealth in the 1980s and '90s.

General news magazines like *Newsweek,* although not particularly sympathetic to workers, were nonetheless forced to admit, like the business press, that workers had not received their share of profits during the boom years. *Newsweek* argued that beyond "union politics, the strike will affect millions of Americans, even those who have never shipped a package or joined a local, for it goes to the heart of large national questions. Will wages finally begin to go up, as the Dow and productivity have risen?"[4] The article had a chart titled "Will you ever get a raise?" to show that although profits had gone up, the median household income had stayed flat or gone down. In a rare moment of reversal, the terms *Americans* and *you* in this article referred to workers rather than consumers. The well-kept secret of rising profits coexisting with stagnant wages was finally exposed.

National Public Radio did a story on part-time and contingent work that included interviews with several researchers. Even though the story began by stating that UPS's hiring of part-time workers was an anomaly and that the overall growth in part-time work was minimal, the guests shed light on the extent of the problem.[5] Eileen Appelbaum of the Economic Policy Institute (EPI) explained that twenty-three million people, a significant percentage of the workforce, held part-time jobs. She argued that this trend had led to the creation of a "two-tiered economy" that was unfair because part-time workers were paid less and denied benefits, even though they do the same work as their full-time counterparts. Tom Djurovich of the University of Massachusetts at Amherst discussed the corporate practices of outsourcing, hiring temporary workers, and independent contracting and how these policies had led to the overall erosion of steady, well-paying jobs.

Local television stations and newspapers also carried stories about the strike's significance. Local venues tend to be more sympathetic to workers during a strike because the striking workers have ties to the community, which is also the station's or newspaper's immediate customer base.[6] Matt Witt and Rand Wilson, who read stories about the union in local newspapers from around the country, assembled for them by the Burrelle News Service, told me that the best coverage of the strike was in local newspapers and on local television. Wilson cited the *Pawtucket (R.I.) Weekly News* and the *Kansas City Star* as examples of local newspapers that were very favorable to workers.

WCVB-TV in Boston interviewed Northeastern University professors, who legitimated the strike by arguing that the reason Americans supported the Teamsters was that they could relate to their concerns. Several city newspapers, whose coverage during Phase Two and afterward was likely to have been as favorable, if not more so, to the workers than the *New York Times* and the *Washington Post,* wrote about the strike's importance in highlighting working-class issues. An article in the *Boston Globe* stated that the "strike dramatized the whole set of trends captured in the antiseptic phrase, 'contingent work'—temps, part-timers, contract workers, outsourcing, downsizing—all of which mean lower pay and less job security for millions not yet represented by unions. The front page and TV network attention to these issues was worth millions of dollars of free publicity."[7]

The *Cleveland Plain Dealer* wrote that, according to labor experts, "The Teamsters won the public relations war during the two-week UPS strike because the union focused on issues that resonate with workers who feel alienated by a corporate culture focused on cutting full-time jobs and pushing work to outside suppliers." In Minneapolis, the *Star Tribune* wrote that a "strong economy, a bullish stock market, a Democrat in the White House and a growing public belief that corporate America has not shared its good fortune with workers all suggested that the time was ripe for the union movement to regain some measure of the momentum it lost when President Ronald Reagan crushed a strike by Professional Air Traffic Controllers Organization (PATCO) in 1981."[8]

Several newspapers, like the *Orlando Sentinel* and the *Baltimore Sun,* picked up a Reuters story that quoted labor supporters, like Nelson Lichtenstein. He argued that the strike was a huge step forward for the union movement and working people in the United States: the "Teamsters union's success in waging the nation's biggest strike in two decades gives the fragile labor movement a shot in the arm and may mark the start of a new era of union strength."[9]

Other papers, like the *Philadelphia Inquirer* and the *Portland Oregonian,* ran a story by the Knight-Ridder news service. It stated that the "agreement announced in the wee hours yesterday ending the Teamsters' two-week strike against UPS is a clear victory for the union. . . . And perhaps more significantly, the settlement displayed the influence of strong public sentiment that—at a time of economic prosperity—companies should share the wealth of profits with workers."[10]

Knight-Ridder, however, like other media conglomerates, seems to have taken a two-pronged approach. Its news service constructed at least two different stories. On August 20, while the *Philadelphia Inquirer* ran the positive story mentioned above, some of Knight-Ridder's other papers, like the *St. Paul Pioneer* and the *Miami Herald,* ran stories that minimized the strike. These papers ran the "UPS exceptionalism" story, based on the idea that the strike was so atypical that it was unlikely to be reproduced in other labor struggles. The *Miami Herald* article stated: "The circumstances that caused the strike by 185,000 UPS workers were so special and the gains so limited that it is unlikely to have much larger effect for labor leaders hoping to halt a steady decline in membership." The *St. Paul Pioneer,* in a slightly different article with the same byline, drew almost identical conclusions. The *San Diego Union-Tribune* also picked up this story.[11] All three ran on the front page.

Knight-Ridder and Gannett, which owns *USA Today,* led the trend to gloss over the strike's significance. This is not surprising since both companies had themselves faced strikes in Detroit in the years 1995–97, at Gannett's *News* and Knight-Ridder's *Free Press.* The Detroit newspaper strike, involving twenty-five hundred workers, began over management demands to wipe out work rules and seniority provisions. Rather than negotiate, Gannett and Knight-Ridder took a combative stance in an all-out attempt to destroy the unions.

Despite the best efforts of these giants, the UPS strike and general proworker public opinion forced a wide range of mainstream news media to acknowledge class polarization and to criticize the corporate practices, that is, the strategy of neoliberal globalization, that led to it. This reversal from the typical probusiness stance that has become standard practice in the mainstream media was truly significant.

This chapter sets out to explain why the media were forced to incorporate the interests of workers into their discussion of the strike and the economy. As discussed earlier, the media are contradictory institutions. Under normal circumstances they uphold the status quo, but during times of social upheaval they can be pressured to include dissenting voices. The media are one site among many in which the struggle between various social forces is fought out.

The major contending forces in this strike were UPS and the Teamsters. Supporting these key players were several other groups. UPS could initially rely on

- the corporate media
- business-related academics, "experts," and think tanks
- the political elite

The Teamsters had

- alternative media
- liberal and left-wing academics and think tanks
- labor supporters and other unions

This is indeed an asymmetrical power relationship. This chapter explores how, over the course of the strike, the Teamsters and their supporters were able to shift the balance of power by winning both public support and relatively favorable media coverage. We start by trying to understand the state of public consciousness in relation to the economy; that is, if the public, composed largely of workers, was to play a crucial role in shifting the balance of power in the direction of the Teamsters, it becomes necessary to understand the degree of openness to proworker arguments.

Workers' Experience and Public Opinion Polls

In chapter 1, I discussed the impact of the employers' offensive on the American working class. The very process that capital needs to restore its vitality—globalization as a policy involving government-enforced laws and corporate restructuring—is undermining its foundation by increasing class polarization. If, in the 1970s, the gap between the average wage of a worker and that of a CEO was 1:45, by the late 1990s, it had increased to 1:531. Not surprisingly, this inequality has given rise to growing anger and bitterness toward corporations. A cover story in *Business Week* found that 80 percent of people surveyed stated that corporations have "too much power."[12] This level of suspicion and skepticism increased after a stream of corporate scandals began to break in 2001. Although the level of class struggle, as measured by the number of strikes and other overt expressions, has been low and continues to remain that way, generalized discontent toward the priorities of corporate America is growing. I describe this discontent below using both quantitative and qualitative research. Together, both the numbers and lengthy interviews present us with a picture of how the economic realities of the last quarter of the twentieth century were experienced by working people in the United States.

The mainstream media addressed some of this discontent prior to 1997. Although, by and large, they ignored globalization's impact on workers, some news media outlets did run stories on its consequences for their target audiences. For instance, the *New York Times* ran a series titled "The Downsizing of America," which was later published as a book. These articles ran in the summer of 1995 and looked at the effects of downsizing on white-collar and, by extension, blue-collar workers; the "hook" was that white-collar workers, part of the *Times* customer base, were experiencing job losses and job insecurity, a predicament that was once mainly limited to blue-collar workers.

The book begins with the story of Steven A. Holthausen, a loan officer for more than two decades, who drew a salary of one thousand dollars a week. After surviving three bank mergers, he was told one day that he no longer had a job. At the age of fifty-one, he found himself as a tourist guide earning one thousand dollars a month. His marriage fell apart, and his children lost contact with him.

Holthausen's story was neither unique nor extraordinary. According to a *New York Times* analysis of Labor Department numbers, nearly forty-three million jobs were lost between 1979 and 1995. Even though far more jobs were created than lost during the same period, their quality left much to be desired, so that only 35 percent of laid-off workers were able to find jobs that paid the same as, or more than, the old job. For the vast majority, conditions only deteriorated. *The Downsizing of America* documents the real suffering, both mental and material, that these workers experienced. Their stories are poignant and heartbreaking.

Robert Muse was a machinist in the aerospace industry until forced to accept a job as maintenance technician, paying half his earlier wage. The following is a description of what his life was reduced to: "Over the days, as he talked about the layoff and what it had cost, he fluctuated between sadness, bitterness, and anger, usually short-lived, beaten back by natural cheerfulness. Before his layoff, he was an infectiously happy man, said his friends and family, and the ghost of that is still here. But as he stared out on the street, he was disgusted, helpless: 'I don't want to cry about it. But I feel like I've been stabbed in the back.'"[13]

Though men like Muse were particularly affected by wage cuts and downsizing, all working-class people were affected, and a majority of this class, more than 60 percent, are minorities and white women.[14] In addition to blue-collar workers, historically the group most frequently laid off, white-collar and government employees began to be downsized in the 1990s.

The experience of downsizing combined with wage stagnation, increased hours, and the rise in contingent employment has had a deep and wide impact on the consciousness of working people, resulting in growing anger and bitterness. One bank employee, a woman in her early twenties, put it this way: "I think there is going to be a backlash. Maybe not this year, maybe not next year, but there's going to be one. People aren't going to give 100% anymore. I see this with a lot of my friends. I'm not going to be like my dad and work till ten o'clock at night and never see the kids. What for? So I'll be thanked with a pink slip?"[15]

The series notes that the "aggregate effect seemed to be a deep-seated pessimism in many Americans, causing people to question what dreams of possibility were available to them and to succeeding generations."[16] If the American dream was a possibility for some workers in the 1950s and 1960s, after the 1970s it evaporated—hard work could not guarantee reaching the middle class.

In her book *Declining Fortunes: The Withering of the American Dream,* Katherine Newman describes how the economic realities of the 1980s and 1990s were experienced by working people. Based on extensive interviews with 150 people from a particular suburban community, she shows that the optimism fostered in the post–World War II era, and the belief in the American dream, was all but eroded by the reality of people's lives. One person she interviewed put it this way:

> I've always killed myself for a reason. I killed myself in school to get good grades, and that was the reward, thank you very much. I got my A's. All the way along, I was rewarded in just the way I was supposed to be. . . . That was what the book said. And then you get out here to the real world and suddenly the last chapter is a sad joke. You're told you work hard for a living and you can buy a house in [your hometown], or the next town down the line that's a little cheaper. But it's not true and it's really very perturbing.

This sentiment is widespread in U.S. society. Newman argues that regardless "of what politicians may have to say about the future of the American economy, the public has long since concluded that all is not well."[17]

A number of people have rightfully targeted their anger at corporations. Respondents to the *Times* survey indicated their dissatisfaction with their employer. For instance, when asked if companies were more or less loyal than they were ten years ago, 75 percent answered "less loyal"; 64 percent believed that workers have become less loyal as well. Many workers felt alienated from their jobs, perceiving little or no control over working conditions. A study by Richard Freeman and Joel Rogers found that 63 percent of workers polled would like more of a say in the decisions about production and operations at their workplace. They also found that the workplace had become more stressful. Of those polled, Freeman and Rogers found that 70 percent of workers felt the need to compete more today than previously. Not surprisingly, 53 percent of workers thought that the mood at the workplace had become angrier, whereas a mere 8 percent said that it had become friendlier. A significant percentage of workers seemed alienated from their work and showed openness to joining unions. Freeman and Rogers found that 32 percent of nonunion workers were willing to join unions, despite the constant bombardment of corporate propaganda and the absence of prounion information. All of these responses reveal a significant growth in class consciousness.[18]

However, the growing anger toward corporations has not translated into increased class struggle. Class anger has to be organized if it is to move from the level of consciousness to activity. The legacy of "business unionism" has meant that the translation of anger into activity has been slow to materialize. In the ideological vacuum left behind, many scapegoats have been produced. As the *Times* study notes, "Polls have shown this anger directed at targets as diverse as immigrants, blacks, women, government, corporations, welfare recipients, computers, the very rich, and capitalism itself." In Newman's study, sections of the people she interviewed blamed immigrants or those on welfare for the overall decline in economic security. As one person said: "Every house on my mother's block has been sold to an Oriental. That's a little depressing at times. It's not that they're second-class citizens. But now you're being alienated from your own town. You're not given a chance to move into your own town."[19] Thus, anger and disappointment at one's own circumstances can be transferred onto "others" in the immediate environment or mythical "others" such as undeserving welfare recipients.

Although it is hard to predict where class anger will be directed in the future, the UPS strike focused blame where it belonged—on corporate America. A national strike for decent jobs brought to the fore and focused attention on the problems of Americans *as workers,* both blue and white collar. Globalization, as a policy to renew corporate profitability, has had both a material and an ideological impact on the American working class. The strike put a spotlight on these problems by raising such issues as decreased job security, loss of benefits, declining wages, mounting debt, and economic polarization. A poll taken after the strike asked, "Do you think American workers have received or not received their fair share of financial benefit created over the last few years by the improved national economy?" The majority of respondents, 65 percent, replied that they had not received a fair share.[20] I argue below that workers' experiences in the job market, together with other contingent influencing factors, produced a heightened class consciousness that came to be expressed in the form of solidarity with the striking Teamsters. The key issues in the strike resonated with the concerns of working people in an economy that had not benefited them.

Public Opinion on the Strike

Several polls showed that a majority of the public supported the strikers.[21] One widely cited poll found that 55 percent of the public supported the strikers, as opposed to 27 percent in favor of the company.[22] Polls, of course, cannot be accepted uncritically, as they can be distorted by a variety of factors, from polling techniques to corporate sponsorship.[23] Furthermore, several scholars have pointed out that polls do not so much represent an independently existing opinion but rather create an opinion through the process of polling.[24] Following Justin Lewis, I take the view that although polls are not neutral, they are also not biased or "ideologically fixed" in every instance. During the UPS strike, the aforementioned poll captured in numerical terms, with all its limitations, the sense of solidarity produced by working people's own experiences.

What makes this poll interesting, and in some ways unique, is also its representation in the media. For instance, as discussed in the previous chapter, the *New York Times* and the *Washington Post* gave the poll fair coverage. Typically, when polls that represent a liberal or left-of-center perspective find their way into the media, they are neutralized, balanced out with opposing views, or downright contradicted by the overall news story.[25] *USA Today,* which was one of the media organizations that had sponsored the survey, reported the poll results but then went on to point out in the same story that 31 percent of Americans disapproved of unions and that 28 percent were inconvenienced by the strike, followed by stories of this inconvenience.[26] However, in the aftermath of the strike, several media outlets would represent the strike as a real shift in public sympathy.

What sections of the public were sympathetic to the strikers? The aforementioned poll does not give us a clear picture of the class composition of those who supported labor. However, the poll broken down by household income is more revealing. Income is not the best indicator of class, but it does help us understand how economic insecurity played a role in public support. Among those with household incomes less than $20,000, 61 percent supported the workers, while 19 percent supported UPS. Of those earning between $20,000 and $29,999, 66 percent supported the workers and 15 percent UPS. Of those earning less than $50,000, 50 percent supported the Teamsters. Among those with incomes higher than $75,000, 35 percent supported the union, while 48 percent supported UPS.[27]

Interestingly, people from various parts of the political spectrum supported labor. One would expect that those who identify as liberal are likely to support labor, while those who consider themselves conservative would support corporations. However, in this instance, 77 percent of liberals supported labor and 14 percent UPS, 53 percent of moderates supported UPS workers and 27 percent the company, and contrary to expectation 46 percent of conservatives supported the workers while 36 percent UPS.[28] What this points to is the mixed and contradictory ideas that individuals may hold at any point in time. This is not surprising. In a society dominated by procorporate ideas, not only in the media but in all venues, workers are encouraged to think of themselves as happy consumers, united in national solidarity with the employing class.

However, the experience of work and life in a capitalist system constantly conflicts with this rosy picture. For the vast majority of workers in the 1990s, the American dream had become a myth. They adapted to this reality in different ways, often holding contradictory ideas that festered in relative silence due to the lack of serious discussion in the public sphere. Class anger in the United States has a subterranean existence because labor does not have a voice in the political sphere.[29] In several nations, prominent liberal-left parties such as the Labour Party in Britain or the Socialist Party in Spain represent, at least in theory, the interests of the working classes. There are no such equivalents in the United States, only much smaller parties, such as the Greens, which can easily be marginalized. In this vacuum, the largely capitalist-funded Democratic Party poses as the party of workers and minorities. Without a party primarily funded by workers, a means through which they can pressure their representatives to publicly support them against capitalist encroachment, workers' interests will continue to be sidelined in the media. This neglect leads to a dynamic in American history in which long periods of rising class anger but low struggle are followed by major social upheavals. For instance, the 1920s was a period of low struggle and great class polarization, followed by the massive labor uprising of the 1930s. From the 1990s to the present, we have witnessed a period in which developing class anger has not been accompanied by a corresponding rise in struggle. In such a period, a national strike by 185,000 UPS workers that made headline news in most media outlets captured the attention of American workers, and gave legitimate expression to their concerns.[30]

Thus, the struggle over ideas is important in winning the allegiances of various groups, despite their stated political affiliations. Additionally, ideas change over time. Whereas in 1981, 52 percent supported management and 29 percent the striking workers during the air-traffic controllers' strike, in 1989 during the Eastern Airlines strike, 57 percent supported the strikers and 23 percent the airline.[31] There are various objective and subjective factors that explain these differences. We will now examine some of the subjective factors, that is, how UPS and the Teamsters prepared for this strike.

Competing Strategies: Big Brown versus the Teamsters

During the period of negotiation that preceded the strike, neither UPS nor the Teamsters union leadership anticipated a strike. Both reasoned, based on their respective assessments of the power balance, that they would achieve their goals at the bargaining table. However, both sides prepared for a strike (see table 6 for their communication strategies). The Teamsters adopted the "contract campaign" strategy, which, while geared to winning solidarity within the union and gaining public support, does not necessarily aim for a strike. Ron Carey had hoped to use it to pressure management in the negotiation process.

UPS, too, prepared for the strike, even though in public statements it claimed to have been unprepared. Jennifer Jiles, corporate PR manager at UPS, writing about the strike's lessons, notes, "Our focus was on labor-management negotiations, not on devising a public relations strategy in the event of a strike."[32]

When an agreement could not be reached by the strike's deadline, Carey granted an extension. He "tried up through the last weekend of negotiations

Table 6. Communication strategies

UPS	Teamsters
Internal and external communications	Contract campaign
1. Prework communication meetings	1. Rank and file involvement
2. PR department prepares and hires more personnel	2. Public support
	3. Media attention

to avoid a strike by crafting a proposal that included the bare minimum," notes David Moberg.[33] But UPS overplayed its hand and refused to settle. Carey found himself in a position in which he had raised the workers' expectations through the contract campaign, and when the negotiations failed to yield the expected results, he was forced to call a strike. In the context of the strike, the Teamsters' preparations paid off.

UPS Miscalculates

UPS had reasoned that it would easily win a strike both ideologically and on the picket lines. Consequently, it had a modest internal communication and public relations strategy. Its internal strategy involved keeping supervisors informed of the negotiation process through audiotapes and holding "prework communication meetings" with the workers. However, the UPS magazine, *Inside UPS,* barely addressed the upcoming contract. As John Alden, vice chair of UPS, noted after the strike, "In our employee communications, contract issues were not the kind of thing we [talked about] in the past— that's certainly a lesson we learned the hard way."[34] UPS was so overconfident about its control over workers that at several hubs, managers were ill-prepared and not sure what they were supposed to talk about at the prework meetings. They read hesitantly from notes and did not have a method to control workers who disagreed with management's perspective. Shaun Harkin, a part-timer at UPS during the strike, told me that at some hubs, these meetings were taken over by rank-and-file workers, who used them to discuss the contract. Managers who had risen from the ranks were sympathetic to the workers' problems; they even legitimated the workers' demands during these prework meetings.[35]

Overall, UPS's internal communication strategy was weak because it took workers for granted. Jiles explained that UPS relied on company surveys that showed that workers had no "significant dissatisfaction" with "critical" issues, such as job security and wages.[36] Clearly, the surveys did not accurately gauge the employees' anger, which is not surprising since many willfully lie on them. As Harkin pointed out to me, for workers at a company that monitors their every movement, self-preservation tells them not to give away more information than necessary on company surveys.

However, UPS's miscalculations were not the product of bungling. Rather, the multinational enterprise with yearly profits of more than a billion dollars assumed that it could continue to increase its profits at the cost of its workers. After all, the strategies of lean production, particularly the use of part-time labor, were basic to the economy as a whole. UPS failed to understand the growth of class anger in the 1990s. As UPS vice chair Alden would state at the end of the strike, "If I had known that it was going to go from negotiating for UPS to negotiating for part-time America, we would've approached it different."[37]

UPS's assessment of its position was based on its history with the Teamsters union. Since the company had never faced a national strike at the end of a contract period, it relied on its past relationship with the union as an accurate gauge for the present. This calculation seemed appropriate given that, for much of its existence, Teamsters union leaders had connections to organized crime, which meant rampant corruption and a complete lack of interest in members' problems, except when forced to deliver by rank-and-file pressure. Dan La Botz describes the extreme levels of corruption at the top of the union that led to the formation of the rank-and-file caucus, Teamsters for a Democratic Union (TDU). He explains that apart from the outright theft of union dues, the union's money was most atrociously squandered on lavish banquets for Teamster officials, at which company officials were often present. For example, the Teamsters convention of 1986 cost more than a million dollars. Needless to say, this leadership, referred to as the "old guard," put up little resistance to attacks from the corporations at which their membership worked. La Botz points out: "The union leadership has not resisted this employers' offensive. As the employers bullied the union, taking away and tearing up one clause of the contract after another, the union leadership organized no show of strength, no work stoppages, no Teamster strikes. Quite the contrary; throughout the 1980s Teamster officials collaborated with management in foisting concession contracts on the union's members."[38] In 1962, UPS got union approval to start using part-timers, and in 1982, the union agreed to a starting wage freeze of eight dollars an hour for part-timers.

Largely through the efforts of TDU, which mobilized and organized rank-and-file resistance to the old guard, Ron Carey, a reform candidate, won the 1991 elections and became president of the International Brotherhood of Teamsters. In the 1993 UPS contract negotiations, he was able to win some concessions, but on the question of part-time work, he accomplished little. The steady, gradual shift to part-time work was one of the key elements in UPS's success and profitability. In 1986, 42 percent of its workforce was part-time; by 1993, that figure had increased to 54 percent, and by 1997 to 60 percent.[39] Increasing part-time jobs meant that UPS could pay less for the same work. Since Carey had not made much headway on this issue in 1993, UPS reasoned that he would not be able to do much in 1997 either. A sign of UPS's confidence in the union's impotence was that 83 percent of new jobs created since the 1993 contract were part-time.

To a great extent, Carey's inability to accomplish more in 1993 was a result of divisions within the union. The old-guard locals resented the new leadership and did not want to have anything to do with rank-and-file mobilizations. This would be proved in practice in 1994. When UPS unilaterally increased its package weight limit from 70 to 150 pounds, Carey called a one-day national safety walkout. Many union locals, however, refused to participate and did not inform their members. As a result, only 40 percent of the workforce walked out.[40] UPS calculated that the division between Carey and the old guard would prevent any successful action in the future. In addition, the Teamsters barely had a strike fund because of the old guard's past extravagance.

At the end of the day, UPS reasonably assumed that a union that had never conducted a national strike, willingly accepted concessions, was internally divided, and did not have much of a strike fund was not likely to strike. Even if it did, it would have trouble keeping its members together not only because of internal divisions but also because of the large percentage of part-timers. Due to their high turnover rate, part-timers are thought to have little connection with the union and would therefore be less inclined to honor the picket line. All these factors explain why UPS was firm on its "last, best, and final" offer. The strike and its aftermath took the company by surprise.

Teamster Strategy

If the company could assume a position of strength, the union had much to do to overcome its weaknesses. In the 1996 elections, Carey defeated Jimmy Hoffa, a representative of the old guard, by a small margin. For him to continue as leader, he would have to prove himself in the UPS contract fight, as UPS Teamsters are a majority of members. Carey recognized that to succeed in the UPS contract negotiations he would have to go *around* the leadership of the old-guard locals and mobilize the rank and file. He therefore adopted the "contract campaign" strategy, developed by TDU in the 1980s, and hired a few TDU members to work on the campaign.

The contract campaign was designed with three objectives: to build solidarity among the rank and file, to win support in the community, and to obtain positive media coverage. All three goals were interrelated. For the first, the rank and file's primary concerns had to be determined. In April 1996, a full year before negotiations began, a survey of five thousand shop stewards explored preliminary bargaining goals. In July, a pamphlet titled *Countdown to Contract* with guidelines and tools to help build the local contract campaign was distributed to stewards, and members were sent "sign-up" postcards and encouraged to volunteer as coordinators (figure 2). The message on both these materials was "Teamster Unity = Strong Union." The Teamsters'

It's Our Contract

WE'LL FIGHT FOR IT!

Contract Campaign Volunteer Sign-up Sheet

The Teamsters National Negotiating Committee has begun bargaining to win a new UPS agreement to replace the one that expires July 31, 1997. Teamster unity and membership involvement will be the keys to getting a good UPS contract.

Volunteers are needed to be work area coordinators so that Teamster members will be kept informed about contract issues and actions. Each work area coordinator will be responsible for individually contacting between 10 and 20 co-workers about important contract issues or information about actions to show Teamster unity. Contact with co-workers would be done in non-work areas before or after work.

I will be a Work Area Coordinator to help get a good contract.

Name: _____
Street address: _____
City/State/ZIP: _____
Phone number: (___) _____
FAX number, if any (___) _____

What is your usual start time? _____
Building Name: _____
Name of Center: _____

What is your primary work classification?
☐ Package driver ☐ Mechanic ☐ Porter
☐ Feeder driver ☐ Clerk ☐ Car washer
☐ Other (please describe): _____

☐ **Part-time** (check classification below):
☐ Preload ☐ Midnight Hub
☐ Day Ramp ☐ Midnight Ramp
☐ Day Hub ☐ Reload
☐ Air Driver ☐ Air Walker

What is your primary work area?
_____

RETURN THIS FORM TO YOUR LOCAL UNION BUSINESS AGENT

It's Our Contract — We'll Fight For More Full-Time Jobs

It's Our Contract — We'll Fight For Better Wages and Pensions

It's Our Contract — We'll Fight For A Safe Place To Work

It's Our Contract — We'll Fight For A Secure Future

Figure 2. Contract Campaign Volunteer Sign-up Sheet

communication department also mailed members the *Teamsters UPS Update* (henceforth referred to as the *Update*), a newsletter with information pertaining to the contract and other timely and relevant information. The content was balanced between information from the international union and feedback from the membership.

The second step in the contract campaign was to devise a general questionnaire based on the responses from the preliminary survey. It was mailed to the membership in October. The October 21 issue of the *Update* explained why members should fill out the questionnaire.[41] It stated that the survey allowed every member to get involved in the forthcoming contract negotiations, thus enabling the negotiators to win the best possible contract. It expressed concern that while full-timers had been active in contract campaigns, part-timers were now also needed. To achieve this goal, a national part-time task force was set up in November. The chief obstacle to part-time worker involvement is high turnover, which makes keeping track of names and addresses hard; in fact, many part-time workers did not receive the *Update*.

A November 15 deadline was set for return of the six-page survey. The early November *Update* encouraged locals to hold meetings in December or January and to send proposals to the negotiating committee.[42] It also highlighted a video, *Make UPS Deliver,* that was designed to kick-start the contract campaign. It showed a discussion between UPS members and Ken Hall, the Union Parcel Division director, and proposed ways in which members could become involved. Stewards were mailed copies of the video, and others were informed that they could obtain it free by contacting the Washington, D.C., Teamsters office.

About forty thousand members, approximately 22 percent of all UPS workers, responded to the survey. From these responses it was determined that the top priorities were pensions, more full-time opportunities, health and safety, and subcontracting. The March *Update* explained these results with charts and bar graphs. As a way to get more members involved in the campaign, the bulletin showed photographs of events organized in various cities along with quotes from members.[43] For instance, Teamsters were photographed distributing flyers to fellow members at the Chicago UPS hub. It included a two-page spread with a string of quotes from members, listing their problems and concerns. Taken as a whole, these quotes captured, in the workers' own words, what it was like to work for UPS. They spurred members to identify with their fellow workers' grievances and to become active participants in the contract campaign. Along with the photos of various actions taken by locals in several cities, it made a strong case for membership involvement.

In addition to rhetorical appeals through the *Update,* eighteen field organizers were assigned to coordinate the campaign in January 1997. Many were local union activists, some linked to TDU. They worked with the locals when possible but had the authority to go around them and contact members directly should the leadership drag its feet. This mandate was necessary to ensure that local leaders who were hostile to Carey and the campaign would not stifle involvement. To allay resentment, Carey appointed several of the old guard to the negotiating committee. About a quarter of the forty-member committee were old officials. Also, for the first time in the union's history, four rank-and-file workers were included.[44]

Much of the contract campaign work until February was preparatory; in March, timed to coincide with the start of negotiations, about a dozen demonstrations and rallies were held around the country. The union then distributed another video to its members titled *What Are We Fighting for in Our New Contract?* which presented the critical negotiating points. In every month that followed, the campaign focused on a specific theme. Organizers distributed educational material and mounted actions at the hubs.

The media strategy involved inviting local media to cover these events. When the events were covered, the communication department then collected all the articles from local sources and sent clips to other media outlets, including the national media, to demonstrate "newsworthiness," so that anyone not covering the Teamsters might feel compelled to do so. As Matt Witt, who coordinated the communications work, told me, they were "using sections of the media to stimulate other media." He added that the strategy was successful, as many local news media, particularly television, covered the rallies.[45] These clips were also sent to sympathetic academics to keep them up-to-date on contract negotiations, so when the media contacted them, they could offer the latest information.

In April, the campaign emphasized job safety. Grievance forms were distributed to members to fill out whenever they had to handle packages weighing more than seventy pounds without assistance or improperly labeled packages. In two weeks, about five thousand grievances were filed. At the end of the month, the Teamsters held rallies in parking lots under the theme "UPS: Don't Break Our Backs." *Update* reported that several dozen such rallies were held across the country.[46]

In May, the campaign focused on threats to job security, such as subcontracting and supervisors doing workers' jobs. On May 22, at rallies across the country, whistles were distributed so that management could literally hear workers "blowing the whistle" on them. Rand Wilson, of the Teamsters communication department, stated that ninety-six rallies were held in the United States and a total of forty thousand whistles distributed.[47] These rallies received significant media attention, particularly from local television affiliates.

In addition to the domestic rallies, actions were organized at UPS facilities in nine other countries. For instance, in Italy, UPS workers held a one-hour strike, in Spain a two-hour strike, and a protest at UPS's European headquarters in Brussels.[48] These actions followed from a February meeting of all unions worldwide that represented UPS workers, organized by the International Transport Workers Federation.

None of this protest seemed to impress UPS. Negotiations were suspended on April 22 and did not resume until May 13. UPS was proposing more subcontracting, more use of part-timers, no increase in starting pay for part-timers, and a company pension plan that would replace the union's plan. They also wanted to convert the feeder driver job—the workers who drive ground packages around the country—into a nonunion job that would be independently subcontracted. On the main issues that the contract campaign had identified, UPS refused to concede.[49]

The *Update* revealed the details of the negotiations and urged members to take part in rallies, talk to coworkers about the campaign, and display the Teamster stickers, buttons, T-shirts, hats, and bumper stickers produced for the campaign. The message was one of union solidarity and strength; the T-shirt read, "It's our Contract, we'll fight for it." To Carey, it was very important that members wear these items in order to show management that the union was united and backed the negotiating committee.

To build members' confidence, the *Update* featured photographs of "blow the whistle" rallies around the country as well as the solidarity actions in Europe. A new video, *Power at Work: Building a Member-to-Member Action Network,* was also produced to explain a mechanism by which information could be distributed across the union through a membership network. This system was based on a network in which every steward or network member was responsible for staying in touch with about twenty other workers. They had to pass on information, answer questions, and collect feedback. The network's goal was to counter management meetings that tried to win workers to its side.

The June focus was on the fight for full-time jobs. The union research department released a report, *Half a Job Is Not Enough,* that showed how part-time jobs affected all UPS workers. At the same time, more than one hundred thousand members signed a petition demanding that UPS stop increasing part-time jobs and create more full-time jobs. Local unions were encouraged to organize community events to discuss the problem of part-time jobs.

By the beginning of July, the union decided to take a strike-authorization vote, since UPS had not budged on the key issues. It refused to create the number of full-time jobs that the union deemed necessary, it proposed using part-timers to replace full-timers in the air operation, it offered raises of thirty cents per hour every other year for a seven-year contract, and pushed for subcontracting the feeder jobs. These proposals would have weakened the union. The July 1 *Update* explained why a strike vote would give the negotiating committee more power. However, it also took care to point out that the "authorization vote does not mean we are automatically going on strike." UPS workers voted overwhelmingly (95 percent) in favor of this strategy. Carey declared that the vote proved that the Teamsters were "united and ready to fight for a good contract." Again, the *Update* noted that the vote did "not *require* the committee to call for a strike."[50] As the deadline approached, UPS offered two versions of its "last, best, and final offer" to the union, neither of which was satisfactory. More than a dozen parking-lot rallies were held in July.[51]

The contract campaign was a team effort involving many departments of the International union, from research to communication, and many local unions. The overall work was coordinated by the Parcel and Small Package Division. Eighteen field organizers responsible for the actual implementation of the plan reported to the director of field services. The communication department produced the *Update* and handled the media campaign, which had three aspects: sending regular press releases through a media service to interested media organizations, sending information packets to the academic community, and inviting the local media to cover prestrike rallies and other events. It did not have a specific PR strategy. Matt Witt explained its "anti-PR strategy": not trying to manipulate public opinion but rather relying on workers to explain their grievances against the company to their customers and the community.

The contract campaign was a good strategy in theory, but its implementation was somewhat uneven.[52] More than two hundred locals represent UPS workers around the country. Until 1991, these locals were controlled mostly by the old guard, who had established a culture that was antithetical to rank-and-file participation in contract negotiations. Their policy was one of cooperation and collaboration with management. They held meetings with management without stewards being present, traded off grievances, refused to involve or to inform members, and even socialized with management.[53] In the 1996 election, Carey won by a slim margin. Though some sections of the old guard were hostile, others backed Carey and did shift their attitude to rank-and-file participation. However, Joe Allen, shop steward at Local 705 in Chicago, told me that, in his estimation, this change applied to about half the locals; in the other half, implementation of the contract campaign was almost nonexistent.[54] Carey tried to persuade these locals to cooperate in strongly worded messages and e-mails. As late as May 15, 1997, he still had to fight with local officials, as this excerpt from a message suggests: "It has come to my attention that some local unions are not complying with the Teamster national Negotiating Committee's policy and strategy regarding UPS contract negotiation. . . . It is the responsibility of each and every local official representing UPS members to provide members with information they need to make informed decisions and to be an integral part of the negotiating process."[55] Yet despite the rank-and-file orientation of his rhetoric, Carey appointed a number of old-guard officials to the national committee, while keeping the number of rank and filers low. He himself was somewhat lax at his local in New York. He canceled the membership meeting in June and in March ended the meeting in less than an hour, even though several workers were still in line to speak.[56]

Implementation of the contract campaign varied from city to city, from enthusiasm at locals associated with TDU to a complete lack of actions at old-guard locals. In some cities, like Détroit, locals headed by old-guard figures allied to Carey at least tried to carry out the campaign. This was aided by a rank-and-file newsletter, *Contract Connection,* which was distributed throughout the area and helped to lay the groundwork for the strike.[57] Yet even in locals that supported the campaign, implementation was sluggish. For a union leadership that had no practice in mobilizing the rank and file, the contract campaign was a challenge. Joe Allen stated that Chicago Local 705 officials held a few meetings and distributed flyers—far short of what was needed, since they represented eleven thousand UPS workers.

To compensate for this sluggishness, rank-and-file workers in many cities took the initiative, often going around the local leadership. In New York, fifteen part-time workers in Local 804 took it upon themselves to petition every night. Soon they had more than two thousand signatures. In Providence, Local 251 leaders did little, but rank-and-file workers obtained copies of campaign literature from the International. In Oakland, Local 70 leaders were slow to act, but the rank and file mobilized and got involved in the campaign. In Washington, D.C., the leadership of Local 631 called a contract campaign meeting as late as May 1997, but only because rank and filers put enormous pressure on them. At the meeting, the leadership distributed copies of *Contract Forum,* a rank-and-file newsletter, to give the impression that they were really interested in the campaign.[58]

This unevenness explains why, in April, only five thousand grievances were filed. The pace picked up in May, when more than ninety "blow the whistle" parking-lot rallies were held around the country. By June, more than one hundred thousand workers had signed a petition for more full-time jobs, but in July, only a dozen or so parking-lot rallies were organized. Still, a significant number of workers became involved in the campaign and by their actions and conversations with coworkers helped to build the strike.

This groundwork prepared the workers to argue their position on the contract negotiations with confidence and clarity, both with the community and with the media. The prestrike rallies held at various hubs were covered by local media, and rank-and-file workers spoke out about their problems at UPS. Matt Witt commented that a "lot of Teamster members became articulate speakers" and were the "ambassadors" of their own cause. Local news media outlets received much of their information from the workers.

Coverage in local media enabled the public to get a sense of what was at stake for UPS workers, even before the strike began. Those who watched or read this coverage probably recognized the similarities between their own work conditions and those faced by UPS workers and began to identify with the workers. The community outreach that was conducted as part of the contract campaign also helped. However, both local media coverage and community outreach were quite limited. It would take a strike to raise the stakes and focus national attention on the struggle between the Teamsters and UPS.

Without the strike, it is very unlikely that UPS would have budged, for two reasons. First, it cost the company about forty million dollars a day. Although the workers also lost money in the form of wages, the company had significantly more to lose, in terms of not only its customer base but also its revenues. Second, a strike makes public what is normally a private negotiation between a company and a union. The advantage of a mass strike is that it draws national media attention, if for no other reason than the "inconvenience" caused to the public. Thus, UPS was forced to defend itself in a very public arena, an arena where the vast majority had experienced problems similar to those of UPS workers.

Here, UPS lost the battle. It failed to deliver its message, despite a media environment slanted in favor of corporations. The Teamsters won two-to-one support because they were able to craft a message that resonated with the public. This battle was not merely about PR, where the side with the best arguments won. The basis of the Teamsters' support was the *experience* of workers and their pent-up anxieties. The Teamsters succeeded not because of clever rhetoric but because they gave voice to workers' frustrations and anger at their conditions in an otherwise booming economy. The following section describes how the battle over ideas and for public opinion played out over the course of the strike.

The Struggle for "Hearts and Minds"

At the start of the strike, who would win the hearts and minds of the American public—UPS or the Teamsters—was not immediately obvious. UPS, a company with vast resources, was able to respond quickly to the demands of a strike. The Teamsters union, mired in corruption, had a meager strike fund but had led a partially successful contract campaign. At the very least, the campaign kept a check on the old guard and created a space for rank-and-file militants to get involved in strike preparations. It was the first time that UPS workers were involved in a national strike. In a climate of simmering class anger, the Teamsters were able to spotlight class inequality in a way with which most workers could identify. And along with their allies they waged a struggle for ideological domination.

When the strike began on August 3, 1997, the first workers to stand in solidarity with the Teamsters were the more class conscious, that is, those who were already in unions. The American Postal Workers Union (APWU) flatly rejected a proposal by management to increase part-time workers so that the postal service could deliver the packages normally shipped through UPS. Recognizing that a strike can be effective only if it shuts down production and that this strike was about part-time jobs, APWU workers rejected management's demand. The union's president stated in no uncertain terms that the postal workers' union "fully support[ed] the Teamsters in their struggle with UPS."[59] UPS pilots, who are organized under a different union, pledged their solidarity and honored the picket line.

Several UPS pilots, postal workers, and electrical workers joined the picket lines in Colorado and Wyoming. Teamster bakery drivers dropped off baked products at UPS picket lines all across New Hampshire.[60] In Boston, more than five hundred people, members of several unions, including the Union of Needletrades, Industrial, and Textile Employees, the International Brotherhood of Electrical Workers, and the Service Employees International Union, participated in a rally. Outside a major UPS air facility in Rockford, Illinois, a rally of about 250 people drew UPS pilots, members of the United Auto Workers union, the National Association of Letter Carriers, and Teamster Local 325.[61] As the strike progressed, 2,000 telephone workers, members of the Communication Workers of America, marched in solidarity with UPS workers at the Manhattan hub.[62] Prior to this march, twenty vans of Nynex workers drove out on their lunch break to the UPS hub in Maspeth, Queens.[63] By the middle of the strike, AFL-CIO president John Sweeney declared support for the Teamsters and offered money to keep the strike going, putting the weight of the entire union movement behind the Teamsters.

In addition to support from unionized workers, members of the community and labor supporters joined rallies organized by locals across the country. In Seattle, more than 2,000 people participated in a rally organized by Teamster Local 174 and Jobs with Justice. In Warwick, Rhode Island, about 1,300 participated in a rally.[64] In Atlanta, more than 2,000 attended a rally organized by the Teamster locals and the Central Labor Council. In Portland, Oregon, between 400 and 500 people rallied. More than 1,200 workers, their families, and other unionists turned out in Springfield, Missouri. Members of the community brought food for the striking workers, and in several cities, cookouts were organized for the strikers and their families.[65] These actions and rallies, which took place across the country, although modest in size and scale, were a huge step forward for the labor movement after the defeats of the 1980s. They expressed a solidarity that won larger segments of the working class to the Teamsters' side.

Before the strike began, the contract campaign and the rallies held at various hubs engaged the wider community. They also attracted the local media in several cities, giving the public some grasp of what was at stake in the contract negotiations. But it was the *strike* that focused national attention on the workers and their struggle. The story was on the front pages of local and national newspapers and headline news on television and radio. This sustained attention spotlighted the Teamsters' struggle and captured the public's imagination. Seventy-seven percent of the public was following the strike "closely" or "very closely."[66] Initially, public support was probably based on some knowledge of the workers' grievances combined with the general goodwill that American society feels toward UPS workers. However, as Carey and the rank-and-file workers at picket lines all over the country spoke out about the reasons for the strike and explained their situation to news media reporters, this support acquired a distinct class character. Workers and union representatives emphasized two key points: the struggle was about part-time jobs, and it was being waged on behalf of all American workers.

The emphasis on part-time work cast the striking workers in a sympathetic light. For instance, the *Chicago Tribune* wrote about Rosalind Williams, a mother of two who, because of her status as a part-time worker, was not able to secure a loan to buy a house. The *San Antonio Express News* quoted Ontario, California, part-timer Vito Palmisano, who had to work two jobs and still could not make ends meet: "You can't pay the bills on part-time wages." Scott Wabals told a similar story to a *Philadelphia Inquirer* reporter. He worked two jobs, one at UPS and the other as a roofer, and as a result slept for only four hours a night. He had worked seven years for UPS and, despite his desire for a full-time job, had not yet received one. Tammisha Jordan explained that she woke up every morning at one thirty to make it to her shift from three o'clock to eight o'clock at UPS. She barely saw her daughter and then had to leave for her second job as a clerk. When she returned home in the evening, she had a few hours with her daughter, and the routine would start again. Kelly Anglim explained that she and her four year old lived with her grandmother and ate "noodles a lot." She said, "I can't give them everything they want, everything they deserve [because she had so few hours as a part-timer] but I need the job for the benefits."[67]

Such stories about part-time UPS workers appeared in local media all over the country. Even the national media, despite the antistrike tone in Phase One and the emphasis on inconvenience, ran several stories on the part-time problem. Not only did these stories construct UPS workers in a sympathetic light, but many other workers were able to identify with their plight. Preston Conner, president of the National Association of Part-Time and Temporary Employees, explained that the "disparity in wages and benefits is like a big economic secret that people have refused to talk about. The UPS workers have given part-timers a voice."[68]

When Carey was interviewed in the national media, he emphasized concerns about part-time work and said that the strike was being waged not just for UPS workers but for all American workers. He argued that the Teamsters' "fight for good jobs in America mark[ed] an historic turning point for working people in this country."[69] As chapter 3 noted in some detail, Carey took every opportunity on national television to argue that the struggle was for all American workers. It greatly helped the Teamsters' cause that Carey was an experienced union leader and speaker, while his nemesis, James Kelly, the CEO of UPS, had almost no media experience.[70] Overwhelmingly, the articulate Carey was seen, heard, and read in the mainstream media. The message was clear and powerful: the UPS strike was for the rights of all workers.

Some rank-and-file workers also took pains to deliver the same message and were given modest coverage in newspapers. Matt Witt said, "I think that the biggest reasons that the public supported the strike was that workers rather than union officials did so much of the talking, and when they did, they showed how they were standing up for working people generally and not just themselves." Joe Brown of Cleveland argued that, given the state of affairs for workers, "somebody in America had to take a stand, and the Teamsters finally did." His coworker Mike McBride stated that the struggle "isn't just about us, it's about the American work force. If you're a working family, this strike is for you." Edward Stoess of Clarksville, Indiana, said that the UPS strike was "a defining moment" in that it would determine the answer to the question, "Can a person make a living at a blue-collar job?"[71] In this way, some rank-and-file workers were able to generalize their struggle to that of America as a whole. However, by and large, it was Carey who amplified this message in the media.

If sections of the rank and file were able to articulate the key issues of the strike with clarity and confidence, it was due not only to the work of the contract campaign but also to the act of striking. Strikes give the workers involved a sense of their collective power, and this confidence in their power was reinforced by the solidarity rallies that brought out other unions and labor supporters. Even workers who did not participate in the contract campaign would soon be changed through the act of collective struggle. The strongest indication of this transformation comes from the fact that even though only about 64,000 workers participated in the strike vote, as Rand Wilson told me, once the strike was called more than 175,000 honored the picket line.

In addition to speaking to the news media during the strike, some full-timers went on their regular routes with a part-timer to explain the situation to the customers.[72] The union produced a leaflet titled *Your UPS Driver Is Fighting for America's Future,* which was handed out to UPS customers and members of the community (figure 3). The leaflet argued that the UPS strike was a struggle to determine whether the future would hold "good jobs with secure health and pension coverage" or if corporations would continue the "race to the bottom" in the shift to low-wage, part-time jobs. This message struck at the heart of globalization policies, particularly corporate restructuring and the trend toward "lean and mean" corporations.

The union's ability to deliver this message was strengthened by academics who understood the impact of globalization policies on the working class.

Your UPS Driver Is Fighting For America's Future

Will our children and grandchildren be able to look forward to good jobs with secure health and pension coverage?

Or will corporations continue their "race to the bottom" by shifting to low-wage, part-time jobs with few benefits?

That's the issue in the largest union contract negotiations in the United States this year.

This summer, 185,000 workers led by Teamsters President Ron Carey will negotiate a new contract with United Parcel Service — an international powerhouse which makes more than $1 *billion* per year in profits.

In these negotiations, Teamster members are challenging the corporate game plan that many working families are facing today:

■ **The shift to low-wage, part-time jobs.** More than half of UPS's work force is part time, with starting pay of only $8 per hour. In these negotiations, workers are seeking more full-time job opportunities and higher pay and benefits for part-timers.

■ **Subcontracting to low-wage companies.** Like many U.S. companies, UPS is using "contracting out" and nonunion subsidiaries to avoid providing workers with a decent wage and secure health and pension coverage.

■ **Unsafe conditions.** Workers at UPS file more complaints with OSHA than at any other company. Not surprisingly, UPS has been the leader in giving PAC contributions to members of Congress in an attempt to cut OSHA's budget and powers.

Here's how you can help UPS workers fight for the future:

1 Let your driver know that he or she has your support.

2 Call or write your local UPS office and tell them our economy needs good full-time jobs.

3 Share this information with your coworkers, friends, and family.

If you would like a packet of information about the Teamsters' fight at UPS, please contact:

 **Teamsters Union**
c/o Parcel Division
25 Louisiana Avenue N.W.
Washington, DC 20001

Figure 3. Flyer handed out to the public explaining the Teamsters' case

When the strike began, several were contacted as "experts"; Harley Shaiken, Chris Tilly, Kate Brofenbrenner, Nelson Lichtenstein, Stanley Aronowitz, Michael Belzer, Elaine Bernard, Francois Carre, and Peter Rachleff, among others, were quoted often by local and national news media.[73]

Harley Shaiken explained that over "the last five years, part-time work has shifted from being an occasional strategy to being a way of life at U.P.S. That's why there is the anger right now. For U.P.S. workers it represents, in effect, a hidden downsizing." Chris Tilly argued that businesses "have charged off in the direction of flexibility without fully evaluating the costs in terms of worker commitment and productivity. My concern is that with unions weak and labor laws weak, the burden of achieving flexibility gets put on workers rather than being shared by employers." For Kate Brofenbrenner, the UPS strike represented "a sea change in the labor movement. It will put a restraint on employers who thought they had free rein to contract out, outsource and turn good full-time jobs into bad part-time jobs. Employers have been shown there's a cost if you push employees too far."[74] These sorts of arguments were made by several academics who were cited, quite frequently, in city and national newspapers.

The Economic Policy Institute, a liberal, prolabor think tank, was also quoted often during the strike, particularly on part-time employment. Edith Rasell, an EPI economist, explained that nonstandard workers usually earn lower wages and are less likely to have benefits and pensions. She argued that this practice amounts to discrimination. Eileen Appelbaum argued that the strike resonated with the public, because it was "getting harder and harder to find a regular full-time job." She added that there were "lots of people that want full-time employment but [couldn't] get it. There [were] also lots of people in full-time jobs that [were] concerned that their employer might replace them with two part-time employees or a contractor or temporary worker."[75] Thus, groups like the EPI and academics reinforced the message coming from the rank and file and Carey.

Additionally, alternative media were instrumental in putting forward proworker arguments. The radio news program *Democracy Now,* broadcast in many major cities around the country, ran several updates on the strike. On August 5, the show had interviews with UPS workers who explained what the strike was about. The interviews were prefaced by the statement: "If you tried to find out what the strike is about in much of the media, you might have a hard time." On August 11, the program reminded its listeners that one of the key issues in the dispute was part-time work, pointing out that "all but 8,000 of 46,000 new jobs at UPS have been low paid, part-time jobs—jobs which the union would like to see transformed into full-time." The program went on to add that the "strike comes as UPS has been hitting record profits, taking in some $1.1 billion last year."[76] Later, several prolabor academics and columnists such as Bob Fitch of New York University and Alexander Cockburn of the *Nation* magazine were interviewed.

Cockburn, in his column "Beat the Devil," in the mid-August issue of the *Nation,* wrote about the *Wall Street Journal*'s campaign to force a new Teamster election. He defended Carey's reelection, arguing that the victory was not due to illegal campaign contributions but rather the product of a struggle "fought out and won in hundreds of union locals." The newsletter *Labor Notes* ran an article in the August issue explaining why the Teamsters might go on strike, pointing to the problems of part-time jobs at UPS. Leftist newspapers like *Socialist Worker* carried several articles in the lead up to and during the strike highlighting the key issues and making a case in support of the workers. In June 1997, a special supplement was published with several articles on topics such as the issues involved in the contract negotiations, how workers were fighting racial and sexual discrimination at UPS, and the role of rank-and-file workers in organizing against UPS. The August 15 issue ran a front-page story with the headline, "UPS Strikers Take a Stand: Part-Time America Isn't Working."[77] Finally, the Internet was another source of alternative information. In addition to the Teamsters' Web site, supporters had also posted material on the Internet.[78]

Together, the Teamsters and its allies—other unionists, members of the community, academics and groups like the EPI, and alternative media—constructed a powerful message.

UPS Counterarguments

Even before the strike began, UPS deployed its vast resources to wage the battle over ideas. It first phoned its customers in the last week of July to inform them that after July 31, it could not guarantee delivery of packages. By highlighting the inconvenience caused to customers, UPS sought to build support for an antistrike position. When the strike began, the tone of coverage in the national media was consistent with the company's position. In addition to its own efforts, UPS could rely on the corporate media to create a business-friendly atmosphere, on probusiness "experts" to further bolster its case in the media, and on politicians of both stripes to do the same.

UPS also took out full-page advertisements in several newspapers to make its case to the public. Its first series of ads focused on presenting its offer as generous. The August 1 advertisement in the *New York Times* titled "An Open Letter to UPS Customers" argued that UPS had offered the union a fair contract with wage increases, a new pension plan that would increase benefits by 50 percent, five hundred–dollar bonuses for part-timers, guarantees that drivers would not be eliminated through subcontracting, better health care, and opportunities for more than ten thousand new full-time jobs. The advertisement went on to urge the union leadership to "do the right thing" and allow their workers to vote on the contract. Many of these claims were misleading. UPS failed to mention that the wage increases offered were lower than in the previous contract. The offer to create ten thousand full-time jobs was not based on creating new jobs; rather, these were promotions that the company routinely made when full-time jobs became vacant.

During the middle of the strike, UPS took out ads that tried to reshape the debate. The August 12 advertisement in the *Los Angeles Times* titled "What's Really at Stake in the Teamsters Strike: A Few Facts" argued that the strike was not about part-time jobs, because UPS had promoted thirteen thousand workers into full-time positions and created eight thousand new full-time jobs. It went on to state that in a period of downsizing, UPS had actually created forty-six thousand new jobs. The implication is that even though only eight thousand were full-time jobs, UPS should be lauded for creating jobs at all. The ad went on to claim that part-time jobs at UPS were "great jobs with great benefits" that college students and homemakers actually preferred over full-time jobs. They also argued that part-time workers played an important role in the delivery business, because they allowed "UPS to operate with the flexibility and speed to meet the urgency of our customers' needs."

The real issue in the strike, they tried to stress, was the pension fund. UPS had offered to create a new company-run pension plan that would give its employees 50 percent more retirement benefits. However, the union leadership had turned down this "generous" offer because it did not want to lose control of the billions of dollars in the pension fund. The ad went on to state that if the union leadership was truly concerned about its members, it would present the offer to the membership and end the strike. According to the ad, ending the strike was in the interest of "our people" and "our customers."

The PR department organized a tightly controlled system by which messages were sent to the media. On a daily basis, it read and analyzed news media stories and devised responses. It held two daily press briefings and had a status report for reporters who called after hours. It also organized press conferences and set up a system in which journalists could call in to speak directly with top management, such as Ken Sternad, vice president of corporate public relations, and Dave Murray, the chief negotiator. They received more than six hundred calls on the first day alone. Many of the press phone calls were handled by one hundred field managers, who were trained several months before the strike. In addition, the UPS Web site posted updates on the negotiations to counter those put up by the Teamsters. The Web site offered messages by UPS management, press releases, and strike information. Every morning, briefings were held with Edelman Public Relations Worldwide (the external PR agency), senior management, company representatives, lawyers, representatives from the labor department, and salespeople.[79] In this way, the PR department strategized and coordinated the company's communication with the media and public.

UPS made a number of arguments to justify its position, through both its ads and other avenues. First, it argued that the use of part-time workers was necessary because UPS had to be flexible to compete with nonunion transportation companies in the global economy. It claimed that its surveys showed that many of its workers did not want full-time jobs. Second, UPS tried to frame the strike as being about pensions. It argued that if it withdrew from the Teamsters' multiunion plan and created a company-controlled plan, UPS workers would receive as much as 50 percent more in retirement benefits. Third, they argued that Carey had called the strike in order to deflect attention from campaign-financing problems for which he was under investigation.

Throughout the strike, UPS tried to present itself as more concerned about the welfare of its workers than the union. Claiming that the union was holding the workers hostage and forcing them to strike, it challenged the union to allow the workers to vote on the "last, best, and final" contract offer. This pretense was contradicted by the fact that 95 percent of the workers did not cross the picket lines. UPS's claim that their part-timers did not want full-time jobs also could not hold up against scores of workers describing their harsh economic conditions and their desire for full-time jobs. As Jennifer Jiles would later lament, while the PR department could control and coordinate what was being said by the company, they could not control the "picket lines, what our employees said to reporters, and the negative company image that was beginning to form in the public's mind."[80] *UPS lost the battle, both ideologically and economically, on the picket line.*

Rhetorically, it would have been easier for UPS to vilify the workers and to argue that they were greedy. As discussed in the previous chapter, vilification is one of the conventional mechanisms by which management demonizes its workers and wins public support. UPS could not do this, because the drivers are its public face, and the service that they provide is the product that is sold to customers. Therefore, if UPS had constructed them in a negative light, it would have in turn hurt the company image. As Jiles notes, "We have 90 years of brand equity in the men and women who drive our delivery vehicles. Our drivers are a strategic, competitive asset. Unlike steelworkers or autoworkers, our drivers interface with millions of customers each day. When the strike was over, the drivers would still be the primary contacts to our customers."[81]

The company therefore made a strategic decision to "protect the reputation" of the drivers at "all costs."[82] Under no circumstances could the public image of UPS drivers, carefully cultivated over decades, be undermined. This decision also had an impact on UPS's ability to hire replacement workers. Although some managers were driving trucks, since UPS did not anticipate that a majority of the workers would honor the picket lines, it did not organize replacement workers on the massive scale needed. During the strike, the company threatened to hire scabs but could not because UPS drivers are skilled labor and not that easy to replace and public opinion was on their side.[83]

By the same token, because the drivers are in routine contact with UPS customers and have established relationships with them, they were in a better position to explain the strike. UPS workers have a good deal of credibility in American society. They are perceived as hard workers and are known, liked, and trusted. This credibility and goodwill gave them an advantage over the company in the propaganda war. Although many drivers went on their regular route to explain their side in the strike, even in the absence of such discussion customers were more inclined to believe the drivers because they knew them. This familiarity explains why many small business owners, despite the effects of the strike, came out in support of the workers. They probably felt compassion for them.

Rather than demonize the workers, UPS was careful to construct the strike around issues, such as pensions, and the union. They took aim at the union and tried to dissociate the workers from the union and union leadership. UPS reasoned that it could rely on a general antiunion climate in the United States to win public support. The antiunion argument was based on two themes: that Carey had called the strike to deflect attention from his campaign scandal and that by not allowing the workers to vote on the company's generous offer, the union was holding its members hostage. In short, UPS tried to present itself as the guardian of its simpleminded workers, who were being duped by corrupt union leaders.

This tactic might have worked in a period like the 1980s, when public support for unions was low. However, class consciousness had grown in the 1990s. The "simpleminded" workers on the picket line were able to counter UPS's propaganda, and the conflicts that they raised resonated with the public's experiences. The Teamsters presented American workers with a clear picture of what the economic recovery of the 1990s had meant for the working class as a whole. Kept out of sight and out of public discussion for much of the decade, their conditions were crystallized and given legitimate expression in the mainstream media because of the UPS strike. Thus, public support for the Teamsters was won not so much on the basis of a generalized sympathy for the hardworking UPS worker but on the basis of *class* identification. Although the positive image of UPS workers might have helped initially, as the strike progressed, the debate was not about image but about substantive problems and which side, the union or the company, could better solve them. The public supported the proposition that union workers were in a better position to articulate their problems and to implement the solutions than the corporation. What we saw here then was not just "public support" but class solidarity. American workers sided with their class. This support would then exert pressure on sections of the mass media, as discussed in the previous chapter.

The support for workers was a big shift away from 1980s conservatism. In 1981, when Ronald Reagan fired the air traffic controllers, public opinion polls showed that only 40 percent supported the controllers, while 51 percent supported Reagan's decision. Hyman Berman argues that this was because there was "a public perception that the unions had become too strong, too arrogant, and they needed to be stomped upon." He adds that this perception no longer holds. Public sympathy for the UPS strikers was "based on a perception that corporate greed has gone too far and that the great economic breakthrough of the last 15 or 20 years has seen the ordinary worker fall behind, while CEOs have come away with obscene compensation packages. This has finally penetrated into the public mind as being basically unfair."[84] Thus, the UPS strike served to shift the ideological advantage that corporations had enjoyed in the media and spotlight their greed. Corporate paternalism suffered a blow, as large sections of the working class identified with the Teamsters.

UPS even hired a private opinion-research firm to study public opinion and to devise more persuasive messages, yet nothing helped.[85] Ken Sternad tried to explain UPS's failure to win public opinion by arguing that its PR department was understaffed.[86] While this claim may or may not be true, the size of its department had little to do with its ability to sell its message. As Rand Wilson accurately summed up, "All the spin doctors in the world can't compensate for what people think and feel."[87]

UPS's failure to present a convincing argument meant that some of its allies began to falter in their support. By the second week of the strike, as discussed in chapter 4, several economists and ideologues for the employing class began to turn their backs on the company. With anger mounting against corporate greed, these pundits tried to focus attention on UPS as an anomaly, thus deflecting blame from corporate America as a whole. The story of "UPS exceptionalism" began to be propagated. Additionally, politicians from both the Democratic and the Republican parties, whose campaigns receive significant contributions from UPS and transportation political-action committees, were limited in their ability to stop the strike.[88] Early on, several politicians vainly tried to win consent for the use of the Taft-Hartley Act. However, as it became clear that popular support was with the strikers, several politicians such as Paul Wellstone, Joseph Kennedy, Ed Markey, and others joined the picket lines. Prolabor political figures, including Jesse Jackson and Ralph Nader, also threw their weight behind the strikers, and legislative bodies like the Albany County Legislature in New York, the New York City Council, and the Minneapolis City Council passed resolutions in support of the strike. All of this put pressure on President Clinton's decision to use the Taft-Hartley Act.

Additionally, an ABC poll found that even though fully three-quarters of respondents were affected by the strike, only 26 percent wanted President Clinton to stop it.[89] Clinton, who had intervened in and stopped other potential strikes that year, found the pressure mounting. To call off the strike using the Taft-Hartley Act, the administration would have had to present evidence in federal court that the strike affected an entire industry and endangered "national health or safety." President Carter had last done so, but public pressure and scrutiny seems to have discouraged Clinton. As mentioned earlier, 77 percent of the public was following the strike "closely" or "very closely," making it one of the most followed stories of the year.[90] Apparently, when the news media cover issues the American public finds relevant, they do pay attention; the strike drew more attention than the Clinton sex scandal of the same year. This level of public scrutiny of the strike meant that had Clinton terminated the strike before the Teamsters reached an agreeable contract, it would very likely have been perceived as unfair. Thus, an active citizenry, or rather workers and their allies, were able to influence the decisions of the political elites.

When Clinton declined to use the Taft-Hartley Act because the strike did not present a national emergency, the news media found it progressively harder to define the strike as a major inconvenience. The mainstream media accord a good deal of legitimacy to government sources, particularly the president.[91] Rarely is his view questioned; instead, it usually sets the terms of discussion. In this case, Clinton's refusal to intervene legitimated the strike, preventing the mainstream media from focusing as much attention on the question of inconvenience.

By the second week, UPS was running out of options and had lost several hundred million dollars. Additionally, its key allies—the mainstream media, politicians, and corporate ideologues—had started to switch allegiances or abandon UPS. Ideologically, politically, and economically, UPS was weakened, and when several of its key backers jumped ship or started to falter, it shifted the balance of power toward the Teamsters (see table 7). Thus, the company had to retreat, giving the Teamsters the best contract that they had ever won from the company. In the aftermath of the strike, several media outlets would then open up a discussion of inequality.

Conclusion

The key to the Teamsters victory was the strike. By withholding their labor, the Teamsters demonstrated the economic power that they had over UPS. Not only did they cause UPS to lose money, but they also gained confidence in their collective power. A national strike by 185,000 workers was front-page and headline news around the country. The sustained media attention allowed the rank and file and union representatives, particularly Carey, to make a clear argument that the strike was about decent, full-time jobs, not just for UPS workers but for all American workers. This message was reinforced by academics and representatives from progressive think tanks who discussed how corporate practices and trends, such as downsizing, subcontracting, the shift to lean production and part-time jobs, and so on unfairly affected workers. Alternative media also participated in constructing arguments in support of the workers.

Despite unfavorable coverage in the national media in Phase One, the Teamsters were able to win public support due, in part, to prestrike rallies and other outreach events organized as part of the contract campaign and the local media attention that they received. Initially, UPS workers could also rely on their good public image, but, ultimately, the strike itself and the coverage of the part-time controversy as well as other issues, in both the local

Table 7. Supporting groups switch sides

Teamsters	UPS
1. Unions	1. Media ← (significant sections)
2. Academics and liberal think tanks	2. "Experts" and corporate ideologues ←
3. Alternative media	3. Politicians ←
4. Public	

and the national media, sparked public support in the form of class identification. Even though the national media framed the strike in terms of the
inconvenience it caused, American workers were able to see through the procorporate rhetoric and to understand the issues at stake. The working class,
which is barely conscious of its class identity because of an ideological environment dominated by corporations, recognized that the experiences of the
striking workers were similar to their own. By mobilizing class consciousness,
the Teamsters won public opinion, which then influenced the tone of strike
coverage in several national news media outlets, and, in turn, prevented politicians, who under other circumstances would not have been reluctant, from
using the Taft-Hartley Act to stop the strike. Coupled with the financial losses
from the strike, the pressure was on UPS.

By the second week of the strike, several economists and ideologues for
the employing class began to turn their backs on the company. Isolated ideologically and politically and facing huge losses financially, UPS had to withdraw its "last, best, and final" offer and concede to the union's position. The
defeat of this "model" corporation then opened a space, in the aftermath of
the strike, for a generalized discussion in the media, from the business press
to general interest magazines, of the inequality at the heart of the booming
1990s economy.

Since 1997, the labor movement has seen some victories but, overall, it
has failed to stem the tide of a renewed offensive under the presidency of
George W. Bush. One could conclude from this fact that the UPS strike was
an exception. Certainly, there were things about the strike that were unique:
Ron Carey is one among a few union leaders who had risen through the
ranks, UPS workers have a particularly good public image, TDU's involvement in the contract negotiations made a difference, and so on. There will
always be factors that are unique to different strikes. However, it would be
incorrect to draw the conclusion that the success of the UPS strike cannot be
reproduced. If the Teamsters' general strike in Minneapolis in 1934 had not
been followed by the sit-down strikes, the textile workers' strikes, and the
formation of the Congress of Industrial Organizations later in the decade,
one might have concluded then, too, that 1934 was unique. Yet the events of
1934 would still have been indicative of the potential for mass mobilization.
Similarly, the UPS strike showed what is possible in the context of growing
class polarization and anger today. What is necessary is a labor movement
that can channel this anger and turn it into action.

PART THREE

Theory and Lessons

SIX

Retheorizing Resistance in
Communication and Media Studies

Most scholars who study media and class/labor would agree that coverage is biased in favor of corporations. Several discuss the mechanisms by which this bias is achieved, including William Puette, Michael Parenti, Martin Harrison, and Christopher Martin.[1] However, few, if any, discuss how labor is uniquely situated to resist this construction through struggle. Although Martin's brief analysis of the UPS strike does point out that the Teamsters were able to successfully resist the antilabor frames of labor news, he does not discuss the role played by struggle in this process.[2]

In *Through Jaundiced Eyes,* a study of the ways in which various media have dealt with labor issues, Puette argues that each medium focuses on particular aspects of the union stereotype. Movies connect labor with organized crime. Television drama emphasizes the foolishness of union bargaining goals, whereas television and print news share a preference for employers as the source of their information. Puette arrives at eight lenses that color and distort labor's representation in the mass media: unions protect lazy workers and discourage productivity, union members are uneducated and prone to corruption, unions were necessary during another time but are now obsolete, and so on.

Although Puette has performed a thorough analysis of media representation spanning almost the entire twentieth century, he does not historicize his lenses, casting them instead as enduring facts of media-labor relations. He fails to account for the role that the working class can play in shattering these lenses. Furthermore, he believes that prejudice is a product of ignorance and that the solution to the "jaundice-eyed" media coverage of labor lies in educating individuals. The recourse to education seems to be a tendency in media-labor studies, particularly those that assume a liberal worldview. It eschews discussion of the origin of the jaundice, which is structural.

Studies from other quarters focus on the structural limitations of the corporate media system. In *Inventing Reality,* Parenti aims to demonstrate that the news media's major role is to construct a view of reality that supports the existing social and economic order and the class that holds power.[3] He does take care to point out that the media are contradictory institutions in that they must also serve the public interest, but the thrust of his argument lies in uncovering their power to set the terms of political debate. Although his work is useful and accurate, the failure to systematically address the ways in which the dominant ideology can be resisted leads to a static and undialectical understanding of the media. In other words, a shortcoming of Parenti's work is the limited discussion of the role of the working class, as a collective agent under capitalism, in resisting the corporate media's representation of its interests.

This shortcoming is also evident in works that take a cultural studies approach, such as *Mapping Hegemony* by Robert Goldman and Arvind Rajgopal. In this book, the authors analyze the Bituminous Coal Operators Association and United Mine Workers of America strike of 1977–78 and its representation on the *CBS Evening News.* They aim to uncover the means by which the mass media conceal and deflect the contradictions under capitalism, such as class struggle. Although they situate the discussion of representation within a larger social and political context, a limitation of this and other studies that focus solely on representation is that they do not deal with agency. The authors recognize this problem when they state that "no dialectical analysis of hegemony is complete without analysis of how subordinate groups negotiate and contest the potentially hegemonic frames."[4] However, in this book, resistance to "hegemonic frames" is based on subversive readings of texts and discursive "negotiations" rather than, ironically, collective struggle, which is the subject of their analysis.

The three positions staked out above are symptomatic of the field of media studies and its understanding of issues of agency, resistance and struggle, representation, and democracy. The first stems from the political philosophy of liberalism, particularly the pragmatist tradition, which, while acknowledging the flaws of the current system, provides reformist solutions. The second position, derived from political economy, presents a radical critique of the media but fails to underline the potential for collective resistance. Consequently, it overemphasizes the media's power to perpetuate the dominant ideology and underemphasizes the power of collective struggle. The third, influenced by cultural studies, advances the notion of resistance through individualized subversive readings of texts, which, arguably, has few consequences for the structures of oppression and exploitation.

In what follows, I will discuss each of these positions in greater detail. Although each has contributed to our understanding of media, struggle, and representation, ultimately each, in its own way, fails to provide a realistic mechanism by which the media and society may be democratized. Based on my research, I will propose an alternative vision of resistance in which all voices can be heard in the public sphere. Such resistance is based on the collective agency of the working class derived from its ability to struggle for both reforms under the current system and the revolutionary transformation of capitalism.

Cultural Studies and Individualized Resistance

British cultural studies has always been interested not only in how ideology is transmitted through communication and culture but also in how individuals and social groups receive and experience these texts. Stuart Hall's "encoding/decoding" model opened up new ground for media research because it argued that the dominant messages encoded in a text could be interpreted through one of three codes: the dominant code, a negotiated code, and, most important, an oppositional code. David Morley, in *The Nationwide Audience,* expanded Hall's model to include a variety of positions that social groups could occupy in their readings of texts. Paul Willis's *Learning to Labour* and Dick Hebdige's *Subculture* explore the ways that working-class male youth resist and oppose the dominant culture. However, in much of this early work, resistance through culture is clearly understood as necessarily contradictory, that is, it is not entirely oppositional but accepts aspects of the dominant culture. Perhaps more important, this work acknowledged that cultural resistance could not replace organized resistance to the structures of exploitation. Thus, in *Resistance through Rituals,* John Clarke, Stuart Hall, Tony Jefferson, and Brian Roberts would point out, "There is no "subcultural solution" to working-class youth unemployment, educational disadvantage, compulsory miseducation, dead-end jobs, the routinization and specialization of labour, low pay, and the loss of skills. Sub-cultural strategies cannot match, meet or answer the structuring dimension emerging in this period for the class as a whole."[5]

As cultural studies became more influenced by postmodernism in the 1980s, the analysis of discourse replaced the materiality of lived experience and struggle, and semiotic-symbolic resistance became an end in itself. French postmodernist Jean Baudrillard, developing the concept of implosion, suggested that discursive resistance was the key strategy of the day. He argued that the media do not work ideologically, that is, they do not present a view of the world that mystifies reality. Rather, audiences, or the "masses," by refusing to "make a decision about themselves and the world," exercise a "secret" form of resistance. This refusal is "spontaneous, total resistance to the ultimatum of historical and political reason." When meaning is refused, the audience renounces the position of subject and becomes an object. In place of subject resistance (political action, collective organization, and so on), Baudrillard argued that the "winning" strategy is this self-objectification process that derives from the "refusal of meaning and the refusal of speech."[6] In short, in the face of an aggressive neoliberal assault in the 1980s, Baudrillard presented discursive resistance as an appropriate response.

Several scholars within the British cultural-studies tradition adopted similar positions. In 1986, Angela McRobbie argued that in a postmodern world, it was not possible to talk about "unambiguously positive or negative images," that is, that ideology critique was no longer relevant.[7] This was because audiences were able to take media content and put it "to work for them" through such cultural expressions as black urban music and graffiti. McRobbie concluded that this development was reason enough to reject the "sense of political hopelessness" of the 1980s. Apparently cultural resistance was sufficient to counter the attacks of Thatcherism.

Douglas Kellner summarized this shift in cultural studies as follows: "During this phase—roughly from the mid-1980s to the present—cultural studies in Britain and North America turned from the socialist and revolutionary politics of the previous stages to postmodern forms of identity politics and less critical perspectives on media and consumer culture. Emphasis was placed more and more on the audience, consumption, and reception, and displaced engaging production and distribution of texts and how texts were produced in media industries." In the United States, John Fiske laid the basis for notions of discursive and cultural resistance. Fiske argued for a "polysemic" understanding of texts that stressed individuals' ability to make their own unique meanings and, in the process, resist the dominant ideology through subversive readings. He observed that "exploring the strategies by which subordinate subcultures make their own meanings in resistance to the dominant is currently one of the most productive strands in cultural studies." His study of Madonna led him to conclude that her "image becomes, then, not a model of meaning for young girls in patriarchy, but a site of semiotic struggle between the forces of patriarchal control and feminine resistance, of capitalism and the subordinate." In Fiske's work, polysemic readings by abstract audiences with little in common other than their viewing of the text connote resistance. The end result is an individualized, textual and semiotic notion of struggle, which comes to replace a generalized struggle against the system. This critique of Fiske's work is now well known and well established. In fact, as Jonathan Sterne argues, "Fiske-bashing" has become something of a "fashionable sport in some sectors of the academy."[8]

Yet Fiske was not alone in making this move; feminists and cultural theorists in various international contexts also took a similar route. For instance, Janice Radway's research on how and why women read romance novels led her to conclude that although the texts may be patriarchal artifacts, the women in her study consumed them in resistant ways.[9] A similar logic can be found in a number of other studies.[10] As Carol Stabile points out, even though feminists have critiqued Fiske's theory, many adopted a similar understanding of resistance.[11]

The notion of an active audience capable of resisting the dominant ideologies encoded in media texts can also be found in the work of media scholars interested in refuting the thesis of American cultural domination on a world scale. Tamar Leibes and Elihu Katz studied the ways in which four groups of Israeli viewers read the television drama *Dallas*. They found that each group had its own unique readings of the text and concluded that American media products, far from overwhelming people around the world, are being interpreted in selective ways. Ien Ang's study of *Dallas* viewers in Amsterdam led her to argue that rather than focusing on "American cultural imperialism," it is more important to study the ways in which audiences derive pleasure from their viewing experience. Daniel Miller made a similar argument about how Trinidadians view *The Young and the Restless*.[12] Such work continues to be published today.[13]

Although people's nationality, race, gender, ethnicity, occupation, age, personal history, experience, and other factors will undeniably influence the way they make meaning or take pleasure from media products, to conclude that subversive readings are empowering or liberating in any real sense is to ignore the actual structures of exploitation. As Herbert Schiller points out,

"Whatever the unique experiential history of each of the many subgroups in the nation, they are all subject to the rule of market forces and the domination of capital over those market forces. This is the grand common denominator that insures basic inequality in the social order, an inequality that the pluralist and the active-audience culturalists most often overlook."[14] Although the theorists of cultural resistance attempt to "give voice to" and "empower" disfranchised groups, the logic of their project only serves to legitimate the status quo. The usefulness of the argument that power is equally shared between the producers and consumers of the media to the existing structure is apparent.

To be sure, scholars within cultural studies have critiqued notions of cultural resistance at least since the early 1980s. As Sterne reminds us, Gary Clarke, Judith Williamson, Meaghan Morris, Jim McGuigan, and others have offered critiques of this trend in cultural studies. Sterne also rightly argues that Fiske-bashing has become an all too easy way to make inaccurate generalizations about the field from the work of one scholar.[15] However, the time has not yet come to bid farewell to arguments against cultural populism, because despite these critiques within cultural studies, the field has yet to develop new theories of resistance. Or, more accurately, the field is yet to return to old forms of resistance based on collective agency and class struggle. One of the legacies of the postmodernist turn is that few studies today focus on the working class and the struggle for hegemony. If this is true internationally, it is especially so with American cultural studies, in which the discussion of class has historically been almost nonexistent. To the extent that resistance is even discussed, it remains mired in postmodern thought. Perhaps one may look at the debates over the concept of resistance in cultural studies as the struggle for hegemony within the field itself. For critics of cultural resistance, such as myself, this argument will cease to be relevant only after postmodernist notions have lost their dominance.

The postmodernist Left's rejection of working-class agency has a long history that is closely related to their understanding of Marxism. It has its roots in the movements of the 1960s, that is, the influence of Maoism on the New Left and the displacement of class in favor of the agency of students, the oppressed, and subjects of the third world. This shift also stems from the erroneous equation of Marxism with Stalinism, and the failure to understand the Soviet Union as a form of state capitalism.[16] Disillusionment with the movements of the 1960s, in turn, gave rise in the 1980s to what Ellen Meiksins Wood refers to as "New 'True' Socialism," a form of "Marxist" theory (post-Marxism) that rejects the centrality of class. For the theorists of this tradition, such as Ernesto Laclau and Chantel Mouffe, the struggle against capitalism and for "radical democracy," rather than socialist democracy, is going to be carried out by a "plural" subject, instead of the working class, a "unified" subject.[17]

Wood argues that the post-Marxist rejection of class and the politics of Marxism generally is based on a crude dualism in which the two options are simple, mechanical, and absolute determination or absolute indeterminacy. Laclau and Mouffe, in trying to assess the radical potential of the working class, present a false set of alternatives: "Either the working class appears spontaneously and automatically as an organized revolutionary force (the phantom 'essentialist' view), or there is, in effect, no such thing as 'the working class,' and no working-class interest. There are only people with contingent and discursively negotiable social identities."[18] The emphasis on "discourse" and on "identity" derives, in part, from the influence of postmodernism, which severed the link between politics and economics and replaced the politics of determination with contingency.

The collapse of the Soviet Union only reinforced this theory, leading it further away from class. In the later edition of *Retreat from Class,* Wood observes "an unbroken continuity between early post-Marxism and today's postmodernism—with, among other things, their common emphasis on 'discourse' and 'difference,' or the fragmentary nature of reality and human identity."[19] Much of this analysis accurately applies to the cultural studies approach to media and communication research today.

In contrast to the general cultural studies trajectory, a growing body of literature has sought to retheorize resistance in collective terms, emphasizing class struggle. As mentioned in chapter 2, Mary Triece describes the role of class struggle in enabling early-twentieth-century working-class women to successfully challenge their construction in the mainstream media via alternative media. Michael Denning argues that art and culture in the 1930s were proletarianized within the context of the labor movement and leftist politics. George Lipsitz discusses the role of strike activity after World War II as the context from which the working class voiced radical demands to democratically restructure society.[20]

Like these texts, I have argued that studying a contemporary labor struggle can highlight the continued relevance of class struggle in the early twenty-first century and the importance of collective, as opposed to individualized, struggle. A national strike by 185,000 workers was able to temporarily proletarianize some media outlets through a complex and dialectical relationship between discursive and material forms of struggle. In chapter 1, I noted the conditions that caused the Teamsters to strike—downsizing, pay cuts, speed-ups, and part-time work—conditions that are shared by most of the American working class. This collective experience impacted the ways that people read the news so that 55 percent of those polled favored the strikers and their demands, despite procorporate media coverage in Phase One. Had an audience analysis been performed at the time, a significant number of Americans might have had resistant readings of the news. However, it is important to underscore that this discursive resistance took place *within the context* of a national strike in which the union and its allies took an active role in trying to win the public to its arguments; that is, a proworker sentiment was *mobilized* on the basis of a material struggle.

Consequently, the mobilized class solidarity played a crucial role in transforming strike coverage on ABC and in the *New York Times* and *Washington Post* during the strike and in several media outlets after the strike. In the struggle for hegemony, labor and its allies succeeded in shifting the ideological climate. Thus, in contrast to an internalized, textual, individualistic view of resistance that is seldom translated into practice, this study demonstrates that collective resistance can alter the codes of news reporting. The "nationalist narrative," as the dominant method of framing, gave way to a discussion of workers' interests. In sum, a material struggle—the strike—and its ability to mobilize class solidarity changed the terms of representation, and the ensuing textual struggle transcended the discursive realm to aid in the outcome of the material struggle.

Such an understanding of resistance varies from the individualized analysis in three important ways. First, it underscores the agency of the organized labor movement and its ability to wage material struggles and impact mass consciousness. Second, it sees class consciousness as being dynamic and subject to change depending on the concrete historical conditions. Third, it emphasizes the connections between material struggle and ideological-discursive struggle. I see this work, in many ways, as a continuation of cultural studies before the postmodern turn. It is similar, for instance, to Stuart Hall et al.'s *Policing the Crisis,* in which the authors examine the struggle for hegemony in the context of concrete historic events.[21] Furthermore, by focusing on the working class in the United States, this book attempts to address the historical lack of attention paid to class in American cultural studies.

One of the central arguments of this book has been that despite the seemingly insurmountable odds, resistance within the mainstream media is possible, but merely discursive resistance is limited in its political and economic ramifications. Going beyond subversive readings to a strategy of struggle that both pushes the media to address economic justice and forces corporations to cease their attack on workers is important in advancing the ideological and material interests of the working class. This study has also shown that although achieving this goal is possible, it is neither *inevitable* nor *automatic*. Rather, it has to be organized and fought for both materially and ideologically. Such an understanding of agency, struggle, and representation differs not only from cultural studies' emphasis on textual strategies of resistance but also from the liberal view of media and representation. If postmodern cultural studies downplays the need for material transformation, liberalism sees no necessity for it. Liberalism's position on media and democracy is based on an acceptance of the fundamental soundness of the current media system, despite all of its limitations.

Pragmatism and Liberal Pluralism

Several scholars in the field of communication have been concerned with democracy and the representation of multiple, competing voices in the media and other forums of public debate. Much of this work, either consciously or unconsciously, is dominated by the tenets of pragmatism and its investment in a liberal, pluralist vision of society.[22] In this section, I will discuss the work of a few of these scholars individually and then situate their research within the framework laid out by John Dewey.

Reflecting upon the concentration of ownership of the media and its implications for democracy, Michael Schudson acknowledges that the range of political debate within the mainstream media is very limited in the United States, much more so than in western Europe. Thus, the Left tends to be excluded from the spectrum of political views expressed on a subject. However, Schudson argues that this exclusion is not a cause for alarm, as some "anxious and apocalyptic commentators" may have us believe, since there are institutional resources and constitutional guarantees that enable investigative reporting. Because "hot stories" and scandals are routinely covered, he asserts that there are "multiple voices in the American news media." Furthermore, Schudson concludes that the national news media are "not more left or more right but more muddled and multidimensional," due to various sorts of pressures.[23] Media concentration over the past few decades does not bother him because he views their current limitations as enduring features in media history.

Aspects of Schudson's argument are not inconsistent with the arguments made in this book. First, I too have argued that the media are not monolithic institutions impervious to social pressure. Second, the need to serve the public creates openings for the occasional story that questions the status quo. However, powerful social pressures to change media content and insert antiestablishment stories are rare; they are not part of the *normal* functioning of the news media. Chapter 2 laid out in detail how media institutions' corporate structure and internal mechanisms create a *systematic* bias in favor of the status quo. Chapter 3 explored how this bias was manifested in the UPS strike by studying the framing mechanisms employed. The consistency with which dozens of reporters at the three networks framed the story—that is, through the logic of the nationalist narrative—is neither an accident nor a coincidence.

The fundamental shortcoming in Schudson's otherwise useful work is his failure to acknowledge this systematic bias in the media. Thus, even though he recognizes the disproportionate influence that big business has on the media, his solution is to educate journalists and to encourage them to routinely reveal the connections between corporations and government officials. Perhaps for Schudson, these sorts of stories would be permitted because the mainstream media routinely seek out "hot stories." What he fails to mention is that much of what is considered a "hot story" or a "scandal" does not go beyond the bounds of the accepted political and economic order. When reporters do question the practices of the "powers that be," as in the Monsanto–milk hormone controversy at Fox TV in Tampa or the Chiquita exposé in the *Cincinnati Enquirer,* they find that they are not protected and quite dispensable: these reporters were disciplined and later lost their jobs.

The conditions that enable journalists to expose corporate practices and still hold on to their jobs are those created by mass action. Thus, during the UPS strike, several journalists were able to take advantage of the climate to write reports on pension grabs, productivity versus wage cuts as a source of economic growth, and several other labor-related subjects that otherwise would have been difficult to justify. Although he is keenly aware of flaws in the system, Schudson settles for reformist solutions based largely on the voluntary actions of journalists.

If Schudson fails to highlight the structural limitations of a profit-driven media system, Celeste Condit almost entirely avoids economic structures in her discussion of media and public discourse. She argues that contemporary U.S. society is a "multicultural democracy" composed of different classes and social groups, all with different interests. These interests, she states, are negotiated through the media, and representatives of various groups play the role of mediators until a resolution can be reached. Condit acknowledges that this is not an egalitarian process, since all communications are "inherently more favorable to some groups than others." No explanations are offered about why access to the media is unequal and what role media ownership or corporate sponsorship might play. Focusing strictly on discourse, she argues that decisions are reached and "concord" is established through negotiation within a given set of conditions. She adds that social concord is neither fair nor equitable but "simply the best that can be done under the circumstances."[24]

Drawing on postmodernist theories that reject class and class struggle, she argues that whereas during Gramsci's time a working class may have existed, today this is no longer true of the United States. Based on sheer conjecture and in the absence of any empirical evidence, she asserts that in the United States, fully "two thirds of the populace is overfed, adequately housed, and . . . with leisure time for its desired pursuits."[25] A third of this "overfed" population lives the last quarter of their lives as "capitalists," and thus the "majority white male working class" is not "oppressed" and therefore not an agent of progressive social change. Instead, the "white working class," in conjunction with the capitalists, now oppresses the "underclass," composed of women and ethnic minorities.

This book demonstrates the opposite;[26] I will only add that the UPS strike is a vivid example of the immense solidarity that can exist among white men, people of color, and women in the pursuit of their collective interests as members of the same class. Ultimately, Condit's caricature of the working class only serves to validate her rejection of class struggle in favor of "multiple contesting groups" that come together to reach a compromise. Thus, Gramsci's theory of hegemony, rooted in class struggle, is morphed into a vision of society not that different from that offered by liberalism. As Dana Cloud rightly argues in response to Condit, "Understanding hegemony as concordance is an appropriate critical model only if one is satisfied with the compromises allowed within and by the 'given conditions.'"[27] The conditions that Condit asks us to accept are those created by an unequal economic system and a commercial media.

In his own way, Schudson too asks us to accept these conditions. He states that the "media aim to make money for owners, provide jobs to employees, establish prestige among colleagues, entertain consumers—and these are all legitimate aims." To accept as legitimate a profit-driven media system is to accept that the free market can create a "free marketplace of ideas," as liberal thinkers of the past few centuries have. At the heart of this argument is a justification of capitalism, with all its flaws; this rationale is not unique to Condit and Schudson but is a constant feature in the discussion of democracy within the tradition of liberalism, as Hanno Hardt points out. In particular, liberalism in its pragmatist form, emphasizing individualism, entrepreneurship, community, and pluralism as the bedrock the nation, has come to dominate this discussion.[28]

John Dewey and the pragmatists of the early twentieth century, writing when industrialization had increasingly atomized society, believed that scientific knowledge could create a harmonious democracy. Dewey lamented the "machine age," as it had disintegrated small communities and concomitantly failed to create a "Great Community."[29] He set himself the task of creating a great democratic community, based on the belief that science (experimentation and instrumentalization) would assist in this process.

Dewey viewed the society around him as liberal pluralist, arguing that various social groups could come together to establish a consensus that served the interests of the entire community.[30] Communication enabled the accommodation that forged human fellowship and social bonds. He states, "There is more than a verbal tie between the words common, community, and communication. Men live in a community in virtue of the things which they have in common; and communication is the way in which they come to possess things in common. What they must have in common . . . are aims, beliefs, aspirations, knowledge—a common understanding—likemindedness as sociologists say. . . . Consensus demands communication."[31] This consensus is predicated on an understanding that despite the diversity of interests, a greater common good can be arrived at through the process of communication.

Contemporary pragmatists, such as Richard Rorty, continue this tradition, arguing that human conflicts can be resolved through "democratic institutions and procedures to conciliate various needs, and thereby widen the range of consensus about how things are." Rorty sketches a view of humankind as language-using creatures who are constantly trying to redefine their world, not only because they can but also because they are trying to make it work better for themselves.[32]

The current political crisis of American society, for Rorty, is the crisis of citizenship and national pride. It is due, he adds, to the absence of a vision for a better society. He then goes on to accuse the Left, by which he means the postmodernists, of having become "spectators" with "no projects to propose to America, no vision of a country to be achieved by building a consensus on the need for specific reforms."[33] He therefore proposes that we adopt Dewey's and Whitman's secular vision of a "utopian America," a "casteless and classless" democratic society with the struggle for social justice at its heart. According to this model, progress is measured not against a preconceived notion of what should be achieved but by whether problems have been solved and society has made itself better than it was.

Rorty's vision of social change is based on an evolutionary model, consistent with the influence of Darwinism on early pragmatists like Dewey.[34] He therefore argues that "cumulative piecemeal reform" can lead to revolutionary transformation.[35] In other words, Rorty believes that a nonmarket democratic society should be a goal of human pursuit and can be obtained through reforms.

Dewey held a similar view that was based on two factors: his belief that capitalism could be reformed and made less "selfish" and that there were no alternatives. According to Gary Bullert, Dewey accepted the viability of a "mixed economy"—an economy that allowed a high degree of diversity, experimentation, and decentralized control. Bullert argues that Dewey's vision of social change was based on "guild socialism," in which political power is spread out over a vast number of economic groups and small experiments can be conducted to improve society.[36]

However, rather than a proliferation of economic groups, the trajectory of capitalist development since Dewey has produced what Harry Braverman rightly describes as "monopoly capitalism."[37] Furthermore, as chapter 1 explained, the last quarter of the twentieth century witnessed an extreme class polarization, and internationally the welfare state was eroded. Through the twin processes of neoliberalism and corporate restructuring, or what I refer to as globalization policy, economic power has become even more concentrated in the hands of a few. To compound matters, it has all happened with little or no communication or consensus on a national scale. In other words, the priorities of capitalism as an economic system stand at odds with the needs of the political system of democracy. Pragmatism fails to acknowledge this contradiction.

I began this book by describing the character of capitalism today and asking whether genuine democracy is possible in such a system. I then discussed the structural ways in which the media have closed off public debate in favor of an unabashed legitimation of corporate priorities. Thus, the kind of conversation about how to enrich social life that Dewey and Rorty call for does not seem to be possible in the mainstream media. Rather, as I showed in chapter 3, the discussion of the "national interest" and the "public interest" is coded in terms that justify the priorities of the market. There is little or no consensus.

However, I also argued that this impasse can be broken through the mechanism of collective struggle. Although collective struggle includes social movements, I focused on strikes and class struggle because of the working class's centrality in the fight against capitalism. Restoring the agency of the working class offers the possibility and hope, without guarantees, of a better future, yet this agency is precisely what Rorty asks us to abandon. He states that after the collapse of the Soviet Union, the "leftist use of the terms 'capitalism,' 'bourgeois ideology,' and 'working class' depends on the implicit claim that we can do better than a market economy, that we know of a viable alternative option for complex technologically oriented societies. But at the moment, at least, we know of no such option."[38]

Rorty would be justified in this argument if the Soviet Union had represented a postcapitalist society. However, as Tony Cliff and others have argued, the Soviet Union is better described as a state capitalist society, in which the state bureaucracy played the role of the capitalist class.[39] Although no alternative to capitalism exists right now, Rorty's lack of imagination consigns the vast majority of people to conditions of abject wage slavery. Furthermore, imagining a nonmarket, classless democracy is not wishful thinking but understanding the real, material structure of capitalism in this epoch. With all its technological innovations, capitalism continues to sustain a class-divided society. Therefore, the mechanism of class struggle remains the fundamental motor of progressive economic and social change. The ties that bind pragmatism and liberalism with capitalism lead to a politics that accepts the status quo, despite its flaws, and settles for piecemeal reforms while abandoning the hope for an egalitarian society.

Political Economy and Radical Critique

The intellectual tradition that best understands the mechanisms of capitalism and that holds a glimmer of hope for an egalitarian society—that is, a democratic socialist society—is political economy. By linking politics to economics, it offers us a radical critique of democratic processes under a capitalistic system. Here I address two of its limitations. The first is the tendency to overemphasize the elites' power to manufacture consent. For instance, in contrast to the "propaganda model" of Edward Herman and Noam Chomsky,[40] this book has argued for a more dialectical understanding of consent formation, because it allows us to explain *both* how ruling-class interests dominate in the media *and* how that domination may be collectively resisted. Second, I point to the limitations in the tendency to look to publicly owned media as the solution to corporate domination.

In the propaganda model, Herman and Chomsky set out to explain the ways that wealth and power influence the content of news. They argue that all information must pass through five filters before it can become news. The first filter is the size and ownership of the mass media; the second, advertising as the primary source of income; the third, reliance on information provided by the government and businesses as well as "experts" funded by the same sources; the fourth, "flak," or negative publicity, usually generated by powerful organizations as a means to discipline the media; and the fifth, "anticommunism" as a way to marginalize dissent. Herman has noted that the fifth filter has been less powerful since the collapse of the Soviet Union.[41] Today, however, in the aftermath of 9/11, one could easily replace anticommunism with the framework provided by the so-called war on terror.

Taken as a whole, the model provides a useful guide to explain how the views and interests of the capitalist class dominate the mainstream media, and chapter 2 draws on aspects of it. However, the model is one-sided in that it fails to adequately address the mechanisms by which elite propaganda can be countered. Herman and Chomsky argue that flak includes "letters, telegrams, phone calls, petitions, law-suits, speeches and bills before Congress, and other modes of complaint, threat, or punitive action."[42] They add that when individuals with substantial resources organize flak, it can have a significant impact on the media. Such a definition could be used to encompass the actions of social movements or organized labor, but Herman and Chomsky focus almost exclusively on flak-producing institutions like Accuracy in the Media and the Center for Media and Public Affairs that are supported by big business and politicians. The other mechanism for dissent that they discuss is disagreement among elites, such as during the Vietnam War.

Writing in 1988, during the height of the backlash against the sixties' movements, when Reaganism, neoliberalism, and U.S. imperialism were not challenged to the extent that they were in the previous decade, Herman and Chomsky understandably fail to address the power of organized resistance. Furthermore, the case studies that they present on media coverage of U.S. foreign policy prove the strength of the propaganda model.[43] However, precisely for these reasons, the model is static and undialectical. It is important to recognize that during particular historical periods, the U.S. government and the business class can win consent for their policies and programs. Chapter 1 notes that in the 1980s, there was little resistance to corporate restructuring and neoliberalism. Nonetheless, certain specific historical conditions do not warrant generalized conclusions about the process of consent formation. As the research of Triece, Denning, and Lipsitz shows, forums of public discussion can be proletarianized during other periods. This book argues that such challenges to elite domination are not restricted to an era before "postindustrial" capitalism but can be organized today and in the future.

Herman and Chomsky make little space for this sort of resistance. At several points in *Manufacturing Consent,* they argue that voices of resistance are appropriated and reframed within the range of acceptable political discussion. When this does happen, it is not inevitable. Consider Herman's response to critics who state that the propaganda model does not make room for the constraints placed on the media from various sources. He defends the model on the grounds that it accounts for such limits but does not give them a high priority. He asks, why should these constraints "get first place, except as a means of minimizing the power of the dominant interests, inflating the elements of contestation, and pretending that the marginalized have more strength than they really possess?"[44] While Herman makes a valid point about emphasis, he also reveals his profound pessimism in the ability of the marginalized to successfully resist.

Chomsky shares this pessimism. Even though he has spoken about class struggle on several occasions, he tends to emphasize the mechanisms by which the capitalist class has dominated workers and controlled their minds.[45] He rarely, if ever, writes about the ways in which workers have been able, successfully or unsuccessfully, to organize against these attacks. This is not to say that Chomsky is against collective action; he frequently urges people to organize and to make their voices and actions heard collectively.[46] However, his theory fails to demonstrate how this form of collective action can impact the propaganda machine. Ultimately, this disjuncture between his political advice on radio shows and in lectures and interviews and his theoretical framework of consent formation reveals the static nature of the propaganda model.

Another strand in political economy is the tendency to look to publicly owned media outlets as a means to combat the corporate media. Although nothing is inherently objectionable about more public media, consistently posing media reform as the alternative to corporate media takes the focus away from class struggle and structural transformation. There is a long and rich history of political economists working within the area of media policy research, which has included attempts to reform the media and make them more accountable to the public interest.[47] For instance, Dallas Smythe conducted media policy research arguing for public broadcasting and public control over satellite networks. He was also appointed to the FCC as its first chief economist. Herbert Schiller and other political economists have helped to develop communication policies in Latin American, Asian, and African nations. British scholars like Nicholas Garnham, Peter Golding, and Graham Murdock have argued and agitated against that country's efforts to privatize and deregulate the broadcast media. Garnham, once a trade-union activist within the communication industry, has argued for the creation of an international public sphere to counter the corporate media.[48] Scores of political economists have been involved in policy research and activism. In 2003, a popular movement for media reform, spurred on by the efforts of people like Robert McChesney, came into being in response to the FCC's attempt to revise media-ownership rules.[49] Under pressure from massive public opposition, both Congress and the courts in 2004 rejected the FCC's move to loosen ownership limits. This is indeed a significant victory, and one that can form the basis upon which other demands to reform the media can be made.

The work of media reform is, without a doubt, important. Yet, ultimately, as many political economists will acknowledge, completely transforming the corporate media under a capitalist system is not possible. Thus, the struggle to create a public sphere must be located within the larger struggle against the structures of oppression and exploitation. As McChesney has argued in another context, the project of media reform can succeed only within the context of a broader political movement.[50] As this study shows, the working class continues to be the major source of power against seemingly all-powerful transnational corporations. Studies within political economy do tie media reform to structural transformation and class struggle, but more of such work is clearly needed. Vincent Mosco argues that political economy has tended to neglect the role of "resistance, opposition, and efforts to create counter hegemonic alternatives." Although there is work that "considers the social relations of class, gender, and race, in order to understand the dynamics of resistance and its connections to the wider political economic field," this aspect of political economic research is less developed.[51] This book is a contribution to addressing that gap.

Conclusion

I have argued in this chapter that the existing literature on resistance fails to adequately theorize ways to oppose the neoliberal economic system. The postmodern turn in cultural studies has meant that there is little research on how to mount a structural challenge against a corporate media system that genuflects before global capitalism. The focus on discourse also serves to textualize relations of domination that are extradiscursive. For instance, in the recent mobilizations against the institutions of global capitalism, such as the IMF, World Bank, WTO, Federal Trade Area of the Americas, and the Group of Eight, not only have oppositional views been marginalized in the mainstream media but protestors have also been subject to physical coercion. From Seattle to Genoa to Miami, they have been beaten, teargassed, pepper-sprayed, arrested, and even shot to death. In this context, an obsession with texts and discursive struggle borders on irrelevance, on the one hand, and, on the other, a drift into conservatism shrouded in radical language. After all, talking about resistance and struggle is both safer and easier when the realities of actual struggle are physically remote.

If cultural studies overestimates the possibility for resistance by equating subversive readings with actual struggle, political economists like Herman, Chomsky, and, to some extent, Parenti overemphasize media domination by underestimating the power of collective resistance. In contrast, I argue that although explaining the mechanisms by which elites' interests dominate the media is important, it is equally important to show that this is a *process* that can be resisted. When viewed dialectically—that is, as a process with no guaranteed outcomes—the possibility for resistance is not an afterthought or a footnote but a central part of how we explain the ways that the media frame the news.

Pragmatists approach the problem of inadequate representation in the media through the language of reform. Though aware of the structural weaknesses of the media, Schudson is willing to accept the occasional antiestablishment story and scandal story as evidence of multidimensionality. When he does admit the problems with American democracy, his solution lies in the creation of a "schizophrenic media," by which he means a media system that behaves in two different ways. On the one hand, it should set itself the goal of educating the public to be "shrewd observers of politics and enthusiastic participants in the political process."[52] On the other, journalists should recognize that not every citizen wants to be an active, rational participant in the political process, and therefore they must act as a check on those in power. These goals are useful but ultimately unrealistic, since they place the responsibility on journalists to reform a system that is structurally flawed.

To be sure, goals to reform the corporate media system and to expand the range of political debate should not be rejected out of hand. The recommendations of Michael Schudson and Richard Rorty discussed earlier and those of political economists like Herbert Schiller and Robert McChesney are useful in this regard. Schiller calls for an expansion of publicly supported and noncommercial media. McChesney argues that in addition, the state should support a public broadcasting system, increase its regulation of commercial media in the public interest, and enforce antitrust laws that break up the conglomerates.[53] Although they do not discuss the question in much detail, both Schiller and McChesney recognize that these reforms cannot be enacted without a social movement.

Similarly, this book has been interested in demonstrating that collective action can create a more inclusive public sphere, even under a capitalist system. The question is one of emphasis and strategy. Should the media-reform movement exist outside of other movements that are opposed to oppression and exploitation, or should it exist within larger movements that target the system? I would argue that media activism by itself is not able to adequately address the structural problems of capitalism. This challenge can be met only by locating media reform within the broader class struggle and throwing our energy and time into progressive movements that bring together the struggle against capitalist globalization with anti-imperialist struggles and those for the liberation of women, minorities, immigrants, and gays and lesbians.

The system of capitalist democracy has shown that it can accommodate various interests when pressed to do so in the context of collective struggle. History has also demonstrated that these accommodations will be negated when the struggle dies down. After the UPS strike, Ron Carey was expelled from the Teamsters union and faced a federal perjury suit. Although the Teamsters held on to their pensions and received wage increases, UPS did not create new full-time jobs until several years later. Thus, while reforms and strike victories are important markers of progressive change, they occur in a system that is fundamentally unequal. Similarly, reforming the mass media to become more inclusive and to create an open marketplace of ideas can be only a temporary goal. As the tide of social struggle ebbs and flows, so will the ability of dissenting voices to find a space in the "public sphere."

A necessary precondition for a genuine and permanent public sphere and a truly democratic society is an economic system based on equality, in which conditions for individual development would be the same as those for the development of society as a whole. Only in this context will access to the public sphere not be determined by economic power; only when the majority is in control of society and its resources can we talk about true democracy.

The realization of such a democratic socialist society has been and continues to be a historic possibility. Internationally, since the mid-1990s, mass

174 • THEORY AND LESSONS

political strikes against neoliberal policies have swept the globe: in Indonesia, France, South Korea, Brazil, Argentina, Paraguay, Bolivia, Venezuela, Haiti, and so on. Additionally, the movement against corporate globalization has brought students, environmentalists, unionists, nongovernmental organizations, socialists, and anarchists out on the streets of Seattle; Washington, D.C.; Nice and Millau, France; Quebec City; Genoa; and Cancun. We are at the beginning of a global movement against corporate globalization with prospects in the distant future for a more generalized struggle against the system as a whole. Although this movement has receded somewhat in the aftermath of 9/11, particularly in the United States, the conditions that brought forth this movement continue to exist.

Contrary to Rorty, I would argue that now is not the time to abandon a vision of a more egalitarian society but the time for optimism and *activism*. This is especially so in Bush's America where there is an urgent need to defend the right to resist. As scholars, we should also devote our time and energy to providing analyses that can take the various movements—from antiwar to global justice—forward. This book tries to illustrate the effects of collective struggle on an institution as rigid as the mass media and to underscore the centrality of class struggle to theories of resistance.

SEVEN

Conclusion: Lessons of the UPS Strike

If there is no struggle there is no progress.
—Frederick Douglass

Despite the successes of the UPS and other strikes, the U.S. working class continues to be ground down by neoliberal globalization. For five consecutive years in the new millennium, workers' wages declined while CEO compensation soared. The space that was opened up for questioning the priorities of corporate globalization during the UPS strike, and again after the 1999 Seattle demonstrations, was slammed shut by the machinations of the political elite post-9/11. Capitalizing on the tragedy, the Bush administration clamped down on dissent and gutted civil liberties through the Patriot Act.

Intoxicated by their ability to demonize immigrants, particularly Muslims and people of Middle Eastern descent, the House of Representatives passed a bill in December 2005 that would criminalize undocumented immigrants. Then to the elites' utter surprise, some of the most exploited and vulnerable workers took to the streets in the millions in 2006 to demand fair treatment. For the first time in six decades, May Day, which commemorates the struggle for the eight-hour day, was celebrated in the United States by millions of immigrant workers and their allies.

While the emerging immigrant rights movement is about civil rights, it is also a working-class movement. It is fundamentally about the right of workers to travel across borders in search of decent employment. In the process, the movement has exposed the hypocrisy of neoliberal globalization: while corporations are allowed to cross borders, exploit cheap labor, and destroy local economies and the environment, workers fleeing these conditions are prevented from doing so by anti-immigrant legislation. Rather than accept these double standards, immigrants from Latin American countries, who bring traditions of struggle against neoliberalism with them, have chosen to fight back. These fighting traditions could, in the years to come, be a shot in the arm for the moribund labor movement. There are historical precedents for the role that immigrants have played in U.S. labor history: at key moments they have helped to galvanize class struggle.[1] If the union movement is going to stop its slide into irrelevance, it has to wholeheartedly embrace the immigrant rights movement, organize undocumented workers, and be on the frontlines in the fight for amnesty.

In this context, the UPS strike offers many lessons. Perhaps the key lesson is that where there is repression, there is the possibility of resistance. Whether it is undocumented workers standing up to the powerful U.S. elite or UPS workers with a measly strike fund and no strike experience taking on a multinational giant, exploitation begets struggle. And, contrary to the myth that U.S. workers are bought off by consumerism and will not resist, the strike showed that not only do they have an interest in fighting back, but when they do, they can mobilize class solidarity on the basis of common work experiences. But what the UPS strike also shows is that organization is crucial if a movement or a strike is to succeed. In what follows, I draw out the lessons of the UPS strike for the global justice and the labor movement.

Lessons for the Global Justice Movement

The neoliberal project has met with fierce resistance around the world. In Argentina, President Fernando de la Rúa, who had overseen the implementation of neoliberal policies that led to that country's economic meltdown, was overthrown in a mass revolt in December 2001. In January 2000, rural and urban workers in Ecuador toppled the neoliberal administration of President Jamil Mahuad. Three months later, Bolivian workers, peasants, and coca growers triumphed over government plans to privatize water in the Cochabamba region. In 2003, mass protests against government plans to export natural gas to the United States and enrich a transnational consortium forced President Sánchez de Lozada to flee Bolivia. These examples are only a small fraction of the movements against globalization.

The World Social Forum, a conference that brings together activists, scholars, political leaders, students, and unionists, emerged out of these struggles in Latin America. The goal of the forum is to discuss the problems of corporate globalization and to forge international solutions. Since the forum's birth in Brazil in 2001, many continents have held regional social forums from Africa to Europe. As a participant of the 2004 World Social Forum in India, I had the privilege of learning firsthand about the struggles of activists and unionists in India, as well as several Southeast Asian countries. The experiences are similar to those in Latin America. When the "Asian flu" of the late 1990s, a product of IMF and World Bank policies, devastated several economies, workers and activists stood up and challenged those policies.

The world over, the crisis of neoliberalism and corporate globalization is being met by opposition. Within this movement, workers in the United States have a key role to play. They are situated within the world's most powerful capitalist nation and have the ability to restrain some of the largest multinational corporations. Additionally, the U.S. government, which uses organizations like the IMF, World Bank, and WTO to shred labor and environmental laws in developing countries, began these policies at home. Subjected to the "Washington consensus," workers in the United States have had the dubious distinction of being among the first to experience the consequences of neoliberalism. They, therefore, share similar interests with workers around the globe.

For too long there has been an assumption that workers in the West, and the United States in particular, cannot and will not fight back against capitalism. Even within the global justice movement in the United States, there has been a tendency to look to workers in developing nations, skipping over workers here. For instance, one of the leading voices of the global justice movement, Naomi Klein, barely addresses the role of U.S. workers in the fight against corporate globalization. In her otherwise excellent book, *No Logo,* which documents the rise of the anticorporate movement, there is abundant information on student activism in the West and workers' struggles in developing nations. However, there is little about the union movement in the United States. The UPS strike got barely a page in the almost five hundred–page book.

Understandably, Klein as well as activists in the antisweatshop and fair-trade campaigns have looked to workers elsewhere because of the low level of class struggle in the United States. However, it would be a mistake to equate the lack of struggle to the absence of a willingness to fight. As chapters 1 and 5 show, American workers have more than enough reason to resist their employers. However, the level of class consciousness is yet to catch up with the level of organization. In large part this lag is due to the legacy of business unionism.

Rank-and-file workers and progressive union representatives need to find the strength and will to reform the union movement.[2] At the same time, it is crucial for the global justice movement to recognize the social weight that the organized section of the working class possesses in the United States. The ability to strike or slow down production gives these workers the power to impact profit and thus quickly gain the attention of the employers. One example of this power is the General Motors strike of 1996. When workers at two GM brake production factories went on strike in Dayton, Ohio, GM's entire North American operation ground to a standstill.[3] An unintended benefit of globalization for workers is the interconnectedness between various work sites. The global justice movement can gain in strength and influence by working with the U.S. labor movement and vice versa. Just as surely as the movement was strengthened by the coalition between the "Teamsters and the turtles" in Seattle, so it was weakened when labor held separate demonstrations the following year in Washington D.C.

Lessons for the Labor Movement

The labor movement can stem the decline in membership, and even grow significantly, by showing in practice what unions can do for workers. The UPS strike gave a boost to unions because it showed the power of organized workers to force a multinational giant like UPS to concede ground on wages and work conditions. A national strike catapulted the grievance of UPS workers onto the national agenda and forced a debate on the priorities of corporate globalization. In this context, the union's anticorporate and proworker arguments were able to reach large numbers of workers who could identify with the strikers. In short, the battle over ideas took place in the context of a strike. Unfortunately, the union leadership did not draw these fighting lessons from the strike.

Shortly after the UPS strike, Ron Carey was expelled from the union under charges of campaign-finance corruption. The removal was a politically motivated act; it was meant to send a message about what would happen to labor leaders if they dared to lead strikes. It was incumbent on the AFL-CIO to stand up and fight to defend Carey. A strong union movement that had the courage to resist the onslaught could have taken the momentum of the UPS strike and generated a broader fight back that could have reversed the impact of the three decades–long employers' offensive. Instead, the union bureaucracy passively stood by. Carey was acquitted in 2001, but in the meantime Teamsters leadership had passed into the hands of Jimmy Hoffa. Hoffa brought back the practices of the old guard. He barely mobilized for the 2002 contract, and as a result the contract was far from satisfactory. The lessons for the rank and file are clear: in order to win a decent contract, it is important to organize and put pressure on the leadership; otherwise, the bureaucracy will continue business as usual.

"Business as usual" has meant spending large sums of money on the political strategy of supporting the Democratic Party and on image improvement campaigns divorced from organizing and activity. Tom Buffenbarger of the machinists' union suggests that labor's main problem is "public relations and messaging."[4] If labor were to advocate their message loudly, he argues, they could reverse the decline in membership. Toward that end, he has proposed that the AFL-CIO spend $188 million on publicity outlets such as a Labor News Network on cable television. Labor could certainly use such a cable station. Indeed, it could also benefit from a national newspaper dedicated to labor news.[5] Such avenues would greatly help to counter the pro-corporate propaganda in the mainstream media. However, to be successful in reaching the larger public, these media outlets need to be tied to an active movement. In chapter 2, we saw how the success and failure of the labor and leftist press of the early twentieth century ebbed and flowed with the level of class struggle. Yet it is precisely this connection between ideas and organizing and struggle that the labor leadership has eschewed. As Jo-Ann Mort rightly argues, "Publicity and card signing go hand in hand."[6]

In December 2004, the AFL-CIO announced that it would launch a campaign designed to pressure giant retailer Wal-Mart to improve wages and benefits for its workers. Commenting on the need for such a campaign, Greg Denier, with the United Food and Commercial Workers Union, said that there is "no precedent for [such a campaign]. It's a movement to confront the reality of Wal-Mart-ization. No other company has ever had the global economic impact that Wal-Mart has." Indeed, Wal-Mart, the world's largest company, with outlets in many countries around the world, embodies everything that is wrong with globalization. The Waltons, who own the lion's share of the company, are the richest family in the United States, as rich as Bill Gates and Warren Buffett combined. In fact, their fortune is equivalent to the GDP of Singapore.[7] Yet workers at Wal-Mart do not receive a living wage. Targeting such a company in order to win better wages for workers is a much needed goal for the labor movement.

However, this campaign, which will cost $25 million per year, is not going to organize the 1.2 million workers in the United States; rather, it is a publicity campaign designed to educate Americans about Wal-Mart's low wages.[8] The logic behind such a publicity blitz is that exposing Wal-Mart for the stingy company that it is will create enough public pressure to force the company to increase wages. Contrary to Denier's claim, this is not a campaign without precedent. It is a strategy that has a long history in the labor movement and is known as the "corporate campaign."

Developed by Ray Rogers of Corporate Campaign, Inc. (CCI), the corporate campaign focuses on a company's public image, which is seen as a crucial element in labor disputes. CCI markets itself as being able "to package and disseminate information that will place union adversaries on the defensive and sway public opinion in favor of the union."[9] This is a worthwhile goal, as this study shows winning public support is crucial to any labor struggle. When used alongside workplace actions such as strikes or slowdowns, this can be a useful tool in labor's arsenal. However, in practice, the labor movement has tended to use the corporate campaign as a substitute for workers' actions, such as with the recent Wal-Mart campaign. Ultimately, simply pressuring Wal-Mart through image campaigns is not going to daunt a company that has a notorious reputation for being antiunion. Indeed, the corporate campaign has yielded few results for the labor movement since the time of its inception in the late 1970s. A study of twenty-eight corporate campaigns between 1976 and 1988 showed that they were mostly failures.[10]

To understand why this is the case, we need to look at the strategies and tactics used in this campaign. Rogers explains that "traditional tactics" such as strikes are no longer enough to defeat corporations.[11] Instead, the way to force a company to deal fairly with its workers is to identify the network of companies, such as banks and insurance companies, that it is closely tied to. This network of "key power brokers" is then pressured by the union to send a message to the primary corporation to negotiate fairly. For instance, in the mid-1990s, Staley workers in Decatur, Illinois, relied on a corporate campaign to win their struggle. During the lockout, the corporate campaign focused on putting pressure on corporations financially associated with Staley. The strategy was to boycott the products of Staley's largest customers, such as Domino and GW Sugars, Tate and Lyle, Magna Bank, State Farm Insurance, and PepsiCo, among others (see figure 4). CCI produced pamphlets with protest letters that could be sent to each of these companies.

Additionally, activists across the country were instructed to hold informational pickets outside the local Pizza Hut with a message to customers to tell PepsiCo to pressure Staley. I was involved in these pickets in Providence, Rhode Island, in solidarity with Staley workers. Although all these tactics were creative and useful, they ultimately failed, and the lockout went down to defeat.

They failed because the union leadership counterposed these boycotts,

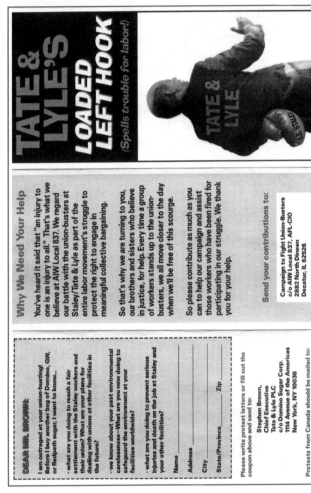

Figure 4. Corporate campaign flyer handed out to the public targeting Tate and Lyle. Reprinted with permission of Corporate Campaign, Inc.

and indirect pressure tactics, to holding strong picket lines that prevented replacement workers from entering the plant. This was a mistake, as the key source of pressure on a company is the workers at that company. By withholding their labor, or by conducting various job actions such as slowdowns, work-to-rule, or by blocking entrance to replacement workers, they can adversely impact the bottom line. When a company is prepared to hire permanent replacements, a corporate campaign-style boycott is at best a secondary strategy to help mobilize solidarity. When production is allowed to resume, there is little financial pressure on the employers. It is therefore not surprising that Staley workers went down to defeat. Yet, despite a string of defeats, the corporate campaign continues to be an official tactic of the union movement.

This is not to suggest that public image is unimportant. In a society saturated by advertising, where the marketing of brand identities has taken the place of marketing products, workers in service industries have a public image that they can leverage to their advantage. For instance, UPS's public image is based on its workers and the service that they provide. UPS presents itself as a company that is able to cater to the hectic pace of the modern world. It embodies the values of a globalized society and its demands. However, in order to sell globalization, UPS uses the faces of its friendly, trustworthy, and honest drivers, thus taming and making acceptable an otherwise impersonal system. UPS workers were able to take advantage of this public image during the strike. Apart from their image, they could also rely on their interpersonal relationships with customers and the trust that is forged through their years of contact.

This sort of public goodwill is not unique to UPS workers but also applies, to varying degrees, to postal workers, department and grocery store clerks, schoolteachers, restaurant employees, airline workers and most workers that perform a service. Unlike their counterparts in the goods-manufacture industry, whose labor is obscured from public view, service workers have a public face. While manufacturing workers labor in factories that are generally far removed from the public, service workers are physically located in the heart of public life. Manufacturing workers are rarely featured in advertisements; it is usually the goods that they produce that are highlighted. One rare exception to this rule is the Saturn ad campaign that highlighted the workers at a "different kind of company." In contrast, service- and retail-oriented corporations like Wal-Mart, Home Depot, and McDonalds routinely use ad campaigns that focus on their labor force. Fast-food chains like McDonalds and Subway have featured their workers in their ads, highlighting their desire to please the customer. Wal-Mart has constructed an image based on cheap products and friendly salespersons. The elderly people often featured in its ads comment on how the store is a home away from home.

These corporate images that are tied to workers can be leveraged by the labor movement. Just like at UPS, a labor action at these corporations will place management in a position in which they cannot easily demonize their workers. Service workers can capitalize on their public image and their proximity to the customer base to win support during contract negotiations, organizing drives, or strikes. One of the key lessons of the UPS strike is that when public relations strategies are used alongside job actions, unions can succeed in winning public support, favorable treatment in the media, and a better contract. However, few in the labor movement have drawn these lessons, returning instead to the corporate campaign at the cost of organizing.

On the other hand, UPS drew the lessons of the strike and corrected several mistakes that it had made. It implemented an internal communication strategy intended to win UPS workers to its side. This strategy even earned praise from the Public Relations Society of America. The "UPS Employee Survey Feedback Systems" was ranked among the top internal communication programs in 1999. UPS also hired five new PR managers and four new administrative aides in addition to a new external PR firm.[12] When the five-year contract expired in 2002, UPS was ready. It had even taken pains to change its brand image. Conscious of their brand image and what that meant during the 1997 strike, UPS switched gears in the lead-up to the 2002 negotiations. Their new advertising campaign, "What Can Brown Do for You?" consciously removed UPS workers from the ads in a not-so-subtle attempt to dissociate the drivers from the company's public image. Once the contract was negotiated, the drivers began to reappear, slowly at first, and by 2004 the company had almost entirely reverted back to its worker-driven image.

Conclusion

In the new millennium, the mainstream media continue to be the key sources of information and entertainment for most working people. Yet the dominance of the corporate media does not automatically guarantee public acceptance of procorporate, proglobalization frameworks. Although the media do have a monopoly over much of our culture, they are not all-powerful. In the context of a strike or other forms of collective struggle, corporate hegemony can be challenged. Herein lies the hope for a better future.

But to make real headway around progressive causes, the Left needs to be organized around an agenda that unapologetically demands everything from an immediate end to the occupation of Iraq, the rebuilding of New Orleans on an equitable basis, amnesty for undocumented immigrants, the legalization of gay marriage, and so on. To do so, it needs to be independent of the procorporate Democratic Party. The Achilles' heel of progressives in the United States is the politics of "lesser evilism," the belief that the Democratic Party is the best that one can hope for despite the fact that, time and again, it has acted against the interests of labor, women, and minorities.[13] History shows that real change takes place only when progressives refuse to accept the terms of discussion set by the mainstream political parties. In this context, alternative media such as the Internet, public access television, community radio, and alternative film and video can play a role in giving voice to and shaping a different set of politics.[14]

There is much to be learned from the UPS strike; at the same time, it is important to keep in mind that the history of the labor movement in the United States is the story of brave and creative men and women. Although the robber barons are back, labor activists like the Elizabeth Gurley Flynns and the Big Bill Haywoods, or even the muckrakers like the Ida Tarbells and the Upton Sinclairs, have yet to rise to their full potential. But just as surely as capitalism is a system based on exploitation and the degradation of work, so is the prospect of resistance. Neoliberalism has few solutions to the international crisis that it has created. Workers around the world have responded through general strikes and by toppling governments. In the United States, the pace of struggle has been much slower. Yet the American working class has an important role to play in the struggle against corporate globalization. The UPS strike gave us a glimpse of workers' power in this country.

Appendix
An Interview with Ron Carey:
The Story of a Militant Union Leader

DEEPA KUMAR: You have a long history with UPS. Your father worked there for forty-five years, and then you joined the company. Broadly speaking, what can you say about the company?

RON CAREY: My father had a great deal of respect for UPS; he also had a great work ethic, and he was a very productive human being. What he didn't like was the way he was treated by the lower management. At that point in time, about 1955, when I started with UPS, the folks that wrote the policy book talked about how employees were the most important product in their company, but that philosophy never trickled down to lower management. The result was daily frustration and anger in the way management dealt with the hourly employees, which was very difficult for me to deal with.

DK: What was it like to work for UPS? Today, the pace of work is very demanding. Did you also experience this as a UPS driver?

RC: UPS does everything to drain you of every ounce of productivity, whether it's mental or physical. For example, keep the key on your finger when you get out of the truck; walk with urgency; if you see the customer ten feet away, holler out so you don't have to go and ring the bell, if it's a private house . . . that sort of thing.

I think they put so much pressure on their management people that they were always angry and frustrated. This was counterproductive. For example, you would never receive credit for an outstanding job. If you ever gave that a thought, you were reminded repeatedly, "But it's your job, you get a good day's pay." So that eliminated the feeling of creativity, of self-worth, and created a sense of "I can contribute more, but why should I? They don't care anyway."

DK: After you became shop steward, you ran for the position of business agent in your union local (Local 804) in 1963. You did this because you were

Interview conducted June 3, 2004, in Washington, D.C.

concerned about the state of things at UPS. Can you say more about what your particular concerns were?

RC: In 1955 when I got out of the marines, I was looking for a good job. I worked with my father first, on the UPS truck, without them knowing. He was teaching me the ropes, how the job should be done. When I finally got a job at UPS it was in Queens, not South Bronx where my father worked. I immediately found that the daily conditions at UPS were not good. It was very frustrating to me, the way they demeaned people, the way they talked to them in such a condescending way. . . . Many times I found myself biting my tongue not to strike out at the manager. I wasn't a shop steward at the time, and I felt like shouting out "Wait a minute! That's a *human being* you're talking to—my God! Give the guy a chance to answer, and get out of his face."

What made it worse was that the union was useless. They were not responsive to the members; they were more interested in the company's problems. Union guys would come down, most of them were six-foot-two characters . . . why would you tell them about your problems, and did they really care? They never came to see the members. The first place they went was into the office to talk to the manager and find out what his beef was, so they could straighten us out when they came outside. That's what we had to contend with. Not just the union officers, but the union itself. During that era, it was the Hoffa years, it was a time of the mobsters and the good old boys. It wasn't about the members. In fact, it was dangerous to speak out against the union leaders. You were actually taking your job and putting it at risk whenever you did that, because there were such strong connections between the union and the company—they worked together.

I hated it, I despised it. All my life I had fought for what was right, so I ran for office, first for steward in the 1950s, then for trustee in 1961, recording secretary in 1964, and then for president in 1967.

The steward I first ran against was a guy who didn't want to rock the boat. His response to any complaint was "What are you complaining about? You're lucky to have a job." We heard the same message from the company and from the union officers.

DK: What were some of strategies you used when you ran [for president] against the incumbent slate?

RC: The incumbents didn't know how to run an election campaign because *no one ever ran against them!* My opponents were out at bars, shaking hands, and associating with the old-boys' network. I held job-site meetings and spoke out against what was wrong with the union, what needed to be done. I told the members I had a plan as to how we could get there. The image that I had was that I was vocal; I had the courage to go out there and say what had to be said. We put together a strong slate with some courageous members and strategized the whole election. We campaigned day and night, and we won! The whole slate, it was a complete upset. And what we promised was that from then on it was going to be about the members.

DK: One of your goals has been to reform the Teamsters union and to fight against business unionism. You mention in an interview with Stephen Brill, "What was wrong with so many people in the Teamster leadership, they see themselves as different once they get elected." And in 1971, you left the international convention early because you were disgusted with the leadership. What did you do to reverse these trends in Local 804?

RC: A man isn't what he *says* he is, he is what his *deeds* say he is. The promises we made in Local 804, we delivered on. The first contract we negotiated (I think we had a twelve-week strike) we won twenty-five years and out, meaning after you work twenty- five years, you can retire. After twenty-five years on the truck, our members were physically worn out, with bad knees, back problems, and the effects of enormous stress.

We put into place a lot of things. First, we made cuts in the union officers' pay, in the local itself. Set up a twenty-four-hour representation. What that meant was that if there were ten of us on the board, each one of us had to work nights for a month. If there was an emergency call, it was your job to get out there and take care of the problem. We set up educational programs for the stewards. What we did was involve them, let them know that this is about *them*. This is their union, not ours; this belongs to all of us. We involved the family in it, the wives, to start planning for the future, for retirement. When you say twenty-five years and out, well, what do you do? How do you make sure that you've saved enough money? We negotiated tax-deferred programs so that our members could leave the union and leave employment with financial security. We represented the members in grievances. We changed the attitude about how union officers were perceived by the members. If I ever heard a BA [business agent] say, "You're lucky you have a job," he'd have a major problem after that. Every union officer, including myself, when we were representing members, we were all the same.

We negotiated innovative health benefit programs. We started training stewards to know their rights, to fight back, to know what to do, what not to do, to protect them legally. Because at this point in time, after the previous union officers lost the election, the company was looking to shoot down anyone who stuck their head above the water, and to somehow embarrass me. But it didn't work. We won our first contract, and everything we had committed to achieving, we achieved. I was happy with that.

DK: Did you think that at some point you would become the head of the Teamsters union?

RC: No. I had no desire to be. My only desire was to do the best I could for the people I represented in Local 804. And to have them involved.

DK: In 1991, after more than twenty years of being president of Local 804 in Queens, you became the president of the International Brotherhood of Teamsters [IBT]. What did it take for your reform slate to win?

RC: It took tremendous hard work and organization, constant traveling throughout the country, campaigning day and night, and putting together a team of rank-and-file members as a slate. TDU was very supportive and instrumental in my success. I promised the members open communication and the courage and willingness to fight for them. To go back to my local union in Queens, it was always communication, communication, communication, keeping the members involved. No secrets. I never hesitated to tell them what I thought and why, a practice I carried over to the International. The members appreciated that kind of openness, and knew I was serious about it.

Here's an example from my local (Local 804): I don't remember what year—the International forced a contract on us requiring a two-thirds vote for rejection of the contract. I took them to court. Just before it was to go to trial, the International sat down with my attorneys and came to an agreement that they would amend the constitution so that future contracts could be rejected by a 50 percent membership vote, which I thought was the fair way, the more democratic way, to do it.

TDU helped with that, but we were the ones that started it. The members appreciated that. They knew that I would not get pushed around by the old guard, and that's why they supported me when I ran for president of the International.

DK: What was your relationship with TDU? You worked with them on several occasions, and they were behind you in your election efforts in 1991. Although you worked with them, you never joined TDU, is that right?

RC: I think TDU has done a fine job. I think they've worked hard, they've got many dedicated people, people who are working for a strong union that puts members first, people who want to see change; without them, I think the Teamsters would just run roughshod over any form of opposition. Even today TDU brings out the things that the International is doing wrong. Without TDU, who would expose the greed and injustices in the union?

I've had some disagreements with TDU, but they have never been of any consequence. I can tell you this: they've always been supportive of me, and I've always been supportive of them. I always found them to be friends. They helped tremendously during my elections—I don't think that I would have been elected without them. While I never joined TDU, I felt close to them and agreed with their so-called radical goals of putting the members first and running the union in an open, democratic way.

DK: What kind of changes did you make to the International once you were elected?

RC: First of all, there was very little money. But everywhere we looked, we found waste. As soon as we took office, we eliminated the wasteful perks of the old guard. We got rid of the limousines, the luxuries, the union's private jet. I cut my own salary from $225,000 to $150,000. We eliminated one of the layers of union bureaucracy, the regional conferences, which were just another way to provide multiple salaries to the top officers. We put the IBT on a financially sound direction and developed programs that would educate the membership. We expanded and strengthened the organizing department. We tried many different strategies to mobilize members, involve them in the union, to make the union stronger.

We had to let the employers know that this was a new day in the Teamsters union. Doing business as usual was out. We were going to fight hard to get our members good contracts and strong representation. The new policy of the Teamsters was about putting the members first.

DK: The Teamsters had a poor image because of the corruption in the union and ties to organized crime. How did this image impact your organizing efforts, and what did you do to counter it?

RC: That was always very difficult because the companies we would try to organize would put information on bulletin boards about what the president of the union was making, plus that he had a plane to fly around in, in addition to his limo, and that's where your union dues are being spent. So all the bad press we received made it difficult. Did we succeed in turning this around? Yes. How did we do it? We said, "Look, that's not us. It doesn't have anything to do with us." Go to one of our union drivers and ask *him* what he thinks of the union, and make a judgment by that.

We instituted an aggressive "member to member" organizing program, which was very successful; we organized a lot of workplaces. Our organizers were able to build on our growing reputation of getting good contracts and providing strong representation for members.

DK: What were your key challenges as president of the International?

RC: I think two of the main challenges were restructuring the union and getting rid of the Mob's influence. The people who were part of the old guard were not willing to easily give up their power, their multiple salaries, their lavish lifestyles. Their continuing bitterness and resentment created great divisiveness within the union, and they opposed every reform and change we tried to institute.

Getting rid of the Mob's influence is STILL a problem plaguing the union.

Finances were a continuing challenge. We supported several long strikes, which depleted our treasury. Before I took office, the delegates at the IBT convention raised strike benefits without providing a way to finance those benefits. The most important thing, I thought, was having a healthy strike fund. That was vital. How do you show strength? How do you show conviction, with no war chest to support strikes? You cannot do without a strike fund, and I was criticized severely by the old guard that giving strike benefits to the members would break the union! Well, who else would we spend the money on? The money is theirs! They deserve it when they strike.

Another big challenge was gaining the confidence of the members, building the support base, building an activist base, so that we could fight the companies and win strong contracts. How were we going to get the image of the fat cats out of the way? The only way to do that is by getting right in the dugout with the members. If there's a strike, being right there with them; giving them the support they need to win that strike; letting them know that you're on their side; communicating, doing what you have to do with the press; making sure that funds were available so they didn't end up on the welfare line. . . . So those were some of the things we did.

DK: Let's go back to UPS. UPS has made a number of changes in the company in order to become the transnational giant that it is today. What were the key issues facing you when you negotiated the contract in 1997? What kind of strategies did you come up with to pressure UPS?

RC: I knew that one of the critical issues was a good retirement plan. Another one of the critical issues facing not just UPS workers but workers in general was part-time work. You can't live on part-time wages; it just won't work. So these were some of the issues: providing a secure job for our members, with good wages, good retirement benefits, good working conditions. . . . This is a company that's making terrific profits!

We analyzed these issues and asked, "What are realistic goals here?" Remember, the company has to make money in order to provide for all of this, so there had to be realistic goals.

Going back over the thirty years of experience with UPS, I understood these would be difficult negotiations, it would be a fight; a fight that would have very dangerous consequences. We were confident we had the support of the members in the strike because we had spent a long time communicating with them to get them involved, to get them fully mobilized and engaged in the process. We got their input in formulating our bargaining demands. Rank-and-file members were on the negotiating committee. We knew what they wanted to achieve in the contract.

We also knew that we had to tap into the resources and strengths of other unions around the world. This was a worldwide company. So we put together a worldwide strategy to involve unions in Europe in this fight. We brought them to the bargaining table, to listen to UPS. We had good relationships with most unions. We had the pilots' union participating with us at the bargaining table. We put together a global cooperation strategy.

We also dug up information on UPS. We looked at UPS's financial records and found weaknesses. We developed strategies to gain community support, media strategies, and we were present with the members on the picket lines.

But most of all, it was the members that made the strike a success. It wasn't union officials talking to the press, it was our members and their families, and the public could relate to what they were saying. This dispute was about good jobs and their hopes and dreams. When members feel involved and know the fight is about them, their future, they'll fight for a better contract.

What happens when people feel involved and feel it is their union? They'll take some chances. They'll fight for a better contract. You take on a good legal fight. You strike them, and do everything you can to win it: communication, strategy, being out there and making sure that the officers are down in the trenches with the members, not at a bar somewhere saying, "Good work, guys."

This was about good jobs in America, and we succeeded—we won on every issue.

DK: You did something that had never been done before in the Teamsters union when you brought rank-and-file workers onto the negotiating committee. Yet you also gave old-guard officials positions on the negotiating team. Why?

RC: I guess I'm a trusting person. I felt I could not rebuild the union without reaching out to some of the old-guard officials. And when I reached out, I was hoping they would accept what I was about, what I believed in, and what I was working for. They of course said they agreed with that and did just the opposite. I suspect that if you look at my campaign manager and look at some of the things that happened, you'll come to the same conclusion. . . . I trust people. I put some of the people who told us that they were interested in reforming the union on the committee. That was part of the dialogue, but that wasn't the reality.

DK: As the contract deadline approached it seemed as if UPS had taken a hardline stance and refused to budge on the key issues that the union was pressing for. A strike was inevitable, yet you negotiated past the deadline. Can you explain the reasoning behind this decision?

RC: The company gave us what they claimed was a final offer, and I felt that their strategy was to keep us confused, fearful, and I was not going to let that happen. They were playing the bluff game, and I knew it. Given what was contained in the company's "drop-dead" offer, I knew a strike was inevitable, but it was not going to be on their terms. It was going to be after we had exhausted every possible remedy. I knew that we had to stand firm and think out what the company expected us to do, while having all our preparations in place; otherwise a strike against this giant could be a disaster. We *had* to be able to take on this one, for the whole Teamsters movement.

I knew in my heart at that point in time, if you don't dig down and bring up the courage you need and bring up the foresight to be able to see that this is part of their strategy to get you in a position where you may think a strike would be a disaster. So I played it on my terms.

DK: In pushing for a strike, UPS miscalculated. They assumed that the workers wouldn't go on strike. Why do you think they had such a mistaken view of their workers?

RC: I think they were listening to the old-guard union officials—the good old boys. "These guys aren't going to strike. People don't want to strike." That's what they'd been saying. But members keep a lot to themselves. They don't talk openly unless they feel you're on their side because they're afraid they'll lose their jobs. And you know that when you go out campaigning, and you're shaking hands, and you look in their eyes, and they say to you, "You're going to do the right thing for us, aren't you, Ron?" I knew the members would support the strike.

So did they miscalculate? Yes, I think that was part of it. They did not know that once they made their move, we anticipated their strategy, and we had six moves already planned. I had sat down with groups of people, developing opposition strategy. What if we did this? What would they do? What's their reaction to this? I did it on every issue. Whatever they brought up, I made sure that we had the ammunition, the research, the communication already there. Each move they made, we had to anticipate what their next move would be. Sometimes we didn't have it a hundred percent, but we were pretty close. Knowing them, how they operate, was one of the good intuitions that I had as a UPS driver, knowing them for thirty-odd years.

DK: Several polls found that the public supported the strikers two to one over the company. Why did this happen? Why do you think American workers identified with the Teamsters?

RC: The Teamsters' position was about the great American dream, good jobs, decent wages, health coverage, a job with security. The company's position was about corporate greed and putting dollars over people. When the members got out there with their families, with wives and children on the picket line, and the media picked it up, the public learned that this was about something decent, something good, about the American dream, about what we all are promised. The promise is that if you work hard, you're honest, you do the right thing, you're supposed to succeed. It's what we all believe in. And here it wasn't happening. Jobs were getting scarce, there were economic problems, and part-timers needed to be treated like people too. The public was able to relate to these issues.

DK: After you left the Teamsters union, UPS reneged on many of the issues it had agreed to in the 1997 contract. Why did this happen?

RC: I left in 1997. Those working conditions, restrictions, contract provisions were in place, signed off by the company. They signed them. They did not live up to that and knew they didn't have to after I left. I would have forced them to live up to them. We would have won the sympathy of the people—here's a company that agreed to it and then violated it. That's what contract enforcement is about—they will take advantage of you if you let them.

DK: Do you think the strike improved the public image of the Teamsters and, more generally, presented unions in a favorable light?

RC: Yes, it did. Our strike against UPS was the most successful strike since World War II. We captured the public's imagination and showed that workers could take on a giant corporation and win.

But two days later, the Teamsters election officer proceeded to disqualify me from union office, so that didn't help. I remember the last day, after the negotiations were settled. I was in the room with the secretary of labor, Alexis Herman, and the company. The company's top negotiator, Dave Murray, got up, and said, "You will pay for this. You will be sorry till the day you die." I said, "Are you threatening me?" I turned to the secretary of labor and said, "Did you hear that?" Ms. Herman said, "I didn't hear a thing."

I knew then that my demise was in the works. I had kept telling people that this company would be looking for a victim to pay for this. They would not let it go. And it wasn't just them—look at all the Mob guys I threw out of the union. They weren't happy campers.

In my time at the IBT, I made a lot of enemies. We took on the union's entrenched old guard and some industry giants. We were able to show the country that a union could still wage a successful strike. I have paid a great personal price. But I don't regret any part of it, I really don't. I am proud of what we were able to accomplish. I did what I was elected to do. I take the philosophical view that where I am today is where I should be.

DK: Many have referred to your disqualification from the union as a "witch hunt." It was meant to send a message of what would happen if a union ever dared to take on a company as powerful as UPS. In this context, why didn't the labor movement do more to defend you?

RC: I have a strong feeling that somewhere within this there's a connection to UPS, but I can't prove that. I've searched for the answers, and I think they knew that they could never have the labor movement flexing its muscle. That was *not* to happen.

Why did the labor movement not jump out and defend me? I think they were concerned, but they weren't there. Clearly, behind the curtains was Jimmy Hoffa. I really can't speak for the AFL-CIO—I don't know why they didn't do anything.

DK: Where do you think the labor movement is today? Do you think they have prioritized organizing? What do you think about the labor movement's continued support of the Democratic Party?

RC: I don't know how effective our continued support of the Democratic Party has been. That's what the labor movement does: we tell candidates we'll endorse you early; we don't know what you'll do for us, but we'll endorse you.

I think the problem is that the labor movement doesn't come out swinging. It does not make its positions clear. It permits politicians to take their money and then vote against issues that are important to working families. Labor needs to reevaluate its friends and enemies.

The labor movement has prioritized organizing in recent years, but I don't know how successful we've been. We need to set some examples. We have to show working people why it's important to join a union and what are the benefits of a union. Just signing a card doesn't get at it. How can we make your life better? What can we do to make you feel a sense of belonging, of being a partner in this, that the union is there to fight for you? I don't think this is being done. I think that's a mistake.

The other problem we have today is it's a different generation. They want to belong to something that will help them move forward right now. I don't know if they see the labor movement as the answer to that. It's like all those UPS part-time college kids—good, hardworking folks—I don't think many of them eventually stay. After being abused and after seeing that they are not treated the way a full-timer is treated, they leave. They move on to other jobs. There are some frustrating problems down the road for the labor movement.

There has to be a global strategy as the world becomes smaller, with multinationals proliferating and so on. Unions need to form alliances with each other around the world. But we also need to be careful about protecting union democracy—activism can only thrive where members are free to stand up at meetings and speak their minds. In order for the labor movement to survive, we have to give workers a compelling reason to join us.

Notes

Preface

1. Lawrence Mishel, Jared Bernstein, and John Schmitt, *The State of Working America, 1998–1999* (Ithaca: ILR Press of Cornell University Press, 1999).

2. Aaron Bernstein, "Too Much Corporate Power?" *Business Week,* September 11, 2000, 144–58.

3. Jared Bernstein, Heather Boushey, Elizabeth McNichol, and Robert Zahradnik, *Pulling Apart: A State-by-State Analysis of Income Trends* (Washington, D.C.: Economic Policy Institute, 2001); available online at http://www.epinet.org/studies/Pulling_Apart_2002.pdf.

4. William Grimes, "After Vintage Year, Wall Street Is Ordering Only the Good Stuff," *New York Times,* February 16, 1998, A1.

5. Lydia Saad, "Americans Backed UPS Workers in Strike," August 23, 1997 (http://www.gallup.com/poll/releases/pr970823.asp).

6. See, for instance, Michael Schudson, *The Power of News* (Cambridge: Harvard University Press, 1995).

7. William Puette, *Through Jaundiced Eyes: How the Media View Organized Labor* (Ithaca: ILR Press, 1992); Michael Parenti, *Inventing Reality: The Politics of the Mass Media* (New York: St. Martin's Press, 1986); Martin Harrison, *TV News: Whose Bias? A Casebook Analysis of Strikes, Television and Media Studies* (Hermitage: Policy Journals, 1985); Christopher Martin, *Framed: Labor and the Corporate Media* (Ithaca: ILR/Cornell Paperbacks, 2004).

8. U.S. Department of Labor, Bureau of Labor Statistics, "Union Member Summary," January 21, 2004; available online at http://www.bls.gov/news.release/union2.nr0.htm

Chapter 1. Globalization and the UPS Strike

1. Howard Zinn, *A People's History of the United States* (New York: Harper and Row, 1980), 338.

2. The property at Woodside was under construction for ten years and was completed in 2004 (Carolyne Zinko, personal communication, January 17, 2005). See also Carolyne Zinko and Carrie Kirby, "Larry Ellison's Most Important Merger: Oracle CEO Ties Knot with Novelist at Woodside Estate; Steve Jobs Takes Wedding Photos," *San Francisco Chronicle,* January 14, 2004; available online at http://www.sfgate.com/cgi-bin/article.cgi?file=/chronicle/archive/2004/01/14/MNG-S649LVB1.DTL.

3. Based on a report by Mark Leibovich, "The Outsider, His Business and His Billions," *Washington Post,* October 30, 2000.

4. Paul Krugman, "For Richer: How the Permissive Capitalism of the Book Destroyed American Equality," *New York Times Magazine,* October 20, 2002.

5. Michael Zweig defines *class* in terms of the power that one has at work. By this he means "power over what goes on at work; who will do which tasks at what pace for what pay, and the power to decide what to produce, how to produce it, and where to sell it." Zweig, *The Working Class Majority: America's Best Kept Secret* (Ithaca: ILR Press, 2000), 12.

6. Sharon Smith, *Subterranean Fire: A History of Working-Class Radicalism in the United States* (Chicago: Haymarket Press, 2006).

7. For a discussion of class in the United States today and its representation in the media, see Deepa Kumar, "Media, Class, and Power: Debunking the Myth of a Classless Society," in *Class and News,* edited by Don Heider (Lanham, Md.: Rowman and Littlefield, 2004).

8. Erik Olin Wright, *Class Counts: Comparative Studies in Class Analysis* (Cambridge: Cambridge University Press, 1997).

9. Carmen DeNavas-Walt, Bernadette Proctor, and Cheryl Hill Lee, *Income, Poverty and Health Insurance Coverage in the United States: 2004* (Washington, D.C.: U.S. Census Bureau, 2005); available online at http://www.census.gov/prod/2005pubs/p60–229.pdf.

10. Heather Bouchey, Chauna Brocht, Bethney Gunderson, and Jared Bernstein, *Hardships in America: The Real Story of Working Families* (Washington, D.C.: Economic Policy Institute, 2001); available online at http://www.epinet.org/books/hardships.pdf.

11. Jeremy Rifkin, "Another Wolf at Our Door," *Guardian,* October 24, 2000, 19; available online at http://80-web.lexis-nexis.com.ezproxy.wfu.edu:3000/universe/document?_m=ed5e63e1e2bd21126efa0c0efc660d18&_docnum=2&wchp=dGLbVzzzSkVA&_md5=4a391fefaaf1a303d7c42994eae3864f.

12. DeNavas-Walt, Proctor, and Lee, *Income.*

13. Robert Pear, "Americans Relying More on Prescription Drugs, Report Says," *New York Times,* December 3, 2004, A22.

14. Alex Kuczynski, "Lifestyles of the Rich and Red-Faced," *New York Times,* September 22, 2002, sec. 9, p. 1.

15. A. Hirshberg, D. Ellison, S. Keaton, K. Johnson, and P. Anthony, *Best Practices in Strategic Management: Cases from the Front Lines of Competition,* Research Project 4853–01 (Calverton, Md.: Macro International, 1995).

16. Gary Hartung, "History of UPS," *Wheels of Time* (January–February 1996).

17. Ibid.

18. Dan La Botz, *Rank and File Rebellion: Teamsters for a Democratic Union* (New York: Verso, 1990).

19. Harry Braverman, *Labor and Monopoly Capitalism* (New York: Monthly Review Press, 1998).

20. Kenneth Labich, "Big Changes at Big Brown," *Fortune* (January 18, 1988): 56–64; Jeremy Schlosberg, "Hell on Wheels," *New England Monthly* (January 1988): 60–64; Matthew Maranz, "Signed, Sealed and Delivered: An Inside Look at the

'Tightest Ship in the Shipping Business,'" *Worcester Magazine* (November 25, 1987): 12–14.

21. Hirshberg et al., *Best Practices,* 4–5.

22. Labich, "Big Changes," 56–64.

23. Sylvester, personal communication, March 29, 2004.

24. Stanley C. Wisniewski, *Multinational Enterprises in the Courier Service Industry: Aspects of Employment and Working Conditions in Selected Enterprises* (Geneva: International Labor Organization, 1997).

25. La Botz, *Rank and File Rebellion.*

26. C. L. Kane, *The Tightest Ship: UPS Exposé* (Cogan Station, Pa.: El Dorado Productions, 1993).

27. Cynthia Mitchell, "The UPS Strike Revisited: What Lessons Did They Learn? *Atlanta Journal-Constitution,* August 2, 1998, F1.

28. Katch, personal communication, March 27, 2004.

29. The ILO is located in Geneva, Switzerland. It has a tripartite structure consisting of labor, corporations, and government coming together to discuss labor issues.

30. Wisniewski, *Multinational Enterprises,* 41.

31. Ibid.

32. Ibid.

33. Kate Bronfenbrenner, *Worker Turnover and Part-Time Employment at UPS: Final Report, a Research Project* (Ithaca: New York State School of Industrial and Labor Relations, Cornell University, 1997).

34. *Half a Job Is Not Enough: How the Shift to More Part-Time Employment Undermines Good Jobs at UPS* (a special report by the International Brotherhood of Teamsters Research Department, Washington, D.C., June 1997).

35. Ibid.

36. Sarah Anderson, John Cavanagh, and Thea Lee, *Field Guide to the Global Economy* (New York: New Press, 2000).

37. Michael Dolny, "Think Tanks: The Rich Get Richer," *Extra!* (May–June 2000); available online at http://www.fair.org/index.php?page=1033.

38. Paul Hirst and Grahame Thompson, *Globalization in Question,* 2d ed. (Cambridge: Polity Press, 1999); David Harvey, *A Brief History of Neoliberalism* (Oxford: Oxford University Press, 2005); Robert Brenner, *The Boom and the Bubble: The U.S. in the World Economy* (New York: Verso, 2003); Anderson, Cavanagh, and Lee, *Field Guide;* Lori Wallach and Michelle Sforza, *The WTO: Five Reasons to Resist Corporate Globalization* (New York: Seven Stories Press, 1999); Jeremy Brecher, Tim Costello, and Brendan Smith, *Globalization from Below: The Power of Solidarity* (Cambridge, Mass.: South End Press, 2000); Russell Mokhiber and Robert Weissman, *Corporate Predators: The Hunt for Mega-Profits and the Attack on Democracy* (Monroe, Maine: Common Courage Press, 1999); Kevin Danaher and Roger Burbach, *Globalize This! The Battle against the World Trade Organization and Corporate Rule* (Monroe, Maine: Common Courage Press, 2000); Kevin Danaher, *Corporations Are Gonna Get Your Mama: Globalization and the Downsizing of the American Dream* (Monroe, Maine: Common Courage Press, 1996); Eric Toussaint, *Your Money or Your Life: The Tyranny of Global Finance,* translated by Raghu Krishnan (Sterling, Va.: Pluto Press,

1999); William Tabb, *The Amoral Elephant: Globalization and the Struggle for Social Justice in the Twenty-first Century* (New York: Monthly Review Press, 2001); Alexander Cockburn, Jeffrey St. Clair, and Allan Sekula, *5 Days That Shook the World: Seattle and Beyond* (New York: Verso, 2000); Ralph Nader et al., *The Case against Free Trade: GATT, NAFTA, and the Globalization of Corporate Power* (San Francisco and Berkeley: Earth Island Press and North Atlantic Books, 1993); Lee Sustar, "The UAW: A Union in Crisis?" *Socialist Worker* (May 12, 2000): 15; Doug Henwood, "Post-What?" *Monthly Review* 48, no. 4 (September 1996); "The New Economy and the Speculative Bubble: An Interview with Doug Henwood," *Monthly Review* 52, no. 11 (April 2001); Chris Harman, "Globalization: A Critique of a New Orthodoxy," *International Socialism* 73 (1996): 3–34; Naomi Klein, *No Logo: Money, Marketing, and the Growing Anti-corporate Movement* (New York: Picador, 1999); Sarah Anderson, ed., *Views from the South: The Effects of Globalization and the WTO on Third World Countries* (Chicago: Food First/International Forum on Globalization, 2000); Joseph Stiglitz, *Globalization and Its Discontents* (New York: W. W. Norton, 2002).

39. Toussaint, *Your Money*.

40. Stiglitz, *Globalization and Its Discontents,* 214.

41. Hirst and Thompson, *Globalization in Question,* 6.

42. Harman, "Globalization," 3.

43. Francis Fukuyama, "Is Socialism Making a Comeback?" *Time,* May 22, 2000, 111–12.

44. "Global Capitalism: Can It Be Made to Work Better?" *Business Week,* November 6, 2000, 72.

45. Danaher and Burbach, *Globalize This*.

46. Cockburn, St. Clair, and Sekula, *5 Days;* Brecher, Costello, and Smith, *Globalization from Below;* Danaher and Burbach, *Globalize This*.

47. Danaher and Burbach, *Globalize This,* 9.

48. Tabb, *Amoral Elephant,* 196; emphasis added.

49. Ibid.

50. Stephanie Coontz, *The Way We Really Are: Coming to Terms with America's Changing Families* (New York: Basic Books, 1997).

51. Juliet Schor, *The Overworked American: The Unexpected Decline of Leisure* (New York: Basic Books, 1992).

52. See Lester Thurow, *The Future of Capitalism: How Today's Economic Forces Shape Tomorrow's World* (New York: William Morrow, 1996); Thurow, *The American Corporation Today* (New York: Oxford University Press, 1996); David Gordon, *Fat and Mean: The Corporate Squeeze of Working Americans and the Myth of Managerial "Downsizing"* (New York: Martin Kessler Books, 1996); Mishel, Bernstein, and Schmitt, *State of Working America;* and Paul Krugman, *The Great Unraveling* (New York: W. W. Norton, 2003).

53. See Mishel, Bernstein, and Schmitt, *State of Working America*.

54. Ibid.

55. Lawrence Mishel, Jared Bernstein, and Elise Gould, "Income Pictures: August 31, 2005" (Washington, D.C.: Economic Policy Institute, 2001); available online at http://www.epi.org/content.cfm/webfeatures_econindicators_income2 0050831.

56. See Mishel, Bernstein, and Schmitt, *State of Working America.*

57. A. Bernstein, "Too Much Corporate Power?"

58. Krugman, "For Richer."

59. Gary Strauss and Barbara Hansen, "Median Pay for CEOs of 100 Largest Companies Rose 25%," *USA Today,* April 10, 2006, Money section, B1.

60. Edward Wolf, *Top Heavy: The Increasing Inequality of Wealth in America and What Can Be Done about It* (New York: New Press, 1995).

61. Edward Wolf, "Recent Trends in the Distribution of Household Wealth," in *Back to Shared Prosperity: The Growing Inequality of Wealth and Income in America,* edited by Ray Marshall (New York: M. E. Sharpe, 2000), 57–63.

62. See Mishel, Bernstein, and Schmitt, *State of Working America.*

63. Thurow, *Future of Capitalism,* 24.

64. Gordon, *Fat and Mean,* 202. See also Michael Goldfield, *The Decline of Organized Labor in the United States* (Chicago: University of Chicago Press, 1987); Kim Moody, *An Injury to All: The Decline of American Unionism* (New York: Verso, 1988); and Stanley Aronowitz, *The Politics of Identity: Class, Culture, Social Movements* (New York: Routledge, 1992).

65. Nelson Lichtenstein, *State of the Union: A Century of American Labor* (Princeton: Princeton University Press, 2002), 236.

66. Ahmed Shawki and Joel Geier, "Contradictions of the 'Miracle' Economy," *International Socialist Review* 2 (1997): 6–14.

67. Sharon Smith, "Twilight of the American Dream," *International Socialism* 54 (1992): 3–43.

68. Thomas Ferguson and Joel Rogers, *Right Turn: The Decline of the Democrats and the Future of American Politics* (New York: Hill and Wang, 1986).

69. Bennet Harrison, *Lean and Mean: Why Large Corporations Will Continue to Dominate the Global Economy* (New York: Guilford Press, 1994).

70. In 1944, forty-four delegations from around the world met in Bretton Woods, New Hampshire, to take stock of the events of the previous thirty years and to restore and stabilize capitalism. The two participants who really had a say in drafting the original conference document were the British, represented by John Maynard Keynes, and the Americans, represented by Harry Dexter White. From this meeting, the International Monetary Fund and the World Bank were set up as multilateral international institutions that would deal with global financial problems. Under the new monetary system, all currencies would be tied to the dollar, which was valued at thirty-five dollars per ounce of gold. When Bretton Woods collapsed, currencies were yanked from the dollar-gold standard and allowed to free-float.

71. See Hirst and Thompson, *Globalization in Question;* and Neil Smith, *American Empire: Roosevelt's Geographer and the Prelude to Globalization* (Berkeley and Los Angeles: University of California Press, 2003).

72. Henwood, "New Economy," 72.

73. Daniel Singer, *Whose Millennium? Theirs or Ours?* (New York: Monthly Review Press, 1999), 186.

74. Toussaint, *Your Money,* 3.

75. Hirst and Thompson, *Globalization in Question;* Toussaint, *Your Money;* Tabb, *Amoral Elephant.*

76. John Carson-Parker, "The Options Ahead for the Debt Economy," *Business Week,* October 12, 1974, 121.

77. Edward Herman and Noam Chomsky, *Manufacturing Consent: The Political Economy of the Mass Media* (New York: Pantheon Books, 1988); Moody, *Injury to All.*

78. Moody, *Injury to All,* 128–30.

79. Paul Buhle, *Taking Care of Business: Samuel Gompers, George Meany, Lane Kirkland, and the Tragedy of American Labor* (New York: Monthly Review Press, 1999); S. Smith, "Twilight of the American Dream."

80. Donald Barlett and James Steele, *America: What Went Wrong?* (Kansas City, Mo.: Andrew and McMeel, 1992).

81. Danaher, *Corporations.*

82. Barlett and Steele, *America: What Went Wrong?*

83. David Cook, "Tough Tax Questions Face the Next President: A Growing Unintended Burden on Middle-Income People, and a Dearth of Corporate Receipts Raise Issues of Fairness," *Christian Science Monitor,* April 14, 2004, 2.

84. Hirshburg et al., *Best Practices.*

85. Barlett and Steele, *America: What Went Wrong?*

86. Wisniewski, *Multinational Enterprises,* 42.

87. Moody, *Injury to All.*

88. Coontz, *Way We Really Are.*

89. Goldfield, *Decline of Organized Labor.*

90. James Womack, Daniel Jones, and Daniel Roos, *The Machine That Changed the World* (New York: Rawson-MacMillan, 1990); James Worthy, David Moore, and Ronald Greenwood, eds., *Lean but Not Mean: Studies in Organizational Structures* (Urbana: University of Illinois Press, 1994); Jerome Rosow, John Hickey, and Jill Casner-Lotto, *Lean, Not Mean: Restoring Organizational Trust in a Climate of Downsizing* (Scarsdale, N.Y.: Work in America Institute, 1995).

91. B. Harrison, *Lean and Mean;* Mike Parker and Jane Slaughter, *Working Smart: A Labor Notes Book* (Detroit: Labor Notes, 1994); Ruth Milkman, *Farewell to the Factory* (Berkeley and Los Angeles: University of California Press, 1997); Kim Moody, *Workers in a Lean World* (New York: Verso, 1997); Singer, *Whose Millennium?*

92. B. Harrison, *Lean and Mean,* 11.

93. Ibid., 156.

94. Klein, *No Logo.*

95. Singer, *Whose Millennium?*

96. Wisniewski, *Multinational Enterprises,* 4.

97. Hirshberg et al., *Best Practices.*

98. Ibid.

99. Wisniewski, *Multinational Enterprises.*

100. Ken Cottrill, "Global Gambits: FedEx, UPS and DHL Will Remain Logistics Heavyweights but Others Will Challenge Them," *Traffic World* (June 2, 2003): 10.

101. Moody, *Workers in a Lean World.*

102. Chris Tilly, *Half a Job: Bad and Good Part-Time Jobs in a Changing Labor Market* (Philadelphia: Temple University Press, 1996), 21.

103. Moody, *Injury to All.*

104. Tabb, *Amoral Elephant.*

105. Moody, *Workers in a Lean World.*

106. Moody, *Injury to All.*

107. Ibid.

108. Richard Florida and Martin Kenney. "Transplanted Organizations: The Transfer of Japanese Industrial Organizations to the U.S.," *American Sociological Review* 56 (June 1988): 381–98; Womack, Jones, and Roos, *Machine That Changed the World.*

109. Martin Glaberman, "Building the Japanese Car," *Canadian Dimension* 17, no. 1 (1983): 17–19; John Junkerman, "We Are Driven," *Mother Jones* (August 21–23, 1982): 38–40; Satoshi Kamata, *Japan in the Passing Lane* (New York: Pantheon Books, 1982); Reiko Okayama, "Industrial Relations in the Japanese Automobile Industry, 1945–1970: The Case of Toyota," in *The Automobile Industry and Its Workers,* edited by Steven Tolliday and Jonathan Zeitlin (New York: St. Martin's Press, 1987), 168–89; Mike Parker and Jane Slaughter, *Choosing Sides: Unions and the Team Concept* (Boston: South End Press, 1988).

110. Parker and Slaughter, *Choosing Sides.*

111. La Botz, *Rank and File Rebellion.*

112. Matt Witt and Rand Wilson, "Part-Time America Won't Work: The Teamsters' Fight for Good Jobs at UPS," in *Not Your Father's Union Movement: Inside the AFL-CIO,* edited by Jo-Ann Mort (New York: Verso, 1998).

113. *Rank and File Power at UPS* (Michigan: Teamster Rank and File Education and Legal Defense Fund, 2000), 27.

114. Parker and Slaughter, *Choosing Sides,* 28, 19.

115. James Rinehart, Christopher Huxley, and David Robertson, *Just Another Car Factory: Lean Production and Its Discontents* (Ithaca: ILR Press, 1997), 201.

116. B. Harrison, *Lean and Mean,* 190.

117. See Bernstein, "Too Much Corporate Power?"

118. S. Smith, "Twilight of the American Dream."

119. For a discussion of the labor union bureaucracy and its betrayals, see Buhle, *Taking Care of Business.*

120. S. Smith, "Twilight of the American Dream."

121. Lichtenstein, *State of the Union.*

122. See also Elizabeth Fones-Wolf, *Selling Free Enterprise: The Business Assault on Labor and Liberalism, 1945–60* (Urbana: University of Illinois Press, 1994).

123. S. Smith, *Subterranean Fire.*

124. Steven Brill, *The Teamsters* (New York: Simon and Schuster, 1978), 13.

125. See Phillip Foner, *Organized Labor and the Black Worker, 1619–1981* (New York: International Publishers, 1982).

126. Dan Georgakas and Marvin Surkin, *Detroit: I Do Mind Dying* (Boston: South End Press, 1998).

127. S. Smith, "Twilight of the American Dream."

128. Ibid.

129. Lee Sustar, "The New Employers' Offensive: Labor's War at Home," *International Socialist Review,* no. 28 (2003): 61–67.

130. U.S. Department of Labor, Bureau of Labor Statistics, "Work Stoppages Summary," released March 19, 2004; available online at http://www.bls.gov/news.release/wkstp.nr0.htm.

131. S. Smith, *Subterranean Fire.*

132. Sustar, "New Employers' Offensive."

133. U.S. Department of Labor, Bureau of Labor Statistics, "Union Member Summary" (Washington, D.C., January 20, 2006); available online at http://www.bls.gov/news.release/union2.nr0.htm.

134. *Human Development Report* (New York: Oxford University Press, 1998).

135. Robert McChesney, *Corporate Media and the Threat to Democracy* (New York: Seven Stories Press, 1997), 14.

Chapter 2. Understanding the Corporate Media

Epigraph: Quoted in Noam Chomsky, *Profit over People: Neoliberalism and the Global Order* (New York: Seven Stories Press, 1999), 53.

1. I use the terms *telecommunication, media,* and *information industries* interchangeably, because many of the same conglomerates that own the media also have a stake in communication technology. For instance, AT&T, in addition to telecommunications, owns TCI cable and dominates cable. The AOL–Time Warner merger demonstrates vividly the trend among media corporations to try to capitalize on the Internet. Thus, even before the dust from the merger frenzy has settled, some patterns point to the correlation of media and information technology.

2. Herbert Schiller, *Living in the Number One Country: Reflections of a Critic of American Empire* (New York: Seven Stories Press, 2000), 101.

3. Steven Liplin, "Corporations' Dreams Converge in One Idea: It's Time to Do a Deal," *Wall Street Journal,* February 26, 1997, 1.

4. Jill Carroll, "AOL–Time Warner Merger Clears FCC—Final Regulatory Approval of $103.5 Billion Deal Is Won after Year Wait," *Wall Street Journal,* January 12, 2001, A3.

5. Ben Bagdikian, *The New Media Monopoly* (Boston: Beacon, 2004).

6. Richard A. Gershon, *The Transnational Media Corporation: Global Messages and Free Market Competition* (Mahwah, N.J.: Lawrence Erlbaum Associates, 1997.)

7. Quoted in ibid., 22.

8. Robert W. McChesney, *Rich Media, Poor Democracy: Communication Politics in Dubious Times* (Urbana: University of Illinois Press, 1999).

9. Edward Herman and Robert McChesney, *The Global Media: The New Missionaries of Corporate Capitalism* (Washington, D.C.: Cassell, 1997).

10. Ibid., 50.

11. Gerald Sussman and John Lent, eds., *Global Productions: Labor in the Making of the "Information Society"* (Cresskill, N.J.: Hampton Press, 1998), 1; Lent, "The Animation Industry and Its Offshore Factories," in ibid., 239–54; Janet Wasko, "The Magical-Market World of Disney," *Monthly Review* 52, no. 11 (2001): 56–71; Ewart Skinner, "The Caribbean Data Processors," in *Global Productions,* edited by Sussman and Lent, 57–90.

12. Herman and Chomsky, *Manufacturing Consent;* Douglas Kellner, *Television and the Crisis of Democracy* (Boulder: Westview Press, 1990); McChesney, *Corporate Media* and *Rich Media;* J. Eldridge, ed., *Glasgow Media Group Reader,* vol. 1, *News Content, Language and Visuals* (New York: Routledge, 1995); R. Entman, *Democracy without Citizens* (New York: Oxford University Press, 1989); James Winter, *Democracy's Oxygen: How Corporations Control the News* (New York: Black Rose Books, 1997); Dennis Mazzocco, *Networks of Power: Corporate TV's Threat to Democracy* (Boston: South End Press, 1994).

13. McChesney and Herman, *Global Media,* 37.

14. Ibid.

15. George Lipsitz, *Rainbow at Midnight: Labor and Culture in the 1940s* (Urbana: University of Illinois Press, 1994), 1.

16. Robert Goldman and Arvind Rajgopal, *Mapping Hegemony: Television News Coverage of Industrial Conflict* (Norwood, N.J.: Ablex, 1991).

17. Walter Lippman, *Public Opinion* (1922; reprint, New York: Macmillan, 1930), 350.

18. Robert McChesney, "Why We Need *In These Times,*" *In These Times,* January 18, 2002; available online at http://www.inthesetimes.com/issue/26/06/feature1.shtml.

19. Diane E. Schmidt, "Public Opinion and Media Coverage of Labor Unions," *Journal of Labor Research* 14, no. 2 (1993): 151–65.

20. See also Martin, *Framed;* and Justin Lewis, *Constructing Public Opinion* (New York: Columbia University Press, 2001).

21. It can also be referred to as a dialectical model of the media.

22. Robert Cirino, *Don't Blame the People: How the News Media Use Bias, Distortion and Censorship to Manipulate Public Opinion* (New York: Vintage Books, 1971); Gaye Tuchman, *Making News: A Study in the Construction of Reality* (New York: Free Press, 1978); Herbert J. Gans, *Deciding What's News: A Study of "CBS Evening News," "NBC Nightly News," "Newsweek," and "Time"* (New York: Pantheon Books, 1979); Herman and Chomsky, *Manufacturing Consent;* Joseph Turow, *Media Systems in Society: Understanding Industries, Strategies, and Power,* 2d ed. (New York: Longman, 1997); Mazzocco, *Networks of Power;* Winter, *Democracy's Oxygen;* McChesney, *Corporate Media* and *Rich Media.*

23. "Fear and Favor in the Newsroom," http://www.fair.org/ff2000.html, 1.

24. According to the estimates for 2006, $427 billion will be spent on advertising ("Zenith Sees 5.9% Boost in '06 Global Ad Spending," *Advertising Age* [December 5, 2005]: 1); Mercedes Cardona, "Forecasts: U.S. Will See Modest Boost in Ad Spending, Gains for Most Media, Global Totals to Rise," *Advertising Age* (December 16, 2002): 22.

25. Edward Herman, "Media in the U.S. Political Economy," in *Questioning the Media,* edited by John Downing, Ali Mohammadi, and Annabelle Sreberny-Mohammadi, 2d ed. (Thousand Oaks, Calif.: Sage Publications, 1995), 77–93.

26. Felicity Barringer and Laura M. Holson, "Tribune Company Agrees to Buy Times Mirror," *New York Times,* March 14, 2000, A1, C16.

27. Oscar Gandy, "Tracking the Audience," in *Questioning the Media,* edited by Downing, Mohammadi, and Sreberny-Mohammadi, 227.

28. Jim Boothroyd, "Media: Can Two Reporters Take on Murdoch and Win?" *The Independent* (London), September 1999, 13.

29. "We Paid $3 Billion for These TV Stations. We Will Decide What the News Is," *Extra! Update* (June 1998): 1.

30. Herbert Schiller, *Culture, Inc.* (New York: Oxford University Press, 1989), 8; Mazzocco, *Networks of Power,* xiv.

31. Gans, *Deciding What's News.*

32. This has been true for well over a century. Since at least the late nineteenth century, the search for profit has dominated the process of news production. See Gerald Baldasty, "The Rise of News as a Commodity: Business Imperitives and the Press in the Nineteenth Century," in *Ruthless Criticism: New Perspectives in U.S. Communication History,* edited by William Solomon and Robert McChesney (Minneapolis: University of Minnesota Press, 1993).

33. James Fallows, *Breaking the News: How the Media Undermine American Democracy* (New York: Vintage Books, 1997), 8, 83.

34. Phillip Gaunt, *Choosing the News: The Profit Factor in News Selection* (New York: Greenwood Press, 1990), 4–5.

35. See also Gene Roberts, Thomas Kunkel, and Charles Layton, eds., *Leaving Readers Behind: The Age of Corporate Newspapering* (Fayetteville: University of Arkansas Press, 2001).

36. David Barboza, "Reporters Try on Many Hats in Chicago News Experiment," *New York Times,* March 15, 2000, A1, A21.

37. Herman and Chomsky, *Manufacturing Consent.*

38. James Carey, "The Communications Revolution in the Professional Communicator," in *Sociology of Mass-Media Communicators,* edited by Paul Halmos, Sociological Review monograph no. 13 (Keele: University of Keele, 1969), 23–28.

39. John Stauber and Sheldon Rampton, *Toxic Sludge Is Good for You: Lies, Damn Lies and the Public Relations Industry* (Monroe, Maine: Common Courage Press, 1995).

40. Herman and Chomsky, *Manufacturing Consent.*

41. See also Kristina Borjesson, *Into the Buzzsaw: Leading Journalists Expose the Myth of a Free Press* (New York: Prometheus Books, 2004).

42. Herman and Chomsky, *Manufacturing Consent.*

43. Ibid.

44. Michael Dolny, "Study Finds First Drop in Think Tank Cites: Progressive Groups See Biggest Decline," *Extra!* (May–June 2006); available online at http://www.fair.org/index.php?page=2897.

45. Hanno Hardt and Bonnie Brennen, *Newsworkers: Toward a History of the Rank and File* (Minneapolis: University of Minnesota Press, 1995).

46. Puette, *Through Jaundiced Eyes,* 56–57 (see preface, n. 7).

47. Robert W. McChesney, *The Problem of the Media: U.S. Communication Politics in the 21st Century* (New York: Monthly Review Press, 2004).

48. James Carey, "Communications Revolution"; Dan Schiller, *Objectivity and the News: The Public and the Rise of Commercial Journalism* (Philadelphia: University of Pennsylvania Press, 1981); McChesney, *Corporate Media* and *Rich Media.*

49. McChesney, *Corporate Media,* 14.

50. Ibid., 13–14.

51. Schudson, *The Power of News,* 55, 54 (see preface, n. 6).

52. Quoted in Herman and Chomsky, *Manufacturing Consent,* 19.

53. Brent Cunningham, "Re-thinking Objectivity," *Columbia Journalism Review* (July–August 2003).

54. Douglas Kellner, "Overcoming the Divide: Cultural Studies and Political Economy," in *Cultural Studies in Question,* edited by Marjorie Ferguson and Peter Golding (Thousand Oaks, Calif.: Sage Publications, 1997), 109, 102–20. Kellner's "hegemony model" of the media is very similar to the one presented here. See, for instance, chap. 2 of Douglas Kellner, *The Persian Gulf TV War* (Boulder: Westview Press, 1992).

55. Antonio Gramsci elaborated his ideas on hegemony while in jail and trying to evade prison censorship. Thus, his language is Aesopean and at times seemingly contradictory. In this book, I have read Gramsci from a historical materialist-classical Marxist perspective. Gramsci, *Selections from Prison Notebooks,* edited and translated by Quintin Hoare and Geoffrey Nowell Smith (New York: International Publishers, 1989), 57–58.

56. Ibid., 12.

57. Deepa Kumar, "Media, War, and Democracy: Strategies of Information Management during the 2003 Iraq War," *Communication and Critical/Cultural Studies* 3, no. 1 (2006). There are many excellent essays and books, too numerous to mention here, that arrive at this same general conclusion. See, for instance, Lee Artz and Yahya Kamalipour, eds., *Bring 'em On: Media and Politics in the Iraq War* (Lanham, Md.: Rowman and Littlefield, 2005); and Yahya Kamalipour and Nancy Snow, eds., *War, Media and Propaganda* (Lanham, Md.: Rowman and Littlefield, 2004).

58. John Barry, "Exclusive: The Defector's Secrets," *Newsweek,* March 3, 2003; available online at http://stacks.msnbc.com/news/876128.asp.

59. Michael Dobbs, "U.S. Had Key Role in Iraq Buildup," *Washington Post,* December 30, 2002, A1.

60. Kumar, "Media, War, and Democracy."

61. For ways in which the New Left in the 1960s was marginalized in news coverage, see Todd Gitlin, *The Whole World Is Watching: Mass Media in the Making and Unmaking of the New Left* (Berkeley and Los Angeles: University of California Press, 1980). Herman and Chomsky, in *Manufacturing Consent,* in their analysis of media coverage of the Vietnam War, argue that the views of the antiwar movement were largely ignored, and the only acceptable debate was that between elites over tactical issues. Daniel Hallin presents a similar assessment of media coverage prior to the Tet Offensive. He suggests that only dissenting views that fell into the "sphere of legitimate controversy," that is, debate between the two major political parties, were allowed. However, after the Tet Offensive this would change dramatically due to pressure from many sources, including the antiwar movement. See Hallin, *The "Uncensored" War: The Media and Vietnam* (Berkeley and Los Angeles: University of California Press, 1986). For the representation of the global justice

movement, see Andy Opel and Donnalyn Pompper, eds., *Representing Resistance: Media, Civil Disobedience, and the Global Justice Movement* (Westport, Conn.: Praeger, 2003).

62. Mary Triece, *Protest and Popular Culture: Women in the U.S. Labor Movement, 1894–1917* (Boulder: Westview Press, 2001).

63. Ibid., 195.

64. Michael Denning, *The Cultural Front: The Laboring of American Culture in the Twentieth Century* (New York: Verso, 1996), xiv, 414.

65. Lipsitz, *Rainbow at Midnight,* 300.

66. Fones-Wolf, *Selling Free Enterprise.*

67. McChesney, "Why We Need *In These Times.*"

68. See John Graham, *Yours for the Revolution: The Appeal to Reason, 1895–1922* (Lincoln: University of Nebraska Press, 1990).

69. Figures taken from ibid.

70. This number is based on circulation figures put out by the Audit Bureau of Circulation and can be found at the *New York Times* online: http://www.nytco.com/investors-nyt-circulation.html.

71. Matthew Klam, "Fear and Laptops on the Campaign Trail," *New York Times Magazine,* September 26, 2004, 43–49.

Chapter 3. "Us" and "Them"

Epigraph: Quoted in Nancy Bernhard, *U.S. Television News and Cold War Propaganda, 1947–1960* (New York: Cambridge University Press, 1999), 10.

1. Kenichi Ohmae, *The End of the Nation-State: The Rise of Regional Economies* (New York: Free Press, 1996).

2. Vivien A. Schmidt, "The New World Order, Incorporated: The Rise of Business and the Decline of the Nation-State," *Daedalus* 124, no. 2 (1995): 75–107.

3. Vincent Cable, "The Diminished Nation-State: A Study in the Loss of Economic Power," *Daedalus* 124, no. 2 (1995): 23–53.

4. The Lexis-Nexis database was searched, and after the short "teasers" and promotions were excluded, 269 stories (ABC had 75, CBS 114, and NBC 80) were counted. Lexis-Nexis provides their entire transcripts.

5. Quoted in Stephen Vaughn, *Holding Fast the Inner Lines: Democracy, Nationalism and the Committee on Public Information* (Chapel Hill: University of North Carolina Press, 1980), 25.

6. At the beginning of the twentieth century, the only form of mass communication was the newspaper, but none was truly national. Woodrow Wilson was particularly dismayed at this absence, commenting that it made countering the provincialism of local papers harder (see ibid.). It was a problem during the Spanish-American War and more so during World War I, when the Wilson administration sought to inculcate feelings of nationalism and patriotism to combat the lack of popular support for U.S. involvement. It was clear to the administration that if the vast majority were to be won to the idea of the war, then it had to be articulated as being in everyone's interest, that is, as the "national interest."

This is why the CPI, also known as the Creel Committee, was set up as a large-scale propaganda agency whose primary task was the construction of the nation and the legitimation of the U.S. version of parliamentary democracy. Its task was urgent, particularly in light of massive late-nineteenth-century immigration. Around the time of World War I, 14.5 million out of a total of 100 million people in the United States were foreign born (ibid.). Immigration as well as class conflict prevented any sense of ideological or attitudinal cohesion regarding the war, and the task of the CPI was to form an "imagined community" with a shared set of interests.

7. Ibid.

8. Lynn Spigel, *Make Room for TV: Television and the Family Ideal in Postwar America* (Chicago: University of Chicago Press, 1992); William Boddy, *Fifties Television: The Industry and Its Critics* (Urbana: University of Illinois Press, 1990).

9. Jonathan Sterne, "Television under Construction: American Television and the Problem of Distribution," *Media, Culture and Society* 21 (1999): 508.

10. Kellner, *Television and the Crisis of Democracy*, 49.

11. Godfrey Hodgson, *America in Our Time* (Garden City, N.Y.: Doubleday, 1976), 151–52, 139–40.

12. Schudson, *The Power of News*, 172.

13. Moss quoted in Sterne, "Television under Construction," 520.

14. Bernhard, *U.S. Television*, 1.

15. Quoted in ibid., 25; see also Fones-Wolf, *Selling Free Enterprise*.

16. For similar arguments, see Glasgow Media Studies Group, *Bad News* (London: Routledge and Kegan Paul, 1976).

17. In the following chapter I discuss Sonnenfeld's role as an "expert" in more detail. Elizabeth Vargas, *Good Morning America,* August 4, 1997, Lexis-Nexis.

18. Linda Vester, *NBC News at Sunrise,* August 7, 1997; Joan Lunden, *Good Morning America,* August 1, 1997, both Lexis-Nexis.

19. Dan Rather, *CBS Evening News,* July 31, 1997; Ann Curry, *Today Show,* August 1, 1997; Lunden, *Good Morning America,* August 1, 1997; Sara James, *NBC Nightly News,* August 10, 1997; John Roberts, *CBS Evening News,* August 7, 1997, all Lexis-Nexis.

20. Tom Bergeron, *Good Morning America,* August 4, 1997, Lexis-Nexis.

21. This coincides with Christopher Martin's argument, in *Framed,* that a "consumer ethos" informs the media's coverage of labor-management conflicts.

22. Cynthia Bowers, *CBS Morning News,* August 4, 1997, Lexis-Nexis; Curry, *Today Show,* August 4, 1997, Lexis-Nexis.

23. Lauer and Katie Couric, *Today Show,* August 5, 1997, Lexis-Nexis.

24. Kumar, "Media, Class, and Power" (see chap. 1, n. 7).

25. George Will, Sam Donaldson, and Cokie Roberts, *ABC This Week,* August 10, 1997, Lexis-Nexis.

26. Eric Hobsbawm and Terence Ranger, *The Invention of Tradition* (New York: Cambridge University Press, 1983), 1.

27. John Seigenthaler, *NBC Nightly News,* August 17, 1997, Lexis-Nexis; emphasis added.

28. Lipsitz, *Rainbow at Midnight*.

29. Richard O. Boyer and Herbert M. Morais, *Labor's Untold Story* (Pittsburgh: United Electrical, Radio, and Machine Workers of America, 1997).

30. Jeremy Brecher, *Strike* (Boston: South End Press, 1997), 248; emphasis added.

31. Curry, *Today Show,* August 4, 1997; Joe Vaughn, Mark Mullen, and Asha Blake, *World News This Morning,* August 5, 1997; Couric and Curry, *Today Show,* August 12, 1997; Russ Mitchell, *CBS Evening News,* August 17, 1997; Rather, *CBS Evening News,* August 15, 1997, all Lexis-Nexis; emphasis added.

32. Brian Williams, *NBC Nightly News,* August 15, 1997; Tom Foreman and Forrest Sawyer, *World News Tonight,* August 7, 1997, both Lexis-Nexis.

33. Bowers, *CBS This Morning,* August 14, 1997, Lexis-Nexis.

34. Rather, *CBS Evening News,* August 14, 1997; Couric and Curry, *Today Show,* August 13, 1997, both Lexis-Nexis.

35. Seigenthaler, *NBC Nightly News,* August 17, 1997, Lexis-Nexis.

36. Bob Kur, *Sunday Today,* August 17, 1997; Seigenthaler, *NBC Nightly News,* August 17, 1997, both Lexis-Nexis.

37. Gans, in *Deciding What's News,* argues that "individualism" and the idea that people can successfully overcome adversity are enduring values in the news.

38. Mike Davis, *Prisoners of the American Dream* (New York: Verso, 1986).

39. Dana Cloud, "The Rhetoric of Family Values: Scapegoating, Utopia and the Privatization of Social Responsibility," *Western Journal of Communication* 62, no. 4 (1998): 387–419; Barbara Dafoe Whitehead, "Dan Quayle Was Right," *Atlantic Monthly* 4 (1993): 84.

40. Michael Kelly, "Clinton's Escape Clause," *New Yorker,* October 24, 1994, 43.

41. David Abshire and Brock Brower, *Putting America's House in Order* (Westport, Conn.: Praeger, 1996), 5.

42. Hallin, *"Uncensored" War,* 125.

43. James, *NBC Nightly News,* August 10, 1997, Lexis-Nexis.

44. Bill Ritter, *Good Morning America,* August 17, 1997, Lexis-Nexis.

45. Dana Cloud, "The Null Persona: Race and the Rhetoric of Silence in the Uprising of '34." *Rhetoric and Public Affairs* 2, no. 2 (1999): 177–209.

46. See chapter 5 for a discussion of these solidarity actions.

47. Saad, "Americans Backed UPS Workers" (see preface, n. 5).

48. Jack Ford, *NBC Nightly News,* August 9, 1997, Lexis-Nexis.

49. Rather, *CBS Evening News,* August 8, 1997; Bill Redeker, Jack Smith, and Cokie Roberts, *Nightline,* August 18, 1997, both Lexis-Nexis.

50. Rather, *CBS Evening News,* August 8, 1997; Bob Schieffer, *Face the Nation,* August 10, 1997; Williams, *Meet the Press,* August 17, 1997, all Lexis-Nexis.

51. Jacqueline Adams, *CBS Morning News,* August 19, 1997, Lexis-Nexis.

52. Shaun Harkin, UPS worker in New York City, personal communication, December 2000.

53. Rather, *CBS Evening News,* August 14, 1997, Lexis-Nexis.

54. Bowers, *CBS Morning News,* August 15, 1997; Jane Robelot, *CBS This Morning,* August 15, 1997, both Lexis-Nexis.

55. David Johnston, "United Parcel and Teamsters to Resume Talks," *New York Times,* August 14, 1997, A28.

56. Mullen and Blake, *World News This Morning,* August 19, 1997, Lexis-Nexis.

57. Will, Donaldson, and Roberts, *ABC This Week,* August 10, 1997; Schieffer, *Face the Nation,* August 10, 1997; Lunden, *Good Morning America,* August 19, 1997, all Lexis-Nexis.

58. Lunden, *Good Morning America,* August 19, 1997, Lexis-Nexis.

59. Will, Donaldson, and Roberts, *ABC This Week,* August 10, 1997, Lexis-Nexis.

60. Williams, *NBC Nightly News,* August 15, 1997, Lexis-Nexis.

61. Vargas, *Good Morning America,* August 4, 1997; Couric and Curry, *Today Show,* August 14, 1997; Schieffer, *Face the Nation,* August 10, 1997, all Lexis-Nexis.

62. Tom Brokaw, *NBC Nightly News,* August 4, 1997, Lexis-Nexis.

63. Paula Zahn, *CBS Evening News* August 9, 1997; Schieffer, *Face the Nation,* August 10, 1997; Couric and Curry, *Today Show,* August 14, 1997, all Lexis-Nexis.

64. Williams, *Meet the Press,* August 17, 1997; Ford, *NBC Nightly News,* August 9, 1997; Williams, *NBC Nightly News,* August 12, 1997; Bowers, *CBS Morning News,* August 18, 1997, all Lexis-Nexis.

65. Mullen and Blake, *World News This Morning,* August 19, 1997; Bowers, *CBS Morning News,* August 19, 1997, both Lexis-Nexis.

66. See also the interview with Carey in the appendix.

67. Williams, *Meet the Press,* August 17, 1997, Lexis-Nexis.

68. Robelot, *CBS This Morning,* August 4, 1997; Lunden, *Good Morning America,* August 20, 1997, both Lexis-Nexis.

69. Dana Frank, *Buy American: The Untold Story of Economic Nationalism* (Boston: Beacon Press, 1999).

70. In general, rank-and-file workers are rarely interviewed. See Yorgo Pasadeos, "Sources in Television Coverage of Strikes," *Journal of Broadcasting and Electronic Media* 34, no. 1 (1990): 77–84.

71. ABC had the most sound bites from workers, accounting for about half the number of all stories on the three networks. In all, ABC was the most sympathetic to the interests of workers, and a less than coherent but significant resistance to the nationalist narrative was voiced there. This is discussed in greater detail in the conclusion to chapter 4.

72. Frederick Schiff, "How 'Public Opinion' Is Perceived and Produced by U.S. Newspaper Publishers," *Javnost* 4, no. 2 (1997): 71–90; David Croteau, "Challenging the 'Liberal Media' Claim: On Economics, Journalists' Private Views Are to the Right of the Public," *Extra* (July–August 1998): 4–9.

73. This condescension is not specific to strikes. The "man-on-the-street" is always asked questions of a different kind than the "experts."

74. Linda Vester, *NBC News at Sunrise,* August 7, 8, 1997; Vaughn and Blake, *World News This Morning* August 8, 1997; Roberts, *CBS Evening News,* August 7, 1997, all Lexis-Nexis.

75. Robelot, *CBS This Morning,* August 11, 1997, Lexis-Nexis.

76. Ibid.

77. Rather, *CBS Evening News,* August 8, 1997, Lexis-Nexis.
78. Ibid.
79. Ibid.
80. Fones-Wolf, in *Selling Free Enterprise,* documents in some detail the measures taken by corporations to attack both labor and liberalism (see chap. 1, n. 120).

Chapter 4. Breaking Through

1. Parenti, *Inventing Reality* (see preface, n. 7).
2. Puette, *Through Jaundiced Eyes,* 56–57; Martin, *Framed.* See chapter 1, "How Labor Gets Framed," for a summary of the research on the representation of labor in the media, and chapter 3 for a historical overview of labor and the media.
3. These are among the top five national newspapers in terms of circulation (B. Brunner, ed., *1998 Information Please Almanac* [Boston, Mass.: Information Please, 1997], 750). The *Wall Street Journal* was omitted in this study, as its target audience is the business community and its construction of the news is quite explicitly directed toward that group. The *Washington Post* was selected over the *Los Angeles Times* to get a sense of beltway reporting.
4. Newspaper articles were downloaded from Lexis-Nexis.
5. This summary of the Teamsters' argument is based on press releases sent out by the union before, during, and after the strike. Titled *News from the New Teamsters,* the union sent out hundreds of press releases to major news agencies and organizations telling its side of the story.
6. Whereas the Teamsters union was forthcoming with their PR materials, UPS refused to part with theirs. Margaret Grynastyl, then UPS public relations coordinator, stated that UPS's PR material was "in cold storage in a distant location" and could not be reached easily (personal communication, May 7, 1999). The analysis I present is based on media coverage of UPS's arguments.
7. Schudson, *The Power of News* (see preface, n. 6).
8. Personal communication, June 15, 1999.
9. B. Horovitz and P. Davidson, "UPS Strike Stifles Shippers, So What Happens When We Can't Have It Now?" *USA Today,* August 5, 1997, A1.
10. Advertising's depiction of modern life as frenzied has a much longer history. Roland Marchand talks about this theme in terms of the "parable of Civilization Redeemed." See *Advertising the American Dream: Making Way for Modernity* (Berkeley and Los Angeles: University of California Press, 1985), 223–28.
11. Horovitz and Davidson, "UPS Strike Stifles Shippers," A1.
12. "Gripes about Part-Timers at UPS Just Don't Add Up," *USA Today,* August 7, 1997, A12.
13. Del Jones and James Waggoner, "Strike Targets Two-Tier Workforce: UPS Labor Efforts Could Reshape Flexible Workplace," *USA Today,* August 5, 1997, B1.
14. David Field, "UPS Drivers Start Strike," *USA Today,* August 4, 1997, A1.
15. Personal communication, June 9, 1999.
16. J. Evans and B. Berselli, "UPS, Union Fail to Agree on Contract: Talks Break Off, but Strike Postponed," *Washington Post,* August 2, 1997, F1.

17. J. Evans, "On Day 1 of UPS Strike, Headaches but No Panic: Clinton Sees No Need for Intervention Now," *Washington Post,* August 5, 1997, A1.

18. However, if a reporter really wanted to, she or he could include historical context in the story. But this rarely happens today since most reporters sent to cover strikes are not labor reporters and thus lack this context.

19. D. Schmidt, "Public Opinion and Media Coverage," 151–65 (see chap. 2, n. 17).

20. Brian Duffy, "The Test of the Teamsters Strike," *Washington Post,* August 5, 1997, C1.

21. At the time that I spoke to him in 1999, Greenhouse had been the labor reporter at the *Times* for about three years, prior to which he covered beats ranging from business to government. He stated that a few days into the strike several business reporters were assigned to the strike, freeing him to do the more in-depth coverage (personal communication, June 9, 1999).

22. Stephen Greenhouse, "High Stakes for 2 Titans," *New York Times,* August 5, 1997, A1.

23. Bob Herbert, "A Workers' Rebellion," *New York Times,* August 7, 1997, A31; "Behind the Teamsters Strike," *New York Times,* August 7, 1997, A30.

24. This assertion is incorrect. According to Chris Tilly's research in *Half a Job,* involuntary part-time work has, in fact, been increasing, albeit not dramatically (see chap. 1, n. 100).

25. Stephen Greenhouse, "For Teamsters' Leader, UPS Is an Ancient Enemy," *New York Times,* August 7, 1997, A1.

26. "Teamsters Set UPS Strike Deadline for Midnight, Sunday Night," *News from the New Teamsters* (press release), August 2, 1997. I obtained all the press releases put out by the Teamsters from March 10, 1997, to July 28, 1998, from Rand Wilson, who functioned as the media contact.

27. "Media Update on Teamster UPS Strike," *News from the New Teamsters* (press release), August 6, 1997.

28. Christine Dugas, "UPS Leaders Worked Their Way through the Ranks," *USA Today,* August 5, 1997, B3; David Field, "Where They Part Company: Hours, Wages," *USA Today,* August 5, 1997, B3.

29. Vargas, "Teamsters Walk Away from Bargaining Table," August 4, 1997, Lexis-Nexis.

30. Horovitz and Davidson, "UPS Strike Stifles Shippers," A1; Del Jones, "UPS Part-Timers Hold Solidarity Key," *USA Today,* August 11, 1997, B2. The *Post* did not cite Sonnenfeld. The *Times* has two mentions of Sonnenfeld, both in stories by Stephen Greenhouse. In the story on August 5, 1997, Greenhouse did not identify Sonnenfeld as a UPS consultant ("High Stakes for 2 Titans"), whereas in the August 14 story he did ("Pension Plan Puts Teamsters' Chief in Tight Spot," *New York Times,* August 14, 1997, A28).

31. The *Times* is read mainly in the Northeast, whereas a majority of *USA Today*'s audience is found in the Midwest and the South. The target audience, individuals with annual incomes greater than twenty thousand dollars, constitutes about half the readership of the *Times* (49.1 percent) and *USA Today* (53.9 percent). These individuals are either professionals, managers, or administrators or involved in

technical, clerical, or sales jobs (taken from Simmons Study of Media and Markets [New York: Market Research Bureau, 1994]). The *Post* is read mainly in the Washington, D.C., area. About 78 percent of its readership earn more than thirty-five thousand dollars per year. About 14 percent are blue-collar and service workers, while a majority are "white-collar" professionals, managers, and technical workers (taken from *1998 Scarborough Report* [March 1997–February 1998], available from the *Washington Post*'s Business Department).

32. Saad, "Americans Backed UPS Workers" (see preface, n. 5).

33. Jones, "UPS Part-Timers Hold Solidarity Key," B2.

34. David Field, "Teamsters, UPS Dig in as Talks Fail," *USA Today,* August 11, 1997, B1.

35. David Field, "UPS Warns of Layoffs, Union Fills Strike Fund," *USA Today,* August 13, 1997, B1.

36. Jeffrey Wilder, "UPS Workers against Strike 'Held Hostage,'" letter to the editor, *USA Today,* August 14, 1997, A14.

37. David Field, "Union Chief Will Talk, but Not to Mediator," *USA Today,* August 12, 1997, B1.

38. Donna Rosato, "'Family' in a House Divided," *USA Today,* August 15, 1997, B3.

39. Field, "Union Chief."

40. Jennifer Jiles, "Lessons Learned from the UPS Strike," *Public Relations Tactics* (November 1997): 17.

41. Del Jones, "A Watershed for Labor Legacy Hangs on Line," *USA Today,* August 15, 1997, B1.

42. P. Blustein and C. M. Liu, "Economic Experts: Strike Cuts Wide but Not Too Deep," *Washington Post,* August 14, 1997, E1; Tara Mack, "Business People Try to Make Do without UPS: Strike Sends Many Scrambling," *Washington Post,* August 16, 1997, V1.

43. Frank Swoboda, "Labor's Dilemma on Display at UPS," *Washington Post,* August 12, 1997, A1; Swoboda, "AFL-CIO Pledges Teamsters Support: $10 Million Weekly to Go for UPS Strikers' Benefits," *Washington Post,* August 13, 1997, D9.

44. B. Berselli, "The Bitter End of the Picket Line," *Washington Post,* August 14, 1997, E1.

45. Jeff Madrick, "Strikers Deliver a Message," *Washington Post,* August 10, 1997, C1.

46. D. Rodriguez, letter to the editor, *New York Times,* August 11, 1997, A14.

47. David Johnston, "Pension Concerns Move to the Picket Line," *New York Times,* August 10, 1997, sec. 3, p. 11; Stephen Greenhouse, "U.P.S. and Union Break Off Negotiations," *New York Times,* August 10, 1997, A26; Stephen Greenhouse, "Why Labor Feels It Can't Afford to Lose This Strike," *New York Times,* August 17, 1997, D3; Louis Uchitelle, "What Goes Up Must Usually, Well, Stop Going Up," *New York Times,* August 10, 1997, D1.

48. Mark Levinson, "Turning Point for Labor?" *New York Times,* August 17, 1997, D15.

49. Stephen Greenhouse, "Part-Time Workers at UPS See Cause for Full Scale Fight," *New York Times,* August 12, 1997, A1.

50. Stephen Greenhouse, "A Glass Half Full or Half Empty," *New York Times,* August 18, 1997, A16.

51. Stephen Greenhouse, "U.P.S. Urges Vote by Rank and File," *New York Times,* August 11, 1997, A13.

52. Stephen Greenhouse, "Shift to Labor," *New York Times,* August 17, 1997, A1.

53. Allen Myerson, "UPS Image of Labor Peace Is Being Fractured by the Strike," *New York Times,* August 10, 1997, A26; emphasis added.

54. James A. Champy, "Business 101, the Hard Way," *New York Times,* August 16, 1997, A21.

55. P. Behr and B. Berselli, "UPS, Teamsters Reach Tentative Contract Accord," *Washington Post,* August 19, 1997, A1.

56. Quoted in Donna Rosato and David Field, "UPS Trucks to Roll Today," *USA Today,* August 20, 1997, A1; and Stephen Greenhouse, "UPS Says Fears of Bigger Losses Made It Cut Deal," *New York Times,* August 20, 1997, A1.

57. "Few Winners," *USA Today,* August 25, 1997, A14; J. Lee and B. Nichols, "Labor Secretary Credited for Role in Strike Talks," *USA Today,* August 20, 1997, B5; B. Belton and David Field, "Unions Brandish Renewed Power," *USA Today,* August 20, 1997, B1.

58. Belton and Field, "Unions Brandish Renewed Power."

59. Paul Davidson, "Teamsters Improve Image with Settlement Deal," *USA Today,* August 20, 1997, B5.

60. Del Jones, "Wounds Will Take Time to Heal," *USA Today,* August 20, 1997, B4.

61. Rosato and Field, "UPS Trucks to Roll Today"; ellipsis in original.

62. Behr and Berselli, "UPS, Teamsters"; "The UPS Strike," *Washington Post,* August 20, 1997, A24; Frank Swoboda, "Labor's Win May Be Brief," *Washington Post,* August 20, 1997, A1.

63. Behr and Berselli, "UPS, Teamsters." In all three phases, the percentage of government sources was significantly higher in the *Post* than in the other two papers.

64. Ibid.

65. P. Behr and B. Berselli, "UPS Ready to Roll after 15-Day Strike," *Washington Post,* August 20, 1997, A1.

66. Behr and Berselli, "UPS, Teamsters."

67. "What's Ahead for Working Men and Women," *New York Times,* August 31, 1997, sec. 4, p. 9; David Johnston, "On Payday, Union Jobs Stack Up Very Well," *New York Times,* August 31, 1997, sec. 3, p. 1; Stephen Greenhouse, "Yearlong Effort Key to Success for Teamsters," *New York Times,* August 25, 1997, A1; Patrick Lyons, "Looking for Union Labels, or Boycotts," *New York Times,* September 1, 1997, D4; Jeffrey Sonnenfeld, "Dignity Department," *New York Times,* 24 August 1997, 3:14.

68. Stephen Greenhouse, "Teamsters and U.P.S. Agree on a 5-Year Contract Plan to End Strike after 15 Days, *New York Times,* August 19, 1997, A1; Stephen Greenhouse, "Victory for Labor," *New York Times,* August 20, 1997, A1.

69. Stephen Greenhouse, "Fears of Bigger Losses," *New York Times,* August 20,

1997, A1; "Settlement at U.P.S.," *New York Times,* August 20, 1997, A22; Stephen Greenhouse, "Victory for Labor."

70. Peter Jennings, *World News Tonight with Peter Jennings,* August 4, 1997, Lexis-Nexis.

71. Chris Bury, *ABC World News This Morning,* August 13, 1997, Lexis-Nexis.

72. Lunden, *Good Morning America,* August 13, 1997; Aaron Brown, *ABC World News Saturday,* August 16, 1997; Bill Ritter, *Good Morning America Sunday,* August 17, 1997; Steve Fox, *Good Morning America,* August 13, 1997, all Lexis-Nexis.

73. Joe Vaughn, *ABC World News This Morning,* August 14, 1997; Bill Redeker, *World News Tonight with Peter Jennings,* August 14, 1997, both Lexis-Nexis.

74. Jennings, *World News Tonight with Peter Jennings,* August 19, 1997; Charles Gibson, *Good Morning America,* August 19, 1997, both Lexis-Nexis.

75. Brokaw, "Move towards Hiring More Part-Time Employees," *NBC Nightly News,* August 5, 1997, Lexis-Nexis; Vargas, "Teamsters Walk Away from Bargaining Table."

76. I use this term in the way described by Michael Denning in his study of culture in the 1930s. He argues that, during this period, there was a "laboring of American culture." It involved the widespread use of the term *labor* and its synonyms in the rhetoric of the time, the impact that working-class people would have on culture and the arts and their active participation in this sphere, and the visibility given to the labor involved in cultural production. Although the moment of "laboring" I discuss in this chapter and the next is but a mere shadow of Denning's definition, it offers us a glimpse of what a more dominant role for labor in mass culture might look like.

77. "Union Label Week and the *Wheel of Fortune,*" *BMWE Journal* 106, no. 10 (November 1997); available online at http://glo.bmwe.org/public/journal/1997/11nov/08.htm.

Chapter 5: The Battle for Hegemony

1. Paul Magnusson et al., "A Wake-Up Call for Business," *Business Week* (September 1, 1997): 28.

2. "UPS Settlement," *Financial Times,* August 20, 1997, 15; Jacob Schlesinger and Bernard Wysocki, "UPS Pact Fails to Shift Balance of Power Back toward U.S. Workers," *Wall Street Journal,* August 20, 1997, A1.

3. Bob Rast, "Labor Pains," *Traffic World* (August 25, 1997): 5; Stuart Varney and Deborah Marchini, "Before Hours 7 AM," CNNfn, August 26, 1997, Lexis-Nexis.

4. Michael Meyer, "UPS Strike: Labor's Deliverance," *Newsweek,* August 25, 1997, 26–29.

5. David Molpus, *Morning Edition,* National Public Radio, August 19, 1997, Lexis-Nexis.

6. Puette, *Through Jaundiced Eyes.*

7. "Newscenter 5 at 6:00," WCVB-TV, August 19, 1997, Lexis-Nexis; Robert Kuttner, "And Labor's New Face," *Boston Globe,* August 24, 1997, D7.

8. Sandra Livingston, "Labor Sees Chance for Revival in UPS Deal," *Cleveland Plain Dealer,* August 20, 1997, A1; Eric Black and Steve Berg, "Organized Labor

Seized on Strike as an Opportunity to Revitalize Itself," *Minneapolis Star Tribune,* August 20, 1997, A1.

9. "Labor Feeling Its Oats after Teamster Deal," *Orlando Sentinel,* August 20, 1997, A6; "Union May Get New Lease on Life," *Baltimore Sun,* August 20, 1997, C1.

10. Daniel LeDuc, "UPS Strike: A Win for Fabor," *Portland Oregonian,* August 20, 1997, A14 (a).

11. Larry Williams, "Labor's Victory at UPS May Not Spread to Others," *Miami Herald,* August 20, 1997, A1; Larry Williams, "Despite UPS Win, Labor Faces Tough Times Ahead," *St. Paul Pioneer Press,* August 20, 1997, A1; "Teamsters Win One for Organized Labor—but Will It Turn the Tide?" *San Diego Union-Tribune,* August 20, 1997, A1.

12. A. Bernstein, "Too Much Corporate Power?" (see preface, n. 2).

13. *New York Times, The Downsizing of America* (New York: Times Books, 1996), 103.

14. Wright, *Class Counts* (see chap. 1, n. 8).

15. *New York Times, Downsizing,* 54–55.

16. Ibid., x.

17. Katherine S. Newman, *Declining Fortunes* (New York: Basic Books, 1993), 4, 130.

18. Richard Freeman and Joel Rogers, *What Workers Want* (Ithaca: Cornell University Press, 1999).

19. *New York Times, Downsizing,* 24; Newman, *Declining Fortunes,* 153.

20. "Public: Labor Unions Beneficial for Workers, Not that Good for Economy," *Gallup Poll Monthly* 383 (1997): 18–20.

21. Not only did these people reject the procorporate framing of the strike on network television and in national newspapers, but they also expressed support for an institution that has not typically had mass support, the labor union. When asked about their confidence in organized labor, only 25 percent of the respondents in 1996 replied a "great deal" or "quite a lot." This figure has ranged from the high 30s in the latter half of the 1970s to 28 percent in 1981 and 26 percent between 1993 and 1995. *The Gallup Poll: Public Opinion 1997* (Wilmington, Del.: Scholarly Resources, 1998).

22. Saad, "Americans Backed UPS Workers."

23. See, for instance, Pierre Bourdieu, "Public Opinion Does Not Exist," in *Communication and Class Struggle,* edited by A. Mattelart and S. Siegelaub (New York: International General, 1997), 1:124–29. Following the key sources of distortion that Bourdieu identifies, one could argue that, in this instance, several distorting factors are either absent or minimized. First, the study itself appears to be fairly representative (telephone interviews with 819 adults based on random sampling). Second, the issue being measured was raised not by the pollster but by the strike itself. Third, an analysis of the questions reveals no obvious bias. Finally, given its sponsorship by the corporate media, the poll's results are hardly likely to have been adjusted in favor of labor.

24. For a summary of research critical of opinion polls, see Lewis, *Constructing Public Opinion* (see chap. 2, n. 18).

25. Ibid.

26. David Field, "55% Support Strikers at UPS," *USA Today,* August 15, 1997, A1.

27. *Gallup Poll, 1997,* 134.

28. Ibid.

29. See S. Smith, *Subterranean Fire.*

30. Seventy-seven percent of the public was following the strike "closely" or "very closely," making it one of the most followed stories of the year (Saad, "Americans Backed UPS Workers").

31. *Gallup Poll, 1997.*

32. Jiles, "Lessons Learned," 1-17.

33. David Moberg, "The UPS Strike: Lessons for Labor," *Working USA* (September–October 1997): 11-15, 29.

34. C. Mitchell, "UPS Strike Revisited," F6 (see chap. 1, n. 27).

35. Shaun Harkin, personal communication, August 15, 2002.

36. Jiles, "Lessons Learned," 17.

37. Magnusson et al., "Wake-Up Call," 29.

38. La Botz, *Rank and File Rebellion,* 12 (see chap. 1, n. 18).

39. Moberg, "UPS Strike," 11-15, 29.

40. Ibid.

41. "What Are Your Priorities for the Next National Contract?" *Teamsters UPS Update,* October 21, 1996, 1-2.

42. "Give Your Ideas on the Next Contract at Local Union Proposal Meetings," *Teamsters UPS Update,* November 6, 1996, 1.

43. "Union Contract Proposal Highlights Wages and Pensions, More Full-Time Jobs, Job Security, Safety and Health," *Teamsters UPS Update,* March 17, 1997, 1-3.

44. Arguably, this inconsistent approach to the old guard and the failure to include more rank and filers on the committee came back to haunt Carey when he was expelled from the union for campaign-finance violations. Ultimately, his best chance of reforming the union lay not in temporary alliances with the old guard but rather in empowering the rank and file, which is what the contract campaign was intended to do. However, even the contract campaign has limitations: it is controlled from above. In this case, rank-and-file workers did not develop their own initiative and relied on the leadership. When Carey was fired from the union, the rank and file did not seem to have the ability to mobilize a campaign to defend him.

45. Witt, personal communication, March 12, 1999.

46. "Save Our Backs," *Teamsters UPS Update,* May 5, 1997, 2.

47. Wilson, personal communication, March 12, 1999.

48. Moberg, "UPS Strike."

49. "Members Send Company a Message," *Teamsters UPS Update,* May 30, 1997, 1.

50. "Vote to Show UPS That We'll Fight for a Good Contract," *Teamsters UPS Update,* July 1, 1997, 1; "Teamsters Vote for Strike Authorization by 95 Percent," *Teamsters UPS Update,* July 15, 1997, 1; emphasis added.

51. These rallies were held in Little Rock (Local 878) and Fort Smith (Local 373),

Arkansas; Tucson and Phoenix (Local 104), Arizona; Modesto (Local 386), Oakland (Local 70), Sunnyvale (Local 287), California; Lansing (Local 580), Michigan; Atlanta and Forest Park (Local 728), Georgia; Santa Fe (Local 492), New Mexico; North Carolina (Local 391); Jackson (Local 217) and Memphis (Local 667), Tennessee.

52. My assessment of the contract campaign is based on interviews with Rand Wilson, who was part of the Teamsters communication department before and during the strike; Shaun Harkin, a UPS part-time worker in Providence, Rhode Island, at the time of the strike; Darrin Hoop, a full-time UPS worker in Seattle, Washington; Tim Sylvester, seventeen-year UPS driver in New York; and Joe Allen, shop steward and member of Teamsters Local 705 in Chicago, who worked with the regional contract campaign coordinator. I was also aided by several alternative media sources.

53. *Rank and File Power at UPS* (Detroit: Teamster Rank and File Education and Legal Defense Fund, 2000).

54. Allen, personal communication, July 25, 2003.

55. Lee Sustar, "How to Beat the Big Brown Machine," *Socialist Worker,* special ed. (June–July 1997): 2.

56. "Part-Timers Step Up Contract Campaign," *Socialist Worker,* special ed. (June–July 1997): 2.

57. Ibid.

58. Ibid.

59. "Postal Workers Support Our Fight," *Teamsters UPS Update,* August 6, 1997, 1.

60. "Local Action," *Teamsters UPS Update,* August 7, 1997, 1.

61. "Outpouring of Solidarity for Workers," *Socialist Worker* (August 15, 1997): 12.

62. "Local Action," *Teamsters UPS Update,* August 11, 1997, 1.

63. "Outpouring of Solidarity."

64. "Local Action," *Teamsters UPS Update,* August 13, 1997, 1.

65. "Members, Locals, Step Up Action," *Teamsters UPS Update,* August 15, 1997, 1.

66. Saad, "Americans Backed UPS Workers."

67. John Schmeltzer, "Part-Timers Drive UPS Strike," *Chicago Tribune,* August 5, 1997, 1; "You Can't Pay Bills on Part-Time Wages," *San Antonio Express News,* August 5, 1997, D1; Sarah Knox, "Full-Time Struggle over Part-Timers," *Philadelphia Inquirer,* August 5, 1997, A1; "Part-Time Job, Full-Time Pressures," *Chicago Sun-Times,* August 7, 1997, 6.

68. Matthew Lubanko, "The Problem with Part-Time," *Hartford Courant,* August 10, 1997, A1.

69. Mark Mullen and Asha Blake, *World News This Morning,* August 19, 1997, Lexis-Nexis.

70. Douglas Blackmon and Martha Brannigan, "UPS Struggles in Bid to Deliver Its Message to a Skeptical Public," *Wall Street Journal,* August 14, 1997, A3.

71. Matt Witt, personal communication, March 12, 1999; Sandra Livingston, "UPS Strike Is Personal for Teamster Members," *Cleveland Plain Dealer,* August 8, 1997, C1; Eleena DeLisser, "Two UPS Part-Timers, Two Different Worlds," *Wall Street Journal,* August 14, 1997, B1.

72. *Rank and File Power at UPS.*

73. A keyword search on Lexis-Nexis with the academics mentioned in the text and the organization EPI found that, together, they were cited about one hundred times in newspapers across the country before, during, and after the strike. The search was limited, and if additional academics—that is, those not mentioned in the text list—were included, the figure would be even higher. Additionally, Lexis-Nexis lists only major newspapers; if we include city newspapers, the figure would be significantly higher.

74. Stephen Greenhouse, "High Stakes for 2 Titans"; Jonathan Marshall, "Full-Time, Part-Time Facts and Fiction," *San Francisco Chronicle,* August 15, 1997, B1; Francine Knowles, "AFL-CIO Out Front in the UPS Strike," *Chicago Sun-Times,* August 13, 1997, 61.

75. Sandra Livingston, "Living the Part-Time Life," *Cleveland Plain Dealer,* August 24, 1997, A1; Michael Towle, "UPS Strike Outcome Could Hit Growth of Part-Time Jobs," *Sacramento Bee,* August 7, 1997, F2.

76. Amy Goodman, *Democracy Now,* August 5, 11, 1997.

77. Alexander Cockburn, "The Teamsters and the Journal," *Nation* 265, no. 5 (August 11–18, 1997); "Teamsters May Strike UPS for Full-Time Jobs," *Labor Notes* (August 1997); *Socialist Worker,* June 20 and August 15, 1997; *Socialist Worker,* special ed. (June–July 1997); *Socialist Worker* (August 15, 1997): 1.

78. However, the use of the Internet in this struggle was not as extensive as the 1999 antiglobalization protests in Seattle (see part 3 of Opel and Pompper, *Representing Resistance* [see chap. 2, n. 59]). Although the use of the Internet in social movements began in the early 1990s, with the Zapatista movement in Chiapas, Mexico, employing the Internet to effectively win international support, it was not until the protests in Seattle that the Internet became an integral part of organization and communication in movements in the United States.

79. Jiles, "Lessons Learned."

80. Ibid., 17.

81. Ibid.

82. Ibid.

83. Shaun Harkin told me that had the company organized replacement workers, the Teamsters might have lost the strike, given the weakness of the picket lines. Joe Allen noted that their "festive, picnic-like" atmosphere would not have been conducive to keeping out scabs. This point is significant, because a number of strikes in the 1990s, such as the Detroit newspaper strike, were lost because replacement workers filled strikers' jobs.

84. Black and Berg, "Organized Labor," A1, A11, A1.

85. Blackmon and Brannigan, "UPS Struggles," A3.

86. C. Mitchell, "UPS Strike Revisited."

87. Blackmon and Brannigan, "UPS Struggles," A3.

88. William Roberts, "Transport PACs Give $4 Million in Final Weeks," *Journal of Commerce* (July 9, 1997): A1, A6.

89. David Johnston, "United Parcel and Teamsters to Resume Talks," *New York Times,* August 14, 1997, A28.

90. Saad, "Americans Backed UPS Workers."

91. C. J. Robinson, "Mass Media and the U.S. Presidency," in *Questioning the Media,* edited by Downing, Mohammadi, and Sreberny-Mohammadi, 94–111 (see chap. 2, n. 23).

Chapter 6. Retheorizing Resistance in Communication and Media Studies

1. Puette, *Through Jaundiced Eyes;* Parenti, *Inventing Reality;* M. Harrison, *TV News* (see preface, n. 7); Martin, *Framed.*
2. Perhaps this is because the book focuses on several strikes and is therefore unable to study each in greater depth. Martin's book, and his brief analysis of the UPS strike, draws similar conclusions to that presented in this book. Indeed, when the book was published in 2004, I was delighted to find that another scholar studying the same news stories would arrive at an assessment not dissimilar to mine. If nothing else, it makes the point that critical research is not simply interpretive, but that two scholars working independent of each other can and do find similar themes and arguments (see also Deepa Kumar, "Mass Media, Class, and Democracy: The Struggle over Newspaper Representation of the UPS Strike," *Critical Studies in Media Communication* 18, no. 3 [2001]: 285–302). However, although there are similarities, there are also differences. Perhaps the key difference is one of emphasis. Whereas Martin focuses on mechanisms of media control, this book underscores the potential for resistance. Martin suggests that media coverage of the UPS strike was exceptional, stating that there were "four *unique* factors behind the Teamsters' victory" (*Framed,* 167; emphasis added). The four factors that Martin notes are accurate, but they are, arguably, not unique to the UPS strike. For instance, Martin points out that the "living wage" theme resonated with U.S. citizens. He states that the strike "successfully struck a chord with Americans disturbed by the trend of downsizing: well paid, full-time, family-wage jobs being replaced with low-paying positions with no benefits and little security—while corporate profits soar" (ibid., 168–69). Indeed, this book makes a similar argument. However, Martin's suggestion that this is unique to the UPS strike is problematic because it misses the dynamic of how strikes can mobilize incipient class anger (see chapter 5) in the larger battle for hegemony. Overall, it seems that because the other strikes analyzed in the book conform to the five antilabor frames, Martin concludes that UPS was an exception. This is an undialectical understanding of the media, as it fails to grasp that every strike is a battlefield in which ideological domination must be won through a process of struggle. Although corporations usually find themselves at an advantage, this does not mean that labor is predestined to be marginal.
3. Parenti, *Inventing Reality,* 10.
4. Goldman and Rajgopal, *Mapping Hegemony,* 216 (see chap. 2, n. 15).
5. Stuart Hall, "Encoding/Decoding," in *Culture, Media, Language,* edited by Hall, Dorothy Hobson, Andrew Lowe, and Paul Willis (London: Hutchinson, 1980), 128–38; David Morley, *The Nationwide Audience: Structure and Decoding* (London: British Film Institute, 1980); Paul Willis, *Learning to Labour: How Working-Class Kids Get Working-Class Jobs* (Farnborough, England: Saxon House, 1977); Dick Hebdige, *Subculture: The Meaning of Style* (London: Methuen, 1979); Stuart

Hall and Tony Jefferson, eds., *Resistance through Rituals: Youth Sub-cultures in Postwar Britain* (1976; reprint, New York: Routledge, 2004).

6. This essay was originally a lecture delivered at the University of Melbourne in 1985. Jean Baudrillard, "The Masses: The Implosion of the Social in the Media," in *Media Studies: A Reader,* edited by Paul Marris and Sue Thornham (New York: New York University Press, 2000), 98–108. Quotes are on pp. 105, 107, 108.

7. Angela McRobbie, "Postmodernism and Popular Culture," in ibid., 392, 385–92.

8. Douglas Kellner, "Cultural Marxism and Cultural Studies," 11, available online at http://www.gseis.ucla.edu/faculty/kellner/kellnerhtml.html; John Fiske, "British Cultural Studies and Television," in *Channels of Discourse,* edited by Robert C. Allen (Chapel Hill: University of North Carolina Press, 1987), 270, 272; Jonathan Sterne, "The Burden of Culture," in *The Aesthetics of Cultural Studies,* edited by Michael Berube (Malden, Mass.: Blackwell, 2005), 94, 80–102.

9. Janice Radway, *Reading the Romance: Women, Patriarchy, and Popular Literature* (Chapel Hill: University of North Carolina Press, 1991).

10. See Christine Gledhill, "Pleasurable Negotiations," in *Female Spectators: Looking at Film and Television,* edited by E. D. Pribram (London: Verso, 1988), 64–89; Valerie Hartouni, "Containing Women: Reproductive Discourse in the 1980s," in *Technoculture,* edited by C. Penley and A. Ross (Minneapolis: University of Minnesota Press, 1991), 27–56; and Angela McRobbie, *Feminism and Youth Culture* (Hampshire, England: Macmillan Press, 2000).

11. Carol Stabile, "Resistance, Recuperation, and Reflexivity: The Limits of a Paradigm," *Critical Studies in Mass Communication* 12, no. 4 (1995): 403–22.

12. Tamar Leibes and Elihu Katz, *The Export of Meaning: Cross-Cultural Readings of "Dallas"* (New York: Oxford University Press, 1990); Ien Ang, *Watching "Dallas"* (New York: Methuen, 1985); Daniel Miller, *"The Young and the Restless* in Trinidad: A Case of the Local and the Global in Mass Consumption," in *Consuming Technologies: Media and Information in Domestic Spaces,* edited by R. Silverstone and E. Hirsch (New York: Routledge, 1992), 163–82.

13. See also, for instance, Terence Lee and Christine Giles, "Discursive Realities: Global Media and September 11," *Australian Journal of Communication* 31, no. 1 (2004): 37–57.

14. Schiller, *Culture, Inc.,* 153 (see chap. 2, n. 28).

15. Sterne, "The Burden of Culture."

16. See Tony Cliff, *State Capitalism in Russia* (1948; reprint, London: Bookmarks, 1996).

17. Ellen Meiksins Wood, *The Retreat from Class: A New "True" Socialism* (1986; reprint, New York: Verso, 1998); Ernesto Laclau and Chantel Mouffe, *Hegemony and Socialist Strategy: Towards a Radical Democratic Politics* (New York: Verso, 1985).

18. Wood, *Retreat from Class* (1986), 79; Laclau and Mouffe, *Hegemony and Socialist Strategy,* 197.

19. Wood, *Retreat from Class* (1998), iv.

20. Triece, *Protest and Popular Culture* (see chap. 2, n. 60); Denning, *Cultural Front* (see chap. 2, n. 62); Lipsitz, *Rainbow at Midnight* (see chap. 2, n. 14).

21. Stuart Hall, Charles Critcher, Tony Jefferson, John Clarke, and Brian Roberts, *Policing the Crisis* (New York: Macmillan, 1978).

22. Hanno Hardt, *Interactions: Critical Studies in Communication, Media and Journalism* (Lanham, Md.: Rowman and Littlefield, 1998).

23. Schudson, *The Power of News*, 170, 5, 185 (see preface, n. 6).

24. Celeste Condit, "Hegemony in a Mass-Mediated Society: Concordance about Reproductive Technologies," *Critical Studies in Mass Communication* 11, no. 3 (1994): 211, 210.

25. Ibid., 210.

26. See Kumar, "Media, Class, and Power," 6–21 (see chap. 1, n. 7).

27. Dana Cloud, "Concordance, Complexity, and Conservatism: Rejoinder to Condit," *Critical Studies in Mass Communication* 14 (1997): 197.

28. Schudson, *The Power of News*, 204–5; Hardt, *Interactions;* George Novack, *Pragmatism versus Marxism: An Appraisal of John Dewey's Philosophy* (New York: Pathfinder Press, 1975).

29. John Dewey, *The Public and Its Problems* (Chicago: Swallow Press, 1954), 127.

30. John Dewey, *Intelligence in the Modern World: John Dewey's Philosophy,* edited by Joseph Ratner (New York: Random House, 1939).

31. Quoted in James Carey, *Communication as Culture: Essays on Media and Society* (New York: Routledge, 1988), 22.

32. Richard Rorty, *Achieving Our Country: Leftist Thought in Twentieth-Century America* (Cambridge: Harvard University Press, 1998), 35; Rorty, *Consequences of Pragmatism* (Minneapolis: University of Minnesota Press, 1982).

33. Rorty, *Achieving Our Country*, 15.

34. James Campbell, *Understanding John Dewey* (Chicago: Open Court, 1995).

35. Rorty, *Achieving Our Country*.

36. Gary Bullert, *The Politics of John Dewey* (New York: Prometheus Books, 1983).

37. Harry Braverman, *Labor and Monopoly Capitalism* (see chap. 1, n. 19).

38. Rorty, *Achieving Our Country*, 101.

39. Cliff, *State Capitalism in Russia*.

40. Herman and Chomsky, *Manufacturing Consent* (see chap. 1, n. 75).

41. Edward Herman, "The Propaganda Model Revisited," in *Capitalism and the Information Age: The Political Economy of the Global Communication Revolution*, edited by Robert McChesney, Ellen Meiksins Wood, and John Bellamy Foster (New York: Monthly Review Press, 1998), 191–206.

42. Herman and Chomsky, *Manufacturing Consent*, 26.

43. Except perhaps the discussion of the Vietnam War, in which the antiwar movement in the United States and U.S. soldiers' rebellion in Vietnam are given barely a few sentences.

44. Ibid., 252; Herman, "The Propaganda Model Revisited," 200.

45. Noam Chomsky, *Year 501: The Conquest Continues* (London: Verso, 1993) and "Propaganda and Control of the Public Mind," in *Capitalism and the Information Age*, edited by McChesney, Wood, and Foster, 179–90.

46. Chomsky, *Year 501;* Noam Chomsky and David Barsamian, *Secrets, Lies and Democracy* (Tucson: Odonian Press, 1994).

47. Vincent Mosco, *The Political Economy of Communication: Rethinking and Renewal* (Thousand Oaks, Calif.: Sage Publications, 1996).

48. Nicholas Garnham, "The Media and the Public Sphere," in *Communicating Politics: Mass Communications and the Political Process,* edited by Peter Golding, Graham Murdock, and Philip Schlesinger (New York: Holmes and Meier, 1986), 37–54.

49. For a history of this movement, see chap. 7 of McChesney, *Problem of the Media* (see chap. 2, n. 45).

50. McChesney, *Rich Media* (see chap. 2, n. 7)

51. Mosco, *Political Economy,* 95, 96.

52. Schudson, *The Power of News,* 223.

53. H. Schiller, *Culture, Inc.;* McChesney, *Rich Media.*

Chapter 7: Conclusion

Epigraph: Phillip Foner, *Life and Writings of Frederick Douglass,* vol. 2 (New York: International Publishers, 1975), 437.

1. S. Smith, *Subterranean Fire.*

2. In 2003 several large unions in the AFL-CIO joined together to form the New Unity Partnership (NUP). This was a promising development. The grouping, headed by the Service Employees International Union (SEIU), shook up the AFL-CIO by voicing sharp criticisms of its failure to stem the decline in membership. The NUP proposed several changes, including allotting more money to organizing and merging smaller unions with larger ones. However, by 2005 the NUP had disbanded after accepting a proposal put forward by old-guard Teamsters president Jimmy Hoffa. After dissolving the NUP, a coalition called Change to Win, which included the member unions from the NUP plus the Teamsters and the UFCW, was formed in July 2005. At the end of the day, despite its progressive rhetoric, Change to Win has done little to differentiate itself from the pro-Democrat, business-unionism model of the AFL-CIO. If nothing else, this example points to why it is important for rank and filers to take the initiative rather than wait for change from above. Recently, immigrant workers in SEIU and UNITE-HERE have pressured various locals to endorse and support the immigrant rights movement. This sort of sustained rank-and-file activity can force Change to Win to play a more central role in the immigrants' movement and to organize larger sections of the immigrant workforce.

3. Margaret Warner, "Putting on the Brakes," *PBS News Hour,* March 12, 1996; available online at http://www.pbs.org/newshour/bb/business/gm_strike_3–12.html.

4. Matt Bai, "The New Boss," *New York Times Magazine,* January 30, 2005, 38–45.

5. See, for instance, Sam Pizzigati, "The Case for a National Labor Paper," in *The New Labor Press: Journalism for a Changing Union Movement,* edited by Pizzigati and Fred J. Solowey (Ithaca: ILR Press, 1992): 203–13. See also the rejoinders by Karen Kieser and Jo-Ann Mort.

6. Jo-Ann Mort, "The Case for a National Labor Paper: Rejoinder II," in ibid., 222, 218–23.

7. Stephen Greenhouse, "Unions Push for Better Pay at Wal-Mart," *New York Times,* December 11, 2004, A16; Andy Serwer, Kate Bonamici, and Dorris Burke, "The Waltons: Inside America's Richest Family," *Fortune* 150, no. 10 (November 15, 2004).

8. Stephen Greenhouse, "Unions Push for Better Pay at Wal-Mart."

9. "What Is a Corporate Campaign?"; available online at the Corporate Campaign Web site, http://www.corporatecampaign.org/intro.htm.

10. Paul Jarley and Cheryl Maranto, "Union Corporate Campaigns: An Assessment," *Industrial and Labor Relations Review* 43, no. 5 (July 1990): 505–24.

11. Ray Rogers, "How Labor Can Fight Back," reprinted by Corporate Campaign, Inc., originally appeared in *USA Today Magazine,* July 1984. This article was mailed to me by CCI along with a packet of other corporate campaign materials used during the Staley lockout.

12. C. Mitchell, "UPS Strike Revisited."

13. Joshua Frank, *Left Out: How Liberals Helped Reelect George W. Bush* (Monroe, Maine: Common Courage Press, 2005).

14. In chapter 2, I discussed the importance of alternative media to various social movements of the past. Increasingly today, the Internet has become a vital space for progressive politics and organizing. The protests in Seattle in 1999 were largely coordinated through the Internet, and the antiwar movement in the aftermath of 9/11 continued to use the Internet. It is important to keep in mind, as Richard Kahn and Douglas Kellner point out, that the Internet is a "contested terrain, used by Left, Right, and Center of both dominant cultures and subcultures to promote their own agendas and interests. The political battles of the future may well be fought in the streets, factories, parliaments, and other sites of past struggle, but politics is already mediated by broadcast, computer, and information technologies and will increasingly be so in the future" ("Internet Subcultures and Oppositional Politics"; available online at http://www.gseis.ucla.edu/faculty/kellner/essays/internetsubcultu resoppositionalpolitics.pdf). A media-reform movement tied to the global justice and antiwar movements can play a role in demanding more space for public communication.

Index

Gandy, Oscar, 40
Gannett Corporation, 114, 120
Garnham, Nicholas, 171
Gaunt, Phillip, 42
General Accounting Organization, 20
General Motors, 59, 63, 178
Gerard, Irwin, 68
Giffith, Robert, 63
Gilded Age, 3
Gingrich, Newt, 72
"Global Capitalism: Can It Be Made to Work Better?" (*Business Week*), 13
global capitalist society, 14
globalization: *Business Week* on, 13; and class polarization, 5; during Clinton administration, 30; and corporate restructuring, 94; costs and benefits, 10–14; and declining income, 16; and developing countries, 12–14, 18, 24; effect on labor, 103–4; hypocrisy of, 175–76; as means to restore profitability, 17–19; and the media industry, 33–39, 42–46, 59; and multinational corporations, 24–25, 59–60, 179; and neoliberalism, 18, 175–77; and part-time employment, 25, 143; protests against, 83, 171–72, 174, 176–77, 225n14; and the UPS strike, 92; and Wal-Mart, 179
Globalization and Its Discontents (Stiglitz), 12
global justice movement, 176–78
Golding, Peter, 171
Goldman, Robert, 37, 156
Good Morning America (television show), 64
Gordon, David, 15–16
government: intervention in the UPS strike, 77–78; and nationalist propaganda, 61–62, 208n6; press releases, 43–44; pressure on media industry, 39; social programs, 5, 20
Gramsci, Antonio, 48
Greenhouse, Stephen, 96–97, 104–5, 111, 213n21
Group of Eight, 171
Grynastyl, Margaret, 212n6

Hales, Bobby, 8
Half a Job Is Not Enough (Teamsters' report), 134

Hall, Stuart, 157, 162
Hallin, Dan, 73
Hardt, Hanno, 166
Harkin, Shaun, 128, 219n52, 220n83
Harman, Chris, 12
Harrison, Bennet, 22, 28
Harrison, Martin, 155
Head of the Class (television show), 46
Hebdige, Dick, 157
hegemony, 48–55, 156, 207nn54–55
Henwood, Doug, 17
Herbert, Bob, 49, 97
Herman, Alexis, 77–78, 108–10
Herman, Edward, 35–36, 44, 168–70
"High Stakes for 2 Titans" (Greenhouse), 96–97
Hirshberg, A., 7
Hirst, Paul, 11–12
Hobsbawm, Eric, 67
Hodgson, Godfrey, 62
Hoffa, Jimmy, 30
Hoffa, Jimmy, Jr., 79, 178, 186, 194
Hollywood writers' strike, 45
Holthausen, Steven A., 122
Hoop, Darrin, 219n52
Hooper, Mr., 70
Howard, Rachel, 103
Howse, Alex, 74
Howse, Edward, 74
Howse, Ryan, 74
Howse, Susan, 74
Hurricane Katrina, 49–50
Huxley, Christopher, 28

IBT (International Brotherhood of Teamsters). *See* Teamsters Union
ideological-discursive struggle, 162
ideological domination, 48
ILO (International Labor Organization), 8–9, 119n29
IMF. *See* International Monetary Fund (IMF)
immigrant rights movement, 175–76, 224n2
income, decline of, 14–16. *See also* wages
India, 177
individualized resistance, 157–63
information technology (IT), 23–24
Inside UPS (magazine), 128

International Brotherhood of Teamsters.
   See Teamsters Union
International Labor Organization (ILO),
   8–9, 199n29
International Monetary Fund (IMF): and
   the Asian flu, 177; and developing na-
   tions, 12, 18, 24; establishment of,
   201n70; and the media industry, 35–36;
   protests against, 83, 171
Internet, 55, 220n78, 225n14
"In the Dignity Department, UPS Wins"
   (Sonnenfeld), 110
invented tradition, 67
Inventing Reality (Parenti), 156
"Inventory Express," 24
investigative journalism, 43
involuntary part-time employment, 25
Iraq, 50–51
IT (information technology), 23–24

Jackson, Jesse, 149
Jackson, Tom, 8
Jefferson, Tony, 157
Jennings, Peter, 112
Jiles, Jennifer, 146
Johns, Joe, 66
Johnston, David, 104
Jordan, Tammisha, 140
journalism: decline in investigative, 43;
   firing of reporters, 44, 164; ideology of,
   39; multimedia, 43; objectivity in, 47;
   and procorporate bias, 41, 47; profes-
   sionalism, 46–48; self-censorship of, 38;
   wage gap among journalists, 42
"just-in-time" logistics, 23–24

Kane, C. L., 8
Kansas City Star (newspaper), 119
Katch, Danny, 8
Katrina (hurricane), 49–50
Katz, Elihu, 159
Katz, Harry, 105
Kellner, Douglas, 48, 62, 158
Kelly, James, 69, 76, 109, 111
Kennedy, John F., 17
Kennedy, Joseph, 149
Keynes, John Maynard, 201n70
Klein, Naomi, 177
Knight-Ridder, 119–20

Kozlowski, Dennis, 5
Krugman, Paul, 4, 15, 49

labor: and alternative media, 54; antilabor bias, 89, 155–56; and class struggle,
   161; creation of proletarian culture,
   53, 68; and the Democratic Party, 30,
   184, 224n2; effectiveness of strikes, 69,
   178; effect of globalization on, 103–4;
   increasing number of immigrants,
   176, 224n2; lacking a voice in political
   sphere, 126; media coverage of, 37–38,
   89, 95, 117–18, 155; and nationalism, 80–
   84; public image of, 179, 182–83. *See also*
   UPS strike; working class
Labor Notes (newsletter), 144
labor unions. *See* unions
La Botz, Dan, 7, 129
Laclau, Ernesto, 161
Laing, Susan, 70
language of news reporting, 89
Lauer, Matt, 66
lean production, 21–28, 36
Learning to Chart Spheres of Influence (UPS
   manual), 7
Learning to Labor (Willis), 157
Leibes, Tamar, 159
Lent, John, 36
letters to the editor, 104
Levinson, Mark, 104–5
liberalism, 163–68
Lichtenstein, Nelson, 29, 119, 142
Lippmann, Walter, 37
Lipsitz, George, 37, 53–54, 68, 161, 170
local newspapers, 118–19, 208n6
lockouts, 180
Loomis, Tom, 70
Los Angeles Times, 145
Lozada, Sánchez de, 176

Madison, James, 33
Madonna, 159
Madrick, Jeff, 103
Mahaud, Jamil, 176
Make UPS Deliver (Teamsters' video),
   130–32
management. *See* scientific management
Manufacturing Consent (Herman and
   Chomsky), 170

DEEPA KUMAR is an assistant professor in the Department of Journalism and Media Studies at Rutgers University.

The History of Communication

Selling Free Enterprise: The Business Assault on Labor and Liberalism,
  1945–60   *Elizabeth A. Fones-Wolf*
Last Rights: Revisiting Four Theories of the Press   *Edited by John C. Nerone*
"We Called Each Other Comrade": Charles H. Kerr & Company, Radical
  Publishers   *Allen Ruff*
WCFL, Chicago's Voice of Labor, 1926–78   *Nathan Godfried*
Taking the Risk Out of Democracy: Corporate Propaganda versus Freedom
  and Liberty   *Alex Carey; edited by Andrew Lohrey*
Media, Market, and Democracy in China: Between the Party Line and the
  Bottom Line   *Yuezhi Zhao*
Print Culture in a Diverse America   *Edited by James P. Danky and
  Wayne A. Wiegand*
The Newspaper Indian: Native American Identity in the Press, 1820–90
  John M. Coward
E. W. Scripps and the Business of Newspapers   *Gerald J. Baldasty*
Picturing the Past: Media, History, and Photography   *Edited by Bonnie Brennen
  and Hanno Hardt*
Rich Media, Poor Democracy: Communication Politics in Dubious Times
  Robert W. McChesney
Silencing the Opposition: Antinuclear Movements and the Media in the Cold
  War   *Andrew Rojecki*
Citizen Critics: Literary Public Spheres   *Rosa A. Eberly*
Communities of Journalism: A History of American Newspapers and Their
  Readers   *David Paul Nord*
From Yahweh to Yahoo!: The Religious Roots of the Secular Press
  Doug Underwood
The Struggle for Control of Global Communication: The Formative Century
  Jill Hills
Fanatics and Fire-eaters: Newspapers and the Coming of the Civil War
  Lorman A. Ratner and Dwight L. Teeter Jr.
Media Power in Central America   *Rick Rockwell and Noreene Janus*
The Consumer Trap: Big Business Marketing in American Life   *Michael Dawson*
How Free Can the Press Be?   *Randall P. Bezanson*
Cultural Politics and the Mass Media: Alaska Native Voices   *Patrick J. Daley and
  Beverly A. James*
Journalism in the Movies   *Matthew C. Ehrlich*
Democracy, Inc.: The Press and Law in the Corporate Rationalization of the
  Public Sphere   *David S. Allen*
Investigated Reporting: Television Muckraking and Regulation   *Chad Raphael*

The University of Illinois Press
is a founding member of the
Association of American University Presses.

_____

Composed in 9/13 ITC Stone Serif
with ITC Stone Sans display
at the University of Illinois Press
Designed by Paula Newcomb
Manufactured by Thomson-Shore, Inc.

University of Illinois Press
1325 South Oak Street
Champaign, IL 61820-6903
www.press.uillinois.edu